Decorating Cakes

Decorating
Cakes

STERLING
New York

CONTENTS

Welcome

TO OUR WORLD OF
wonderfully decorated cakes.
WE'VE DIVIDED THIS BOOK
INTO THREE CHAPTERS:
An easy chapter,
WHERE LITTLE OR NO CAKE DECORATING
EXPERIENCE IS NECESSARY;
A mid-range chapter
WHERE SOME SKILLS ARE
REQUIRED; AND FINALLY
A more difficult chapter
WHERE SOME SKILLS ARE EITHER
A MUST-HAVE OR HAVE TO BE
PRACTICED *and* LEARNED.

You'll find the ideas in the easy chapter are charming, easy to follow and the results will be worth the little effort involved. It's a great place to start to build and improve your decorating skills. There is one cake that is covered with ready-to-use fondant, just so you get to practice rolling it out and covering a cake with it.

Macarons are more popular than ever, so we've used them to decorate two lovely cakes. As well, we have a few cakes that could double as glamorous desserts, plus cupcakes and cookies that can be used for many occasions.

We've developed the medium-range chapter for the newly-experienced cake decorator. Most of the cakes in this chapter are covered with ready-to-use fondant so, if you're a first-timer using this product, it's worthwhile buying a packet from the supermarket to get the feel of it. Practice rolling out the fondant and covering a cake pan with it, take the icing off, re-knead and re-roll it and cover the pan again, do this a few times until you feel confident about covering a real cake.

Using smoothing tools on the fondant, once it's been smoothed with your hands, makes a big difference to the finished look of the fondant. When it comes to using ready-to-use fondant to make shapes, such as numbers and flowers, think of it as play dough – it's very user-friendly.

While the last chapter is for experts, many of the cakes are really not that hard – especially if you've had a little experience in cake decorating from the previous chapters. They may seem tricky at first, but practice and it'll soon become easier. In this chapter we teach you how to do some basic piping, how to make a few different flowers out of gum paste, and even how to make an awesome croquembouche.

You should read the final chapter in this book (*The Mechanics*, page 188) before even thinking about making and decorating any of these cakes. We assume when you make these cakes that you have read it, as not all the information is repeated in each recipe, so refer to these pages often. There is so much to know and many tips and shortcuts that will help. There are lists of cake pans, equipment, information about cake boards, how to make tiered cakes, the different types of cake coverings and frostings, and many useful techniques. There are eight charts of excellent cake recipes – all with the quantity of ingredients worked out for you, so whichever cake you choose, the quantity of mixture you'll need to fill the chosen pans is in the chart. It's also a must that you read each recipe through before starting, as most cakes require 3 days to complete – some up to a week. Make as many of the decorations as you can in advance, so you're not doing them at the last minute.

Changing the color of the icing can change the look of the cake, and the occasion for which it can be used. This can be done with all the cakes throughout this book – adjust the color to suit the theme of your celebration.

This is not just a book of wedding cakes. A lot of the cakes can be used for many different celebrations – Mother's day, Valentine's day, christenings, anniversaries, birthdays, as well as weddings and, of course, the many wedding-related occasions often held before the big day.

Decorations

BEAUTIFUL EMBELLISHMENTS WILL ADD A
PROFESSIONAL TOUCH TO YOUR MASTERPIECE

PIPING

PIPING IS NOT THAT HARD – A LITTLE PRACTICE IS ALL
THAT'S REQUIRED. SEE "PIPING TECHNIQUES" ON PAGE 224.

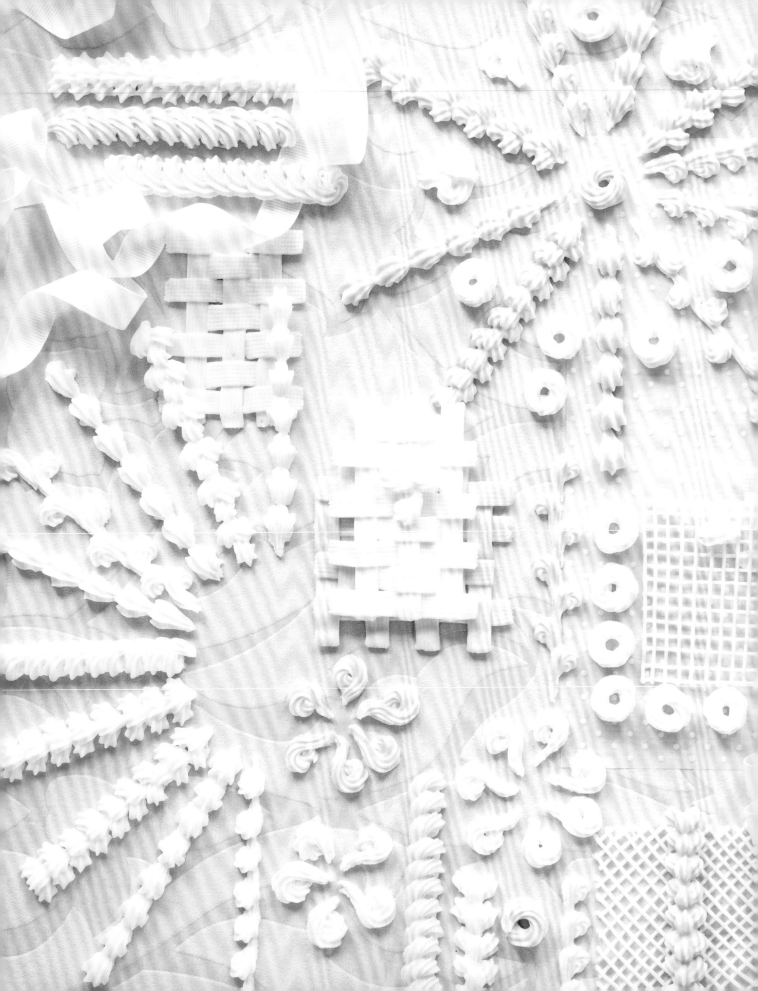

Piping

ALL OF THESE TECHNIQUES WERE
ACHIEVED USING JUST 3 PIPING TUBES

Decorating cakes of all shapes
and sizes is rewarding and fun.
This chapter is a good place to start
to build your skills and confidence.
We minimized the use of piping and
using ready-to-use fondant to cover cakes,
simply because most people think that
these skills are beyond them - however,
trust us - they're not.

CHAPTER ONE

EASY

QUILTED WEDDING
Cake Cookies

THESE PRETTY COOKIES COULD BE USED AT AN ENGAGEMENT PARTY, A BRIDAL SHOWER, OR TAGGED AND USED AS PLACE NAMES AT A WEDDING.

EQUIPMENT
baking trays
4-inch x 4¼-inch wedding cake cutter
pastry brush
small patchwork cutter trellis
fine artist's paint brush
tweezers
COOKIES
1 stick (½ cup) butter
2 eggs
1 teaspoon vanilla extract
⅔ cup superfine sugar
1⅓ cups self-rising flour
1 cup all-purpose flour
DECORATIONS
1 pound ready-to-use fondant
cornstarch
1 egg white, beaten lightly
2 tablespoons tiny silver dragées

1 Have the butter and eggs at room temperature for the cookies.
2 Beat butter, extract and sugar in small bowl with electric mixer only until combined. Beat in eggs, one at a time; beat only until combined.
3 Transfer mixture to large bowl. Stir in sifted flours, in two batches; mix to a soft dough. Knead dough on floured surface until smooth, cover; refrigerate 30 minutes.
4 Preheat oven to 375°F. Grease baking trays; line with parchment paper.
5 Roll dough, in batches, between sheets of parchment paper until ¼-inch thick. Using wedding cake cutter, cut 18 shapes from dough, re-rolling dough as necessary. Place shapes, about 1¼ inches apart, on trays. Bake about 10 minutes or until cookies are browned lightly.
6 Let sit for 5 minutes; transfer to wire racks to cool completely.

7 Knead ready-to-use fondant on surface dusted with a little cornstarch until fondant loses its stickiness. Roll fondant on cornstarched surface into a ⅛-inch thickness. Using wedding cake cutter, cut 18 shapes from fondant; re-roll fondant as necessary. Cover fondant shapes with plastic wrap.
8 Working with one cookie at a time, brush the top of the cookie with egg white. Lift fondant shapes onto cookie. Using patchwork cutter, press onto fondant to make a quilted pattern.
9 Dip paint brush into water, wipe brush almost dry, dab onto one corner in the quilted pattern; use tweezers to position dragée on corner. Repeat with remaining dragées. Stand until set.

makes 18

tip Completed cookies can be made up to 4 weeks ahead; store at room temperature in an airtight container.

Roll out dough between sheets of parchment paper until ¼-inch thick. Using the wedding cake cutter, cut 18 shapes from the dough.

Brush cookies with egg white, top with fondant shapes. Press patchwork cutter firmly onto the fondant to make a quilted pattern.

Dip paint brush into water, wipe brush until almost dry. Lightly dab one corner at a time with brush then position dragée on corner.

SUGAR CONFETTI
Cupcakes

THESE PERFECTLY SIMPLE CAKES ARE IDEAL FOR MANY CELEBRATIONS,
FROM WEDDINGS TO ENGAGEMENT PARTIES.

EQUIPMENT
12 plain white paper liners
large piping bag
½-inch plain piping tube
CAKE
**1 quantity cupcake mixture of
   choice (page 190)**
jam of choice
DECORATIONS
**12 plain decorative cupcake
   wrappers**
**1½ quantities white chocolate
   ganache, whipped (page 210)**
2 tablespoons sugar confetti

1 Divide cupcake mixture into paper liners; bake cupcakes according to recipe. Stand cakes in pan 5 minutes; turn top-side up onto wire rack to cool.
2 Cut a small cavity in the top of each cake; fill with a little jam. Place cakes into cupcake wrappers.
3 Fit piping bag with tube; fill bag ½ full with ganache. Pipe swirls of ganache on top of each cake. Sprinkle ganache with confetti.

makes 12
tips Cupcakes stale quickly, so it's best to use a fruit or chocolate cake if you want to bake ahead. The cakes can be made and frozen for about 3 months. Choose the cake you like, then a type of jam, or a thick fruit puree, to match the cake. For example, any berry jam

or puree goes well with a chocolate cake. To make a puree: Push fresh or thawed frozen berries through a sieve; sweeten to taste with a little sifted icing sugar, and add a little liqueur, if you like. Make sure you cover the tops of the cakes with the ganache to keep the cakes as fresh as possible. The ganache will keep them sealed and fresh for a day or two. Completed cakes should be stored in a cool or air-conditioned room. Sprinkle confetti over ganache up to half a day before they're served.

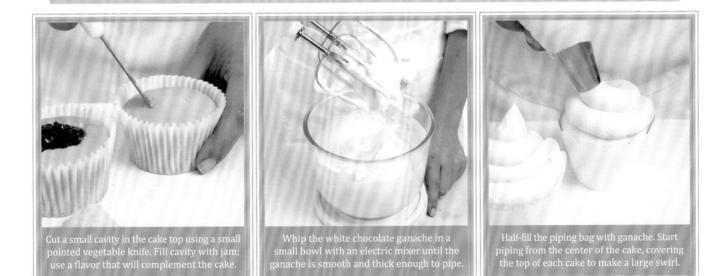

Cut a small cavity in the cake top using a small pointed vegetable knife. Fill cavity with jam; use a flavor that will complement the cake.

Whip the white chocolate ganache in a small bowl with an electric mixer until the ganache is smooth and thick enough to pipe.

Half-fill the piping bag with ganache. Start piping from the center of the cake, covering the top of each cake to make a large swirl.

CHOCOLATE *Box*

WHO WOULDN'T LOVE TO RECEIVE A GIFT AS WONDERFUL, AND AS DELICIOUS, AS THIS CHOCOLATE BOX? IT'S THE PERFECT PRESENT FOR ANY OCCASION.

EQUIPMENT
8-inch square wooden cake board (page 208)
medium metal spatula
craft glue
cheese slicer
CAKE
deep 6-inch square cake of choice (page 190)
DECORATIONS
1 quantity white chocolate ganache (page 210)
8 ounces white chocolate Melts
yellow food coloring
1½ yards wide ribbon
1 pound blocks white chocolate

1 Trim cake (page 209); secure cake to board (page 209). Spread cake all over with ganache.

2 Cut parchment paper into four strips measuring 4-inches x 6½-inches. Melt chocolate Melts in medium heatproof bowl over medium saucepan of simmering water (don't let water touch base of bowl). Remove from heat; tint chocolate with a little yellow coloring.

3 Using spatula, spread chocolate evenly over the parchment-paper strips. Leave chocolate to set for a few minutes, then carefully pick up paper and move to another sheet of parchment paper (this neatens the edges). Stand about 5 minutes or until chocolate sets.

4 Peel parchment paper away from chocolate panels; press panels onto sides of cake. Wrap ribbon around panels; secure ends of ribbon with glue. Make bow (page 226); secure over ribbon with glue.

5 Place one block of chocolate upside down on work surface. Place your hand on the chocolate to warm it slightly. Drag a sharp cheese slicer over the chocolate to make curls. Repeat with remaining chocolate to make enough curls to cover and fill the top of the chocolate box. Fill box with chocolate curls.

tips We found that using a cheese slicer is an easy and effective way of making large chocolate curls. The box panels can be completed at least one week before they're needed; store at a cool room temperature. You can use this recipe as a guide to make the boxes smaller or larger.

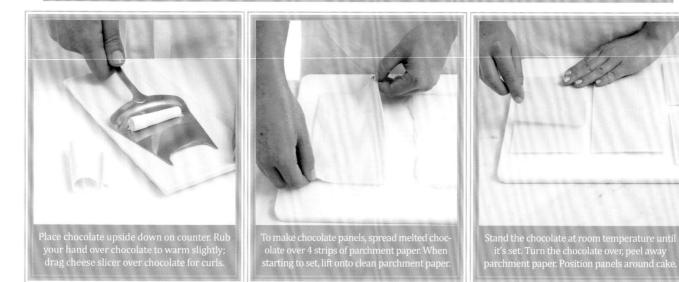

Place chocolate upside down on counter. Rub your hand over chocolate to warm slightly; drag cheese slicer over chocolate for curls.

To make chocolate panels, spread melted chocolate over 4 strips of parchment paper. When starting to set, lift onto clean parchment paper.

Stand the chocolate at room temperature until it's set. Turn the chocolate over, peel away parchment paper. Position panels around cake.

MONOGRAMMED
Cupcakes

JUST THE THING FOR A 21ST, ENGAGEMENT PARTY OR EVEN A CHRISTENING PARTY. THESE MONOGRAMMED IMAGES ADD A PERSONAL TOUCH TO THE OCCASION.

EQUIPMENT
fine artist's paint brush
1½-inch round cutter
12 plain white paper liners
large plastic disposable piping bag
CAKE
1 quantity cupcake mixture of
    choice (page 190)
DECORATIONS
1 pound ready-to-use white
    fondant
cornstarch
1¼-inch monogrammed edible
    images
12 fancy cupcake wrappers
1½ quantities dark chocolate
    ganache (page 210)

1 Knead ready-to-use fondant on surface dusted with a little cornstarch until it loses its stickiness. Roll fondant out on cornstarched surface into about ⅛-inch thickness.
2 Lift 12 monogrammed images off backing paper; brush backs of images lightly with a little water; secure to fondant about ½-inch apart.
3 Use cutter to cut neatly around each image; transfer to parchment-paper-lined tray to dry overnight.
4 Divide cupcake mixture into paper liners; bake cupcakes according to recipe. Stand cakes in pan 5 minutes; turn top-side up onto wire rack to cool.
5 Secure cupcake wrappers around cakes. Fill piping bag ½-full with ganache. Cut the tip from the bag; the opening should be about ¾-inch wide. Pipe a swirl of ganache on each cake; top with monogrammed rounds.

makes 12

tips The cupcakes stale quickly so it's best to use a fruit or chocolate cake if you want to bake ahead. The cakes can be made and frozen for 3 months. The monograms can be prepared at least a month ahead; store them in an airtight container between layers of parchment paper. Position the monograms up to half a day before they're needed. Personalize the cupcakes to suit the occasion — there are lots of similar edible images available at cake decorating shops and online. Make sure you cover the tops of the cakes with the ganache to keep the cakes as fresh as possible. The ganache will keep them sealed and fresh for a day or two. Once completed, the cakes should be stored in a cool or air-conditioned room.

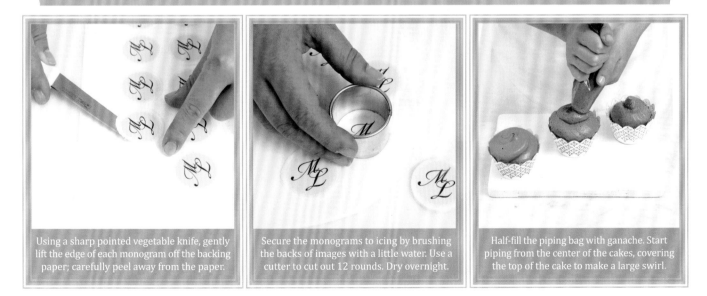

Using a sharp pointed vegetable knife, gently lift the edge of each monogram off the backing paper; carefully peel away from the paper.

Secure the monograms to icing by brushing the backs of images with a little water. Use a cutter to cut out 12 rounds. Dry overnight.

Half-fill the piping bag with ganache. Start piping from the center of the cakes, covering the top of the cake to make a large swirl.

BROWNIE & BLONDIE
Mini Wedding Cakes

THESE MINIATURE WEDDING CAKES WOULD MAKE A LOVELY GIFT TO HAND AROUND TO FRIENDS AT A BRIDAL SHOWER OR ENGAGEMENT PARTY.

EQUIPMENT
2 (9½-inch x 13-inch) baking pans
2-inch round cutter
1½-inch round cutter
1-inch round cutter
paper piping bag (page 221)
DARK CHOCOLATE BROWNIE
9 ounces semi-sweet chocolate
1½ sticks (¾ cup) butter
¼ cup cocoa powder
1 cup firmly packed light brown sugar
¾ cup superfine sugar
2 teaspoons vanilla extract
4 eggs
1½ cups all-purpose flour
WHITE CHOCOLATE BLONDIE
9 ounces white chocolate
1½ sticks (¾ cup) butter
1 cup superfine sugar
3 eggs
1¼ cups all-purpose flour
⅔ cup self-rising flour
DECORATIONS
½ quantity dark chocolate ganache (page 210)
2 tablespoons confectioners' sugar
½ teaspoon edible silver glitter

1 Preheat oven to 300°F. Grease baking pans; line base and long sides with parchment paper.
2 Make dark chocolate brownie and white chocolate blondie.
3 Turn blondie and brownie onto board, trim all sides of both cakes.
4 Using all of the cutters, cut out 12 rounds of each size from both the brownie and the blondie.
5 Make three-tier stacks, alternating rounds of brownies and blondies; securing each tier with ganache.
6 Dust stacks with combined sifted confectioners' sugar and glitter before serving.

dark chocolate brownie Break chocolate into medium saucepan, add chopped butter and sifted cocoa; stir over low heat until smooth. Cool until just warmed; whisk in sugars, extract, eggs and sifted flour. Spread mixture into one baking pan. Bake about 35 minutes. Cool in pan.

white chocolate blondie Break chocolate into medium saucepan, add chopped butter; stir over low heat until smooth. Cool until just warmed; whisk in sugar, eggs and sifted flours. Spread mixture into second baking pan. Bake about 35 minutes. Cool in pan.

makes 24
tips The completed cakes will keep for about 3 days in an airtight container at a cool room temperature, or keep them in the fridge if the weather is hot. The cakes can also be frozen for a month. Dust the cakes with sifted confectioners' sugar and glitter just before serving.

Turn brownie onto a cutting board. Using a long, sharp serrated knife, trim all sides of brownie. Repeat step with the blondie.

Using all 3 of the different-sized round cutters, cut out 12 rounds of each size from both the brownie and the blondie.

Make three-tier stacks, alternating rounds of brownie and blondie. Pipe a dab of chocolate ganache onto tiers to secure.

We decided to use cake mixes just for fun – the cake will keep and cut well and has a fine texture. If you want to make your own cake from scratch, we suggest the deep 10-inch round butter cake recipe on page 190. One quantity of this recipe will be equivalent in volume to one standard cake mix.

POLKA DOTS
and Stripes

WHAT A FUN CAKE THIS IS TO HAVE AT A PARTY – A BURST OF COLOR ON THE INSIDE AND POLKA DOTS ON THE OUTSIDE. THE DOTS WILL ALSO HIDE ANY IMPERFECTIONS ON THE ICING, SO IT'S A GREAT FIRST-TIME CAKE.

EQUIPMENT
10-inch round cake pans
14-inch round wooden cake board (page 208)
smoothing tools
¾-inch, ¾-inch and ½-inch round cutters
fine artist's paint brush
CAKE
4 (15-ounce) boxes butter cake mix
yellow, pink, purple and green food colorings
DECORATIONS
4 quantities white chocolate ganache (page 210)
1½ pounds ready-to-use white fondant
cornstarch

1 Preheat oven to 350°F. Grease cake pans; line base with parchment paper.
2 Make one cake mix according to package directions. Tint mixture with yellow coloring, spread into pan, bake cake about 30 minutes. Stand cake in pan 5 minutes; turn top-side up onto wire rack to cool. Repeat with remaining cake mixes and pink, purple and green coloring. Trim cakes level (page 209), if necessary.
3 Secure one cake to board with a little ganache; top with remaining cakes using about ½ cup of the ganache between each layer. Spread cake evenly all over with remaining ganache (page 210).
4 Knead 1¼ pounds ready-to-use fondant on surface dusted with a little cornstarch until fondant loses its stickiness. Roll fondant on cornstarched surface until large

enough to cover cake. Using rolling pin, lift the fondant onto cake; smooth with hands then smoothing tools. Trim fondant neatly around base of cake.
5 Knead remaining fondant on surface dusted with cornstarch until smooth. Divide into 4 equal portions; color pale pink, green, mauve and yellow. Keep each enclosed in plastic wrap while not using. Roll one color out to ¹⁄₁₆-inch thick. Using cutters, cut rounds from fondant, re-rolling fondant as necessary. Repeat with remaining fondant. Brush backs of dots sparingly with water; position dots on cake. Cut some dots in half to decorate around bottom of cake. Dry cake overnight.

tips We used the end of a ½-inch piping tube to cut out the smallest dots.

Using all 3 cutters, cut out rounds from all 4 colors of fondant. Keep the fondant you're not using airtight by wrapping in plastic wrap.

Brush backs of dots lightly with water and randomly position on cake. Don't use too much water or the dots will slip and slide off.

Position half-dots around base of the cake. Position the dots before they dry so they will more readily take on the contour of the cake.

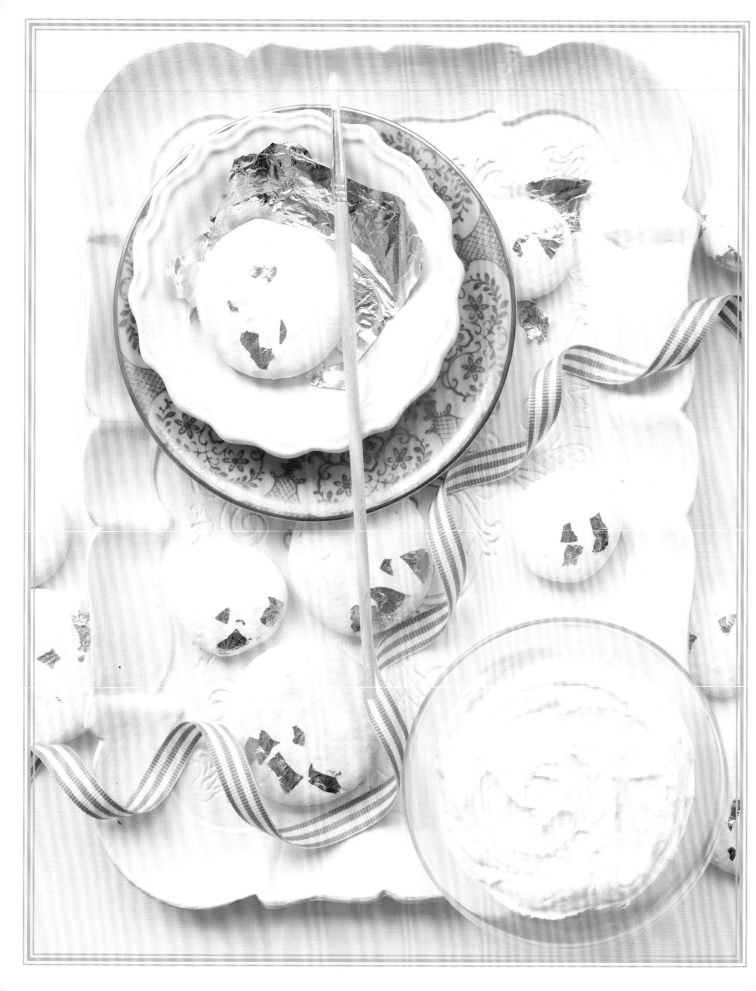

TOWER OF
Golden Macaroons

THIS CONTEMPORARY TOWER CAKE WOULD MAKE A STYLISH WEDDING OR
ENGAGEMENT CAKE – AND THE GOLD LEAF ADDS A TOUCH OF ELEGANCE.

EQUIPMENT
baking sheets
large piping bag
¾-inch plain piping tube
10-inch deep croquembouche
    mold (7¼-inch diameter)
medium-sized ice-cream scoop
10-inch round wooden cake board
    (page 208)
wooden skewer
MACAROONS
6 egg whites
½ cup superfine sugar
2½ cups confectioners' sugar
¼ cup ground almonds
2½ cups desiccated coconut
CAKE
deep 12-inch square coconut cake
    (page 196)
DECORATIONS
2 quantities white chocolate
    ganache (page 210), whipped
gold leaf

1 Grease baking sheets; line with parchment paper.

2 To make macaroons, beat egg whites and superfine sugar in medium bowl with electric mixer until soft peaks form and sugar is dissolved.

3 Meanwhile, blend or process confectioners' sugar, ground almonds and coconut until fine and powdery. Sift through fine strainer; discard solids in strainer.

4 Transfer egg white mixture into large bowl. Fold in almond mixture in two batches.

5 Fit large piping bag with tube. Fill bag with macaroon mixture. Pipe 50 ¾-inch rounds about ¾-inch apart onto trays. Pipe 50 1½-inch rounds about ¾-inch apart onto trays. Pipe 50 1¾-inch rounds about ¾-inch apart onto trays. Refill bag with macaroon mixture as needed. Tap trays on countertop so macaroons spread slightly. Stand macaroons for about 1 hour or until they feel dry to touch.

6 Preheat oven to 250°F.

7 Bake small macaroons, in batches, about 15 minutes. Cool on trays. Bake remaining macaroons, in batches, about 20 minutes. Cool on trays.

8 Line inside the croquembouche mold with plastic wrap.

9 Cut a 2-inch and a 6¾-inch round from the coconut cake. Place the small round of cake inside croquembouche mold. Use the ice-cream scoop to scoop rounds of cake; chop remaining cake coarsely.

10 Using half the ganache, pack the mold with a random mix of cake and dollops of ganache. Top with the large round of cake; press down firmly. Refrigerate tower for 3 hours or overnight until firm.

11 Secure cake tower to board with a little ganache (page 210); remove the croquembouche mold. Remove plastic wrap; spread tower all over with remaining ganache.

12 Using skewer, gently push small pieces of gold leaf onto macaroons. Gently press large macaroons around bottom of the cake, followed by the medium macaroons, then the small macaroons at the top.

tips If you prefer, make the macaroons in 2 or 3 batches – base the proportions on 2 or 3 egg whites (either a third or half of the recipe ingredients) and use a small bowl for beating the egg whites and sugar mixture. Ovens are often inaccurate at low temperatures, so reduce the oven temperature if the macaroons are browning. The tower of cake can be made at least a week ahead, and frozen or refrigerated. The ganache coating and macaroons should be positioned on the day of serving.

Gold leaf is delicate and requires patience to handle, but the results are worth the effort. The coconut cake can be kept at room temperature in an airtight container for a week or frozen for up to 2 months. Choose the best macaroons for the tower. Leftovers will keep in an airtight container at room temperature for at least a week, or can be frozen for about 6 weeks.

Although this tower of macaroons is easy to make – it is time consuming. However, the cake and macaroons can be made well ahead of when the tower is needed. Make sure you have room in the fridge for the cake to set. You need to make about 150 macaroons (we made extra in case of breakages), so it is probably easier to make them in 2-3 batches – make sure you have plenty of baking sheets. Draw circles the size of the macaroons onto the back of the parchment paper to use as a guide when piping the rounds.

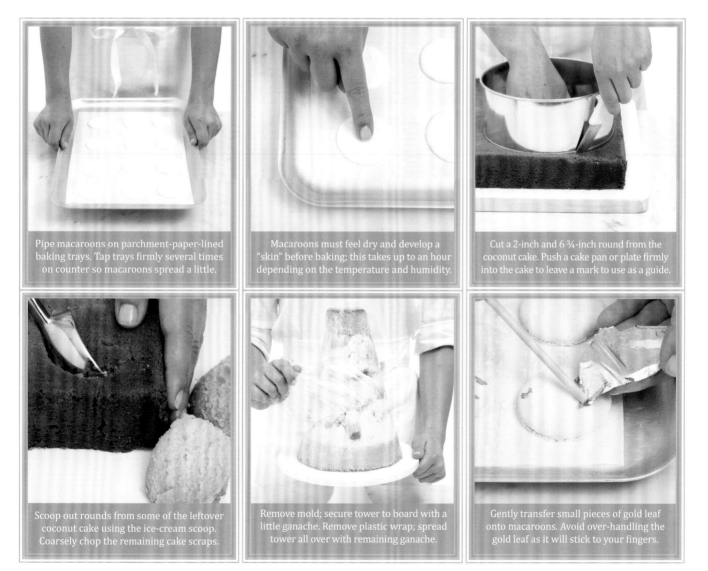

Pipe macaroons on parchment-paper-lined baking trays. Tap trays firmly several times on counter so macaroons spread a little.

Macaroons must feel dry and develop a "skin" before baking; this takes up to an hour depending on the temperature and humidity.

Cut a 2-inch and 6 ¾-inch round from the coconut cake. Push a cake pan or plate firmly into the cake to leave a mark to use as a guide.

Scoop out rounds from some of the leftover coconut cake using the ice-cream scoop. Coarsely chop the remaining cake scraps.

Remove mold; secure tower to board with a little ganache. Remove plastic wrap; spread tower all over with remaining ganache.

Gently transfer small pieces of gold leaf onto macaroons. Avoid over-handling the gold leaf as it will stick to your fingers.

BRIGHT LITTLE
Jelly Bean Cakes

THESE QUIRKY LITTLE CAKES ARE SO EASY TO MAKE, AND ARE IDEAL FOR KIDS'
PARTIES AND BABY SHOWERS. MIX AND MATCH THE COLORS AND FLAVORS
OF THE JELLY BEANS AND THE BUTTER CREAM TO SUIT THE OCCASION.

EQUIPMENT
2 (4-inch) round cardboard cake
  boards (page 208)
4-inch round wooden cake board
  (page 208)
2 (4¾-inch) round wooden cake
  boards (page 208)
6 wooden skewers
CAKE
3 (deep 4-inch) round cakes of
  choice (page 190)
2 (deep 5-inch)round cakes of
  choice (page 190)
DECORATIONS
2 quantities butter cream (page 218)
pink, green and yellow food
  coloring
6 ounces jelly beans,
  approximately, in colors to
  match butter cream

1   Divide butter cream evenly into
three medium bowls; tint pink, green
and yellow.
2   Trim cakes (page 209). Secure two
4-inch cakes to the 4-inch cardboards
with a little butter cream (page 209).
Secure the remaining 4-inch cake to
the 4-inch wooden board. Secure the
two 4¾-inch cakes to the 4¾-inch
boards.
3   Push 3 trimmed skewers into both
4¾-inch cakes to support the top
tiers (page 212).
4   Secure the two 4-inch cakes on
the cardboards to the 4¾-inch cakes
(page 212). You will have 2 two-tiered
cakes and 1 one-tier cake.
5   Spread cakes all over with butter
cream. Using picture as a guide,
decorate cakes with jelly beans to
match the colors of the butter cream.

tip   Use ganache instead of butter
cream, if you prefer. Once the cakes
are covered in butter cream or
ganache, they will keep for about a
week at a cool room temperature.
The jelly beans can be placed on the
cakes as soon as the butter cream
has been applied.

Secure two (4-inch) cakes to 4-inch cardboards
with a little butter cream. Secure remaining
4-inch cake to the 4-inch wooden board.

Using a sharp serrated knife, trim skewers
to the height of the cake. Push skewers into
the largest cakes to support the top tiers.

Once all cakes are on boards, secure two
of the smaller cakes onto the larger cakes
with a little of the butter cream.

EMBOSSED
Lace Cupcakes

DISPLAY THESE ELEGANT LITTLE CAKES ON A CAKE STAND TO SHOW THEM OFF.
WE USED PATTERNED CUPCAKE WRAPPERS TO HIDE THE PLAIN PAPER LINERS.

EQUIPMENT
12 plain white paper liners
texture-embossing mat
2¾-inch round cutter
new large soft-bristled brush
CAKE
1 quantity cupcake mixture of
choice (page 190)
DECORATIONS
1 quantity white chocolate
ganache (page 210)
1 pound ready-to-use white
fondant
cornstarch
12 fancy cupcake wrappers
food-grade white shimmer

1 Divide cupcake mixture into paper liners; bake cupcakes according to recipe. Stand cakes in pan 5 minutes; turn top-side up onto wire rack to cool.
2 Spread tops of cakes evenly all over with ganache.
3 Knead ready-to-use fondant on surface dusted with a little cornstarch until fondant loses its stickiness. Roll fondant on cornstarched surface until about ¼-inch thick.
4 Place textured mat on top of the fondant, using a rolling pin, firmly press and roll pattern onto fondant. Carefully remove mat. Using cutter, cut out 12 rounds from fondant; carefully place rounds on cakes without touching the embossed pattern. Knead and re-roll the fondant and cut out more rounds as needed.

5 Carefully place cakes into cupcake wrappers. Dip brush into shimmer; brush lightly over embossed pattern.

makes 12
tips Ensure you have enough cakes for all the guests. If you like, choose a few different cake recipes, so you get a variety of cakes. The ganache and ready-to-use fondant covering will keep the cakes fresh for a few days in a cool or air-conditioned room. Apply the shimmer to the fondant a few hours before serving; a soft-bristled make-up brush is ideal for doing this.

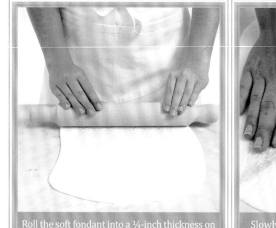

Roll the soft fondant into a ¼-inch thickness on a cornstarched surface. Use rolling pin to press textured mat into fondant to make pattern.

Slowly and carefully remove the textured mat from the patterned fondant to prevent tearing and damaging the embossed pattern.

Cut out rounds from the embossed fondant; carefully position on ganache-topped cakes to prevent marking the pattern.

PINK VELVET
Macaron Cake

PINK VELVET
Macaron Cake

YOU CAN MAKE YOUR OWN, BUT THESE STORE-BOUGHT MACARONS ARE JUST
LIKE HOMEMADE, SO NO-ONE WILL SUSPECT YOU DIDN'T MAKE THEM YOURSELF.
NONE OF THE HARD WORK, YET ALL OF THE COMPLIMENTS – IT'S A REAL WINNER.

EQUIPMENT
deep 9-inch round cake pan
deep 6-inch round cake pan
12-inch round wooden cake board
     (page 208)
6-inch round wooden cake board
     (page 208)
medium offset metal spatula
3 wooden skewers
CAKE
2 sticks (1 cup) butter
4 eggs
2 teaspoons vanilla extract
3 cups superfine sugar
3 cups all-purpose flour
⅓ cup cornstarch
⅓ cup cocoa powder
2 cups buttermilk
2 tablespoons pink food coloring
2 teaspoons white vinegar
2 teaspoons baking soda
CREAM CHEESE FROSTING
1½ sticks (¾ cup) butter
1 pound cream cheese
2 tablespoons strained lemon juice
9 cups confectioners' sugar
DECORATIONS
3 (3½ ounce) packages small
     french macarons

1 Have butter and eggs at room
temperature for cake.
2 Preheat oven to 350°F. Grease and
line cake pans (page 206).
3 To make cake, beat butter, eggs,
extract and sugar in small bowl with
electric mixer until mixture is light
and fluffy. Transfer mixture to large
bowl; stir in sifted flour, cornstarch
and cocoa, and combined buttermilk
and coloring in two batches.
4 Combine vinegar and soda in
small bowl; allow to fizz, then fold
into cake mixture. Divide mixture
between pans. Bake large cake about
1 hour 20 minutes and small cake
about 1 hour.
5 Stand cakes in pans 10 minutes;
turn top-side up onto wire racks to
cool. Wrap cooled cakes in plastic
wrap, freeze about 40 minutes or
until cakes are firm.
6 Make cream cheese frosting.
7 Trim cakes (page 209). Split large
cake into three even layers. Secure
one layer to largest board with a little
frosting. Top with remaining layers
using about ¼ cup of the frosting
between each layer.
8 Split smaller cake into three even
layers. Secure one layer to small board
with a little frosting. Top with the
remaining layers using about ¼ cup of
the frosting between each layer. Use
spatula to spread remaining frosting
over top and sides of both cakes.

9 Push trimmed skewers into large
cake to support the top tier (page 212).
Position small cake on large cake.
Smooth frosting with spatula.
10 Gently twist each macaron to
separate into two halves (or carefully
cut with a small sharp knife if they're
firmly stuck); press the macaron
halves around the sides of both
cakes before the frosting sets.

cream cheese frosting Have butter
and cream cheese at room temperature.
Beat butter, cream cheese and juice
in large bowl with electric mixer
until light and fluffy. Gradually beat
in sifted confectioners' sugar until
frosting is smooth.

tips We bought packaged macarons
from a supermarket (they are available
from the refrigerated part of the
bakery section), but you can make
your own (see page 30, *Tower of
Golden Macaroons* and halve the
recipe); you need about 70 single
macaroons. Homemade macaroons
will keep well in the freezer for about
2 months. This cake freezes well, filled
or unfilled. It's at its best assembled
on the day of serving.

THE COMBINATION OF THIS LUSCIOUS CAKE WITH THE LIGHT SWEET CRUNCH OF THE
MACARONS IS A REAL WINNER. USE THE CAKE FOR A SPECIAL OCCASION DESSERT –
A BIRTHDAY, OR WHEREVER GLAMOUR AND FLAVOR ARE REQUIRED TO IMPRESS.

To make frosting, have the cream cheese and butter at room temperature. Beat butter, cream cheese and lemon juice until combined.

Gradually beat in the sifted confectioners' sugar until the frosting is smooth. Scrape down the sides of the bowl to incorporate all the icing sugar.

Wrap the cakes in plastic wrap and freeze for about 40 minutes or until the cakes are firm. Split each cake into three even layers.

Using a spatula, spread the frosting evenly all over the top and sides of cakes. Smooth frosting after positioning the smaller cake.

Gently twist macarons to separate into two halves or, if they're firmly stuck, carefully cut through the center with a small sharp knife.

Gently press the macaron halves around the sides of both cakes. Arrange the macarons in any color combination you like.

LEMON
Meringue Cupcakes

WHILE IMPRESSIVE AT ANY CELEBRATION, THESE CUTE LITTLE CAKES WOULD LOOK
STRIKING AT A BABY SHOWER. THEY LOOK SPECTACULAR ON A CUPCAKE STAND.

EQUIPMENT
12 straight-sided fancy paper liners
baking tray
large piping bag
¾-inch plain piping tube
craft glue
CAKE
1 quantity cupcake mixture of choice (page 190)
MERINGUES
2 egg whites
½ cup superfine sugar
lemon yellow food coloring
DECORATIONS
1 cup lemon curd
3 yards narrow ribbon

1   Divide cupcake mixture into paper
liners; bake cupcakes according to
recipe. Stand cakes in pan 5 minutes;
turn top-side up onto wire rack to cool.
2   Reduce oven temperature to
200°F. Grease and line baking tray
with parchment paper (see tips).
3   To make meringues, beat egg
whites and sugar in small bowl with
electric mixer until sugar is dissolved
and mixture is thick and glossy. Tint
meringue pale yellow.
4   Fit piping bag with tube, Fill
bag ½-full with meringue; pipe
12 meringues, with bases 2 inches
wide, onto baking tray, about 2 inches
apart, refilling bag as necessary. Bake
meringues about 45 minutes or until
dry to touch. Cool in oven with door ajar.
5   Trim tops from cakes so the
tops are flat and ½ inch below the

top of the paper liners. Spread one
tablespoon of curd over each cake to
completely cover the surface of the
cake. Top cakes with meringues.
6   Position a length of ribbon around
each cake; secure ends with glue. Use
ribbon to make bows (page 226);
secure over joins with glue.

makes 12

tips Use a 2-inch round cutter to
draw circles on parchment paper
about 2 inches apart. Turn the paper
over and use circles as a guide to pipe
the meringues. Cakes can be frozen
for up to 3 months. Meringues can be
made a week ahead and stored in
an airtight container at a cool room
temperature. Assemble the cakes up
to a day before needed.

Pipe meringues onto tray. If you like, draw
2-inch circles, 2 inches apart, on the parchment
paper as a guide; turn paper over before piping.

Trim tops from the cakes so they are about
½-inch below the top of the paper liners to
make room for the curd and meringue.

Using craft glue, secure a length of ribbon
around the cakes. Cover the ribbon ends
with small bows secured with glue.

MANGO ROSE
Cheesecakes

EVERYBODY LOVES THEIR OWN INDIVIDUAL DESSERT – HERE, THE TROPICAL FLAVORS BLEND HAPPILY WITH THE CREAMY CHEESECAKE FILLING. THE MANGO ROSE PATTERN IS SIMPLE TO ACHIEVE, BUT LOOKS IMPRESSIVE ON THE CHEESECAKES.

EQUIPMENT
4 (4-inch) springform pans
CHEESECAKE
8 ounces cream cheese
1 (14½ ounce) unfilled store-bought sponge cake (5¼-inch x 7¼-inch)
1 teaspoon powdered gelatin
2 tablespoons lime juice
2 teaspoons finely grated lime rind
¼ cup superfine sugar
1 cup cream
DECORATION
2 medium firm ripe mangoes

1   Have cream cheese at room temperature.
2   Split sponge cake into two even layers. Using base of one springform pan as a guide, cut out four rounds of cake. Use scraps of cake to patch and complete rounds, as necessary.
3   Line base and sides of springform pans with parchment paper. Place cake rounds into pans.
4   To make cheesecake: Sprinkle gelatin over juice in small heatproof bowl. Stand 5 minutes then place bowl in small saucepan of simmering water, stir until gelatin is dissolved. Cool 5 minutes.
5   Beat cream cheese, rind and sugar in small bowl with electric mixer until smooth; beat in cream. Stir in gelatin mixture.

6   Divide cream cheese mixture evenly between pans; level tops. Refrigerate overnight.
7   Remove cheesecakes from pans, place on serving plates. Slice mango into ⅛-inch thick slices. Starting from the center of each cheesecake, and using small pieces of mango first, arrange slices into a rose shape.

makes 4

tips We used a plain store-bought sponge cake for this recipe; you can make your own, if you like. Grate the rind from the lime before juicing it. The cheesecakes are at their best made one day ahead; keep refrigerated.

Using base of the springform pan, cut out two cake rounds close to the edge. Use scraps to complete second cake round.

You need mangoes that are ripe, but firm enough to slice thinly. Peel mangoes, remove cheeks from seed, and then slice the cheeks.

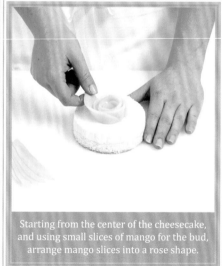

Starting from the center of the cheesecake, and using small slices of mango for the bud, arrange mango slices into a rose shape.

COCONUT DREAM
Cream Cake

THIS IS AN EASY CAKE TO MAKE AND DECORATE – USE ANY CAKE YOU LIKE –
WE PREFER A WHITE CHOCOLATE OR COCONUT CAKE. WHICHEVER TYPE YOU
CHOOSE, THE CAKE WILL BE HEAVY TO MOVE AND LIFT, SO GET SOMEONE TO HELP.

EQUIPMENT
18-inch round wooden cake board
  (page 208)
10-inch round wooden cake board
  (page 208)
8-inch round wooden cake board
  (page 208)
6-inch round wooden cake board
  (page 208)
4-inch round wooden cake board
  (page 208)
12 wooden skewers
small offset metal spatula
CAKE
deep 12-inch round cake of choice
  (page 190)
deep 10-inch round cake of choice
  (page 190)
deep 8-inch round cake of choice
  (page 190)

deep 6-inch round cake of choice
  (page 190)
deep 4-inch round cake of choice
  (page 190)
DECORATIONS
3 quantities white chocolate
  ganache (page 210)
white food coloring
3½ pounds ball-shaped coconut
  chocolates

1 Trim cakes (page 209). Secure
largest cake to the largest board
(page 209). Secure the remaining
cakes to the same-sized boards.
2 Push 3 trimmed skewers into
center of each cake except the
smallest cake to support the next
tier (page 212).

3 Assemble cakes, securing each tier
to the tier below (page 212).
4 Beat ganache in large bowl with
electric mixer. Beat in enough white
coloring to match the color of the
ganache to the coconut chocolates.
Spread cake all over with ganache.
5 Cut chocolates in half, press
cut-sides around each cake, starting
at the bottom of the largest cake.

tips The cake can be completed a day
ahead. It will be fine kept in a cool
or air-conditioned room. Instead of
making the ganache, you could buy
3 (1 pound each) tubs of vanilla
frosting to cover this cake.

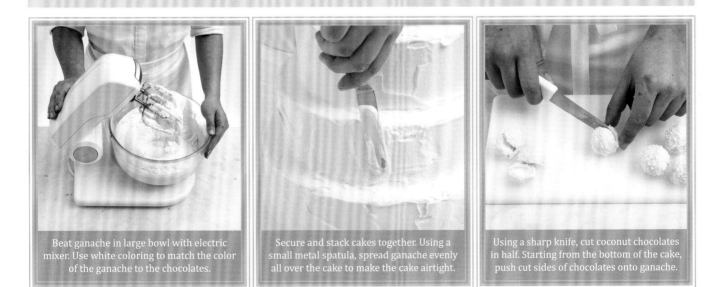

Beat ganache in large bowl with electric mixer. Use white coloring to match the color of the ganache to the chocolates.

Secure and stack cakes together. Using a small metal spatula, spread ganache evenly all over the cake to make the cake airtight.

Using a sharp knife, cut coconut chocolates in half. Starting from the bottom of the cake, push cut sides of chocolates onto ganache.

COCONUT
Ruffle Cake

"SIMPLY STUNNING" BEST DESCRIBES THIS DREAMY CAKE. THE COCONUT
RESEMBLES THE FRILL, OR FLOUNCE, FOUND ON TRADITIONAL WEDDING GOWNS.

EQUIPMENT
**16-inch round wooden cake board
(page 208)**
**12-inch round wooden cake board
(page 208)**
**10-inch round wooden cake board
(page 208)**
**8-inch round wooden cake board
(page 208)**
**6-inch round wooden cake board
(page 208)**
12 wooden skewers
medium offset metal spatula
CAKE
**deep 14-inch round cake of choice
(page 190)**
**deep 12-inch round cake of choice
(page 190)**
**deep 10-inch round cake of choice
(page 190)**
**deep 8-inch round cake of choice
(page 190)**
**deep 6-inch round cake of choice
(page 190)**

DECORATIONS
**5 quantities white chocolate
ganache (page 210)**
white food coloring
2 pounds flaked coconut

1   Trim cakes (page 209). Secure
largest cake to largest board with a
little ganache (page 209). Secure the
remaining cakes to same-sized boards.
2   Push 3 trimmed skewers into
centers of all cakes except the
smallest cake to support the next
tier (page 212).
3   Assemble cake, securing each
tier to the tier below (page 212).
4   Place half the ganache in a large
bowl; whisk in at least 1 tablespoon
of white coloring until the ganache is
as white as possible. Beat ganache
with an electric mixer until light and
fluffy. Repeat with remaining ganache.

5   Spread cake all over with ganache.
Gently press handfuls of the flaked
coconut all over the cake.

tips We used flaked coconut labelled
"coconut chipped" found in health
food stores. Instead of making the
ganache you could buy 5 (1 pound
each) tubs of vanilla frosting to cover
this cake. This cake can be assembled
completely a week before it's
required; It will be fine kept in a cool
or air-conditioned room. Use any
cake recipe you like – our favorite is
the coconut cake (page 196). This five
tier cake is very heavy to move and
lift, so get someone to help you.

Place half the ganache in a large bowl. Whisk
at least 1 tablespoon of food coloring into
the ganache to whiten it as much as possible.

Beat half the ganache at a time in large bowl
with electric mixer until light and fluffy,
scrape down side of bowl during beating.

Once the cake is covered with the ganache,
firmly press handfuls of coconut all over
the cake. Choose long flakes for the top tier.

HEARTS AND
Bows Forever

HEARTS AND BOWS ARE PERFECT TOGETHER. THIS CAKE COULD BE USED FOR A BIRTHDAY, WEDDING OR, FOR A SENTIMENTAL OPTION, VALENTINE'S DAY – THINK WHITE CAKE, RED HEARTS AND RED RIBBON – SO ROMANTIC.

EQUIPMENT
1¼-inch heart cutter
9-inch round wooden cake board (page 208)
small offset metal spatula
CAKE
2 deep (7-inch) round cakes of choice (page 190)
DECORATIONS
4½ ounces ready-to-use white fondant
cornstarch
yellow food coloring
1½ quantities white chocolate ganache (page 210)
1 yard wide ribbon

1   Knead ready-to-use fondant on surface dusted with a little cornstarch until fondant loses its stickiness. Tint fondant yellow with coloring. Roll fondant out on cornstarched surface into ⅛-inch thickness.

2   Using cutter, cut out about 70 heart shapes from fondant, re-rolling scraps as necessary. Place hearts on parchment-paper-lined tray for about 3 hours, or until hearts are firm, but not dried out or hard.

3   Trim cakes (page 209). Secure one cake to board (page 209); top with remaining cake, joining cakes with a little ganache (page 212).

4   Beat remaining ganache in small bowl with electric mixer until light and fluffy.

5   Using spatula, spread ganache all over cake.

6   Starting from the bottom of the cake, press heart shapes onto ganache in rows before the ganache sets.

7   Just before serving, decorate the top of the cake with a bow made from the ribbon (page 226).

tips If you prefer, use butter cream instead of ganache; both will keep the cake airtight and fresh for at least a week in a cool or air-conditioned room.

Cut out 70 heart shapes from the ready-to-use fondant; place on a parchment-paper-lined tray until firm, but not dried out or hard.

Secure one cake to board; join remaining cake to bottom cake with ganache. Spread cake evenly all over with remaining ganache.

Starting from the bottom of the cake, gently press the heart shapes in rows around the cake. Do this before the ganache sets.

WHITE CHOCOLATE
Rose-Print Cake

INSTEAD OF ONE LARGE CAKE, PLACE SMALLER CAKES RANDOMLY ON THE TABLE; DISPLAY THEM ON STEMMED GLASS CAKE PLATES FOR A CHARMING EFFECT.

EQUIPMENT
3 (4-inch) round cardboard cake boards (page 208)
small offset metal spatula
tape measure
plastic ruler
1¾-inch fluted round cutter
1½-inch fluted round cutter
CAKE
3 (4-inch) round cakes of choice (page 190)
DECORATIONS
1½ quantities white chocolate ganache (page 210)
2 (10-inch x 16-inch) chocolate transfer sheets
1½ pounds white chocolate Melts
2 yards wide ribbon

1 Trim cakes (page 209). Secure cakes to boards (page 209). Using spatula, spread cakes all over using two-thirds of the ganache (page 210).

2 Using tape measure, measure the circumference and height of the cakes and add ½ inch to each measurement. Using sharp knife and ruler, cut 3 rectangles from the transfer sheets using these measurements. Reserve any leftover transfer sheet.
3 Melt chocolate in medium bowl over medium saucepan of simmering water (don't allow water to touch base of bowl). Place one cut transfer sheet, print-side up, on a clean surface. Using spatula, spread sheet with one-third of the melted chocolate. Chocolate should be ⅛-inch thick to make it easy to handle. Leave chocolate to set for a few minutes, then carefully pick up transfer sheet and move to a sheet of parchment paper (this neatens the edges). While the chocolate is still wet to the touch, and before the edges have begun to set, carefully pick up the top two corners and wrap the transfer sheet around one

cake, chocolate-side in. Repeat with the remaining transfer sheets, chocolate and cakes. Stand 20 minutes then remove the backing paper. (To remove the backing paper, start from one top corner and carefully peel paper away.)
4 Spread remaining chocolate over any leftover pieces of transfer sheet; leave to set completely before removing the backing paper. Using both fluted cutters, cut out rounds from sheet. Top cakes with remaining ganache, then chocolate rounds. Tie ribbon around cake, finish with a bow (page 226).

makes 3
tips Cakes can be completed at least a week before required. Store in a cool or air-conditioned room. Position the fluted chocolate rounds on top of the cake on the day of serving.

Using a ruler and sharp knife, cut transfer sheets into 3 rectangles large enough to cover the cake. Reserve any transfer scraps.

Cover cake with chocolate-covered transfer sheet; stand 20 minutes, then carefully and gently peel backing paper away from transfer.

Coat transfer sheet with chocolate; remove backing paper when dry, then use both the fluted cutters to cut rounds from transfers.

You can buy the sponge cakes for this recipe – preferably jam and cream filled. You could also buy a large meringue as well, to break up and use to fill and decorate the cake. In this case, you'll need half the meringue ingredients only, to make the meringue sticks. Meringue sticks can be made a month ahead; store in an airtight container at a cool room temperature. Make the large meringue the day before.

MERINGUE
Cloud Cake

ALMOST EVERYONE LOVES THE COMBINATION OF SPONGE CAKE, MERINGUE,
CREAM AND BERRIES, AND THIS SPECTACULAR DESSERT HAS THEM ALL.

EQUIPMENT
baking trays
medium offset metal spatula
large piping bag
¼-inch plain piping tube
12-inch round wooden cake board
(page 208)
6-inch round wooden cake board
(page 208)
3 wooden skewers
craft glue
MERINGUE
8 egg whites
2 cups superfine sugar
2 tablespoons cornstarch
2 teaspoons white vinegar
CAKE
deep 8-inch round cake of choice
(page 190)
deep 6-inch round cake of choice
(page 190)
DECORATIONS
1¼ cups heavy cream (see tips)
4 ounces fresh raspberries
20 inches wide ribbon

1 Preheat oven to 250°F. Line baking trays with parchment paper. Mark a 7¼-inch circle on one tray; turn paper over. Mark 3¾-inch straight lines (you need about 100) on remaining trays; turn paper over.
2 To make meringue: Beat egg whites in large bowl with electric mixer until soft peaks form; gradually add sugar, beat until dissolved between additions. Beat in sifted cornstarch, and vinegar. Using spatula, spread half the mixture inside circle on tray. Shape sides up and in towards the center.
3 Fit piping bag with tube. Fill bag ½-full with meringue; pipe about 100 (3¾-inch) finger-width meringue sticks, about ¾ inch apart, on remaining baking trays. Refill bag as necessary. Bake large meringue about 1 hour and the sticks about 30 minutes, or until dry to touch. Remove from oven; cool on trays.
4 Beat cream in small bowl with electric mixer until firm peaks form; cover, refrigerate until ready to use.

5 Trim cakes (page 209). Secure large cake to largest board; secure small cake to small board (page 209). Push trimmed skewers into large cake to support top tier (page 212). Secure small cake on top of large cake. Spread cakes all over with cream.
6 Position meringue sticks around sides of both cakes. Scoop out large spoonfuls of meringue; place between the tiers and on the top of small cake.
7 Sprinkle cake with raspberries. Wrap ribbon around large cake, secure ends with glue.

tips It is fine to use just 1 (½ pint) carton of cream for this recipe.
If short on oven space, halve the meringue recipe and make the large meringue and the sticks separately. The cake can be assembled and covered with cream one day ahead; store in the refrigerator. Arrange the meringue sticks and spoonfuls of meringue as close to serving as possible. The meringues will soften in about 1 hour.

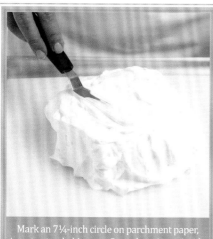

Mark an 7¼-inch circle on parchment paper, invert onto a baking tray. Spread meringue inside the circle, and shape inwards and upwards.

Fit the piping bag with the tube. Pipe finger lengths of meringue, using markings as a guide, onto the baking-paper-covered trays.

Avoiding browned or caramelized meringue, scoop out large tablespoons of soft meringue onto top of cake and around top of large cake.

CHOCOLATE BOX
of Hearts

CHOCOLATE BOX
of Hearts

JUST THE THING FOR A ROMANTIC VALENTINE'S DAY OR ENGAGEMENT PARTY, OR THE PERFECT WAY TO SAY "I LOVE YOU" TO A WONDERFUL MOM ON MOTHER'S DAY.

EQUIPMENT
9-inch round or heart-shaped
    wooden cake board (page 208)
small offset metal spatula
straight-sided metal scraper
paper piping bag (page 221)
cheese slicer
CAKE
1 heart-shaped cake of choice
    (page 190)
DECORATIONS
1 quantity white chocolate ganache
    (page 210) (see step 1)
1 tablespoon instant coffee
    granules
12 ounces white chocolate Melts
6 ounces block white chocolate
15 heart-shaped chocolates,
    approximately
2 yards wide ribbon

1 Make the white chocolate ganache, add coffee granules to the cream while heating; stir until smooth.
2 Trim cake (page 209). Secure cake to board with a little ganache.
3 Use spatula to spread cake all over with ganache until it is about ½-inch thick. Stand cake about 20 minutes or until ganache becomes slightly firmer. Using metal scraper, scrape excess ganache from top and side of cake. Reserve ganache

scrapings in a small bowl; cover with plastic wrap.
4 Using a small knife, cut a ¾-inch deep line right around the cake, ½ inch in from edge of cake. Refrigerate cake 3 hours or overnight.
5 Scoop out cake (with ganache) inside the cut line to make a recess in the cake about ¾-inch deep; discard scrapings. Warm reserved ganache over a small saucepan of simmering water; spread ganache evenly inside the recess (don't fill the recess with the ganache, just use it to cover the base and sides).
6 Trace around base of heart-shaped cake pan onto parchment paper to make a template for the chocolate box lid. Turn paper over onto a flat tray.
7 Melt chocolate Melts in a small heatproof bowl over small saucepan of simmering water (don't let water touch base of bowl). Fill piping bag about ¾ full chocolate, snip end from bag; pipe a thick band of chocolate inside the heart outline. Spread more chocolate in the center of the heart; stand about 10 minutes, or until chocolate is set. Repeat this process using remaining chocolate to

make a thick lid; re-melt chocolate as necessary (page 222).
8 Turn the block of white chocolate upside down; rub your hand over the chocolate to soften slightly. Drag the blade of the cheese slicer over the flat surface of the chocolate to make curls. Position chocolates in box; sprinkle curls between chocolates.
9 Peel paper from back of chocolate lid; tie ribbon around lid, finish with a bow (page 226). Place on top of cake.

tips Ganache will keep the cake airtight for at least a week if stored in a cool or air-conditioned room. A cheese slicer makes curls about 1-inch long; if you don't have one, use a vegetable peeler – it will make smaller curls.

WE USED A WHITE CHOCOLATE CAKE IN THIS RECIPE, AND MADE A
COFFEE-FLAVORED GANACHE TO COMPLEMENT IT AND THE CHOCOLATES,
HOWEVER, A DARK CHOCOLATE HEART CAKE WOULD ALSO LOOK WONDERFUL
FILLED WITH HEART-SHAPED CHOCOLATES IN RED WRAPPERS.

Use a straight-sided metal scraper to smooth the side and top of the heart. Reserve all the ganache scrapings in a small bowl.

Using a small sharp knife, cut a ¾-inch deep line around the cake leaving a ½-inch border. Refrigerate the cake 3 hours or overnight.

Using a large spoon, scoop out the cake and ganache to make a recess in the cake; discard the cake and ganache scraps.

Warm reserved ganache over simmering water until spreadable. Spread ganache evenly over the base and side of the recess.

Pipe melted chocolate around heart outline; evenly spread more melted chocolate in the center of the heart. Repeat to make a thick lid.

Allow chocolate to set at room temperature. Lift the heart from the paper; decorate with a ribbon and bow, place on top of cake.

LAST-MINUTE CAKE
with Fresh Flowers

THIS IS THE EASIEST OF THE TIERED CAKES IN THIS BOOK, BUT THE SIMPLICITY OF THE SNOW-WHITE FROSTING AND BEAUTIFUL FLOWERS MAKE IT AN ELEGANT CAKE.

EQUIPMENT
12-inch round wooden cake board
    (page 208)
8-inch round wooden cake board
    (page 208)
6-inch round wooden cake board
    (page 208)
6 wooden skewers
small offset metal spatula
CAKE
deep 10-inch round cake of choice
    (page 190)
deep 8-inch round cake of choice
    (page 190)
deep 6-inch round cake of choice
    (page 190)
DECORATIONS
2 quantities fluffy frosting
    (page 219) (see tips)
fresh organic flowers
white florist's tape

1 Trim cakes (page 209). Secure large cake to largest board; secure remaining cakes to same-sized boards (page 209).
2 Push 3 trimmed skewers into center of large and medium cakes to support the top tiers (page 212). Secure medium cake on top of large cake; secure small cake on top of medium cake (page 212).
3 Make fluffy frosting.
4 Working quickly, spread frosting all over cake.
5 Trim then wrap flower stems in florist's tape. Position flowers on top of cake.

tips Make the frosting after you have stacked and secured the cakes; you need to work quickly once the frosting is ready as it sets quickly. This frosting colors beautifully if you want a pastel-colored cake to fit in with the color theme of your event. The cakes can be frosted one day ahead, however, the frosting loses its sheen once it has set. The flowers should be prepared and placed on the day of serving.

Beat the fluffy frosting in a small bowl with an electric mixer until it is thick, spreadable and almost cooled to room temperature.

Make sure you're ready to spread the frosting onto the cake as soon as it's ready; you need to work quickly before the frosting sets.

On the day of serving, trim flower stems to lie neatly on top of the cake. Wrap stems in florist's tape; position flowers on top of cake.

Now that you've mastered the Easy chapter, it's time to move on and conquer the fear of rolling out ready-to-use fondant, and of piping. Only a little practice is required to make your efforts look really great. You will be amazed at how quickly you will become proficient in these crafts.

CHAPTER TWO

EXPERIENCED

HEAVENLY HYDRANGEA
Cupcakes

EQUIPMENT
12 plain white paper liners
¾-inch 4-petal blossom cutter
vinyl mat
flower mat
small ball tool
4 paper piping bags (page 221)
fine artist's paint brush
2¼-inch round cutter
CAKE
**1 quantity cupcake mixture of
    choice (page 190)**
DECORATIONS
**3 pounds ready-to-use white
    fondant**
cornstarch
**pink, purple and blue food
    colorings**
1 quantity royal icing (page 220)
pink, green and purple petal dust
**1 quantity ganache of choice
    (page 210)**
12 fancy white paper wrappers

1 Divide cupcake mixture into paper liners; bake cupcakes according to recipe. Stand cakes in pan 5 minutes; turn top-side up onto wire rack to cool.

2 Knead ready-to-use fondant on surface dusted with a little cornstarch until fondant loses its stickiness.

3 Divide fondant into 4 portions. Tint 3 portions shades of blues, pinks and purples; leave remaining portion white. Enclose each in plastic wrap. (Each portion is enough to make 3 cupcakes; you need to make about 14 blossoms for each cupcake.)

4 To make blossoms: Working with one color fondant at a time, roll small portions of fondant on cornstarched surface into ⅛-inch thickness. Using blossom cutter, cut 5 blossoms at a time; cover remaining icing with vinyl mat.

5 Place blossoms on flower mat; using small end of ball tool, roll tool in center of each petal to round and thin the petals. Stand overnight on parchment paper to dry. Repeat with remaining fondant. Re-roll scraps with remaining fondant of same color; reserve, covered with plastic wrap.

6 Divide royal icing into 4 small bowls. Color 3 portions to match colors of blossoms; leave remaining portion white. Cover surface with plastic wrap to keep airtight.

7 Fill each piping bag ½ full with one colored icing, pipe same-colored

dots into centers of blossoms; allow to dry overnight. Reserve all royal icing; cover surface to keep airtight.

8 Mix equal amounts of petal dusts and cornstarch to complement colors of blossoms. Brush dust lightly into centers of blossoms.

9 Spread ganache over cupcakes. Roll out one of the reserved colors of ready-to-use fondant on cornstarched surface into ⅛-inch thickness. Use round cutter to cut out 3 rounds of fondant, position over ganache. Place cakes in fancy wrappers. Repeat with the remaining colors.

10 Secure blossoms to same-colored fondant rounds on cupcakes to resemble hydrangeas using leftover royal icing.

makes 12

tips The blossoms can be completed months ahead. Keep in an airtight container at room temperature. Assemble cakes up to a day before. Use a fruit or chocolate cake for best results if baking ahead.

Cut out several blossoms at a time; place on flower mat. Use ball tool to shape and thin the petals of each blossom; dry overnight.

Pipe centers into blossoms with royal icing; leave to dry. Brush combined petal dust and cornstarch over the centers of the blossoms.

Spread tops of cupcakes with ganache. Top cupcakes with rounds of ready-to-use fondant to seal the cakes as much as possible.

AUTUMN
Leaves

THE AUTUMNAL COLORS OF THIS CAKE AND ITS LEAVES ARE SO SYMBOLIC OF THE SEASON. WE USED LEAVES FROM A JAPANESE MAPLE TREE BECAUSE OF THEIR WONDERFUL SHAPES AND COLORS, AND THEIR LACK OF TOXIC CHEMICALS.

EQUIPMENT
14-inch round wooden cake board (page 208)
8-inch round wooden cake board (page 208)
6-inch round wooden cake board (page 208)
smoothing tools
6 wooden skewers
paper piping bag (page 221)

CAKE
deep 10-inch round cake of choice (page 190)
deep 8-inch round cake of choice (page 190)
deep 6-inch round cake of choice (page 190)

DECORATIONS
2¾ pounds ready-to-use white fondant
cornstarch
orange and brown food colorings
1 quantity royal icing (page 220)
freshly picked organic leaves (see tips)
2 yards narrow ribbon

1 Trim cakes (page 209). Secure large cake to largest board; secure remaining cakes to the same-sized boards (page 209). Prepare cakes for covering with ready-to-use fondant (page 209).

2 Knead ready-to-use fondant on surface dusted with a little cornstarch until fondant loses its stickiness. Divide fondant into three portions: 8 ounces, 1 pound and 1¼ pounds.

3 Use both colorings to tint all the fondant three different autumnal shades. Color the largest portion the darkest, the middle portion the palest and the smallest portion a medium shade.

4 Roll the largest portion of fondant on cornstarched surface until large enough to cover largest cake. Using rolling pin, lift fondant onto cake; smooth with hands then smoothing tools. Trim fondant neatly around base of cake. Use medium portion of fondant to cover medium cake in the same way as the large cake. Use remaining fondant to cover small cake in the same way. Dry cakes overnight.

5 Push 3 trimmed skewers into centers of large and medium cakes to support the next tier (page 212).

6 Assemble cakes, securing each tier to the tier below (page 212).

7 Divide royal icing into 3 bowls; tint with colorings to match cakes. Fill piping bag ½ full with icing; pipe around base of same-colored cake. Use fingertip to blend icing into any gaps where cakes join the boards (page 212). Dry cakes overnight.

8 Wash leaves carefully in cold water; leave to dry on kitchen paper.

9 Wrap and secure ribbon around base of each tier with a dot of royal icing. Pipe dots of icing onto backs of leaves; position leaves on cake.

tips If you choose leaves other than the Japanese maple, check they're organic and free from toxins. Wash, dry and position leaves as close to serving time as possible (4 hours ahead is fine). Use small dried leaves, if you prefer.

Gently wash trimmed leaves in cold water; shake off excess water. Place the leaves on paper towels; leave until dry.

Measure around each cake, cut ribbon into corresponding lengths. Position ribbon around cakes; join ends with royal icing.

Position the leaves on the cake. Use royal icing to pipe tiny dots of icing onto the back of the leaves to secure to the cake.

CHOCOLATE &
Ivory Hearts Cake

EQUIPMENT
3¾-inch heart cutter
8-inch 18-gauge floral wire
wire cutters
14-inch round wooden cake board (page 208)
8-inch round wooden cake board (page 208)
6-inch round wooden cake board (page 208)
smoothing tools
6 wooden skewers
paper piping bag (page 221)
CAKE
deep 10-inch round cake of choice (page 190)
deep 8-inch round cake of choice (page 190)
deep 6-inch round cake of choice (page 190)
DECORATIONS
3 pounds ready-to-use ivory fondant
cornstarch
chocolate brown and ivory food coloring
1 quantity royal icing (page 220)
5 yards narrow ribbon

1 Color 1½ ounces ready-to-use fondant chocolate brown; knead on surface dusted with a little cornstarch until fondant loses its stickiness. Roll fondant out on cornstarched surface into ⅛-inch thickness. Using cutter; cut a heart shape from fondant. Cut wire in half, push one half into the heart shape; place on parchment-paper-lined tray to dry overnight. Make another heart in the same way using 1½ ounces of the ivory-colored fondant.

2 Trim cakes (page 209). Secure large cake to largest board; secure remaining cakes to same-sized boards (page 209). Prepare cakes for covering with ready-to-use fondant (page 209).

3 Knead remaining fondant on surface dusted with a little cornstarch until fondant loses its stickiness.

4 Roll 9½ ounces of fondant on cornstarched surface until large enough to cover small cake. Using rolling pin, lift fondant onto cake; smooth with hands then smoothing tools. Trim fondant around base of cake.

5 Use 1 pound of the fondant to cover medium cake in the same way as the small cake. Use remaining fondant to cover large cake in the

same way. Dry cakes overnight.

6 Push 3 trimmed skewers into centers of large and medium cakes to support the next tier (page 212).

7 Assemble cakes, securing each tier to the tier below (page 212).

8 Tint royal icing ivory to match cake. Fill piping bag ¾ full with royal icing; pipe around base of each cake. Use fingertip to blend icing into any gaps where cakes join the boards (page 212). Dry cakes overnight.

9 Cut ribbon in lengths long enough to go around cakes. Secure around cakes using tiny dots of royal icing. Join ends of ribbon with royal icing.

10 Position hearts on cake by gently pushing wires into cake.

tips The hearts can be made weeks ahead; store in an airtight container. Position them on the day of serving. Positioning and securing the ribbon around these cakes can be challenging, as the ribbon can easily slip out of position. It's best to secure the ribbon after the icing has set completely, which takes about two days.

Roll some of the brown fondant on surface dusted with a little cornstarch. Cut out heart shape. Repeat using some of the ivory fondant.

Cut the length of wire in half. Push one piece of wire about halfway into each heart shape. Dry on parchment-paper-lined tray overnight.

Measure and cut ribbons to go around cakes. Secure ribbons to cakes with tiny dots of royal icing. Join the ends with royal icing.

CAKE POP
Baby Rattles

THEY MIGHT NOT BE FROM TIFFANY'S, BUT THESE CUTE CAKE POP RATTLES ARE
THE HEIGHT OF FASHION – AND SO MUCH CHEAPER THAN THE REAL THING.
GREAT FOR BABY SHOWERS, OR BABY'S FIRST BIRTHDAY CELEBRATION.

EQUIPMENT
18 (12-inch) cake pop sticks
large square styrofoam block
2 paper piping bags (page 221)
CAKE POPS
4 cups firmly packed cake crumbs
(see tips)
½ quantity butter cream,
approximately (page 218)
DECORATION
12 ounces white chocolate Melts
1 quantity royal icing (page 220)
blue and pink food coloring
1½ yards each blue and pink
narrow ribbon

1 Using a fork, combine the cake
crumbs and enough (about ½ cup)
butter cream in a medium bowl to
make ingredients come together.
2 Gently roll level tablespoons of
mixture into balls. Place balls on tray;
freeze 1 hour or refrigerate 3 hours
or overnight.

3 Stir chocolate in medium heatproof
bowl over medium saucepan of
simmering water until smooth (don't
let water touch base of bowl). Pour
into a heatproof bowl.
4 Dip the end of a cake pop stick
into the chocolate, then push the stick
about halfway into a ball of cake. Place
in freezer for 5 minutes to set.
5 Make one cake pop rattle at a time:
Dip the cake pop in the chocolate,
rocking back and forth to coat; don't
swirl the pops, or they'll break. Allow
excess chocolate to drip back into the
bowl. Stand cake pops upright in
styrofoam to set at room temperature
or in the fridge. Repeat with remaining
cake pops. Re-melt the chocolate as
necessary (page 222).
6 Divide royal icing into two small
bowls, tint one batch pale pink, the
other pale blue; cover surface of icing
with plastic wrap to keep airtight.

7 Fill one piping bag ¾ full with
pink royal icing; pipe spirals on top of
half the cake pops, turning the cake
pops in the styrofoam as you pipe.
Repeat with blue royal icing
and remaining cake pops. Stand in
styrofoam until set.
8 Use the ribbon to tie tiny bows at
the base of each cake pop (page 226).

makes 18
tips Use any firm-textured cake to
make cake pops – chocolate, fruit,
coconut or butter cakes all work well.
Cake pop sticks (also sold as 'lollipop
candy sticks') are available from cake
decorating suppliers and craft shops.
Store cake pops, lying down, in a
single layer, in an airtight container
at a cool room temperature.

Dip the end of a cake pop stick into the
melted white chocolate; push the stick
about halfway through into the ball of cake.

Dip each cake pop in the melted chocolate;
rock them backwards and forwards to
ensure that they are evenly coated.

Pipe spirals of pink and blue royal icing
around the tops of the cake pops, turning
the cake pops in the styrofoam as you pipe.

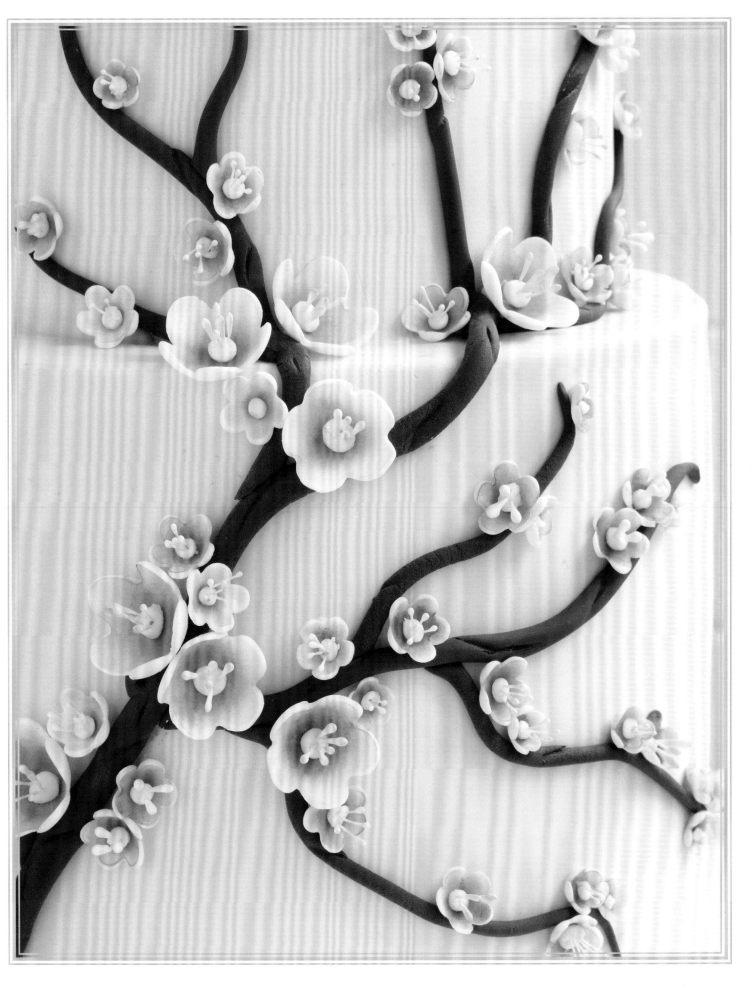

CHERRY BLOSSOMS
in Spring

THE CHERRY BLOSSOM IS THE SYMBOL OF JAPAN, AS WELL AS BEING THE SYMBOL OF SPRING. THE CONTRASTING COLORS OF THIS CAKE – THE PALE PINK OF THE BLOSSOMS AND THE BROWN OF THE BRANCHES – GIVES IT A DRAMATIC EFFECT.

EQUIPMENT
12-inch round wooden cake board (page 208)
6-inch round wooden cake board (page 208)
smoothing tools
3 wooden skewers
2 paper piping bags (page 221)
5-petal plunger cutter set (small, medium and large)
vinyl mat
ball tool
2 fine artist's paint brushes
tweezers
CAKE
2 (deep 8-inch) round cakes of choice (page 190)
deep 6-inch round cake of choice (page 190)
shallow 6-inch round cake of choice (page 190)
jam or ganache of choice (page 210)
DECORATIONS
3 pounds ready-to-use white fondant
cornstarch
rose pink, brown and black food colorings
1 quantity royal icing (page 220)
3 ounces gum paste
magenta petal dust
2 bunches small white stamens

1 Trim cakes (page 209). Secure one 8-inch cake to largest board; top with remaining 8-inch cake, joining cakes with a little jam or ganache (page 212). Secure deep 6-inch cake to smaller board; top with remaining small cake, joining cakes with jam or ganache. Prepare cakes for covering with ready-to-use fondant (page 209).

2 Knead ready-to-use fondant on surface dusted with a little cornstarch until fondant loses its stickiness. Tint fondant pink with coloring.

3 Roll one-third of the fondant on cornstarched surface until large enough to cover small cake. Using rolling pin, lift fondant onto cake; smooth with hands then smoothing tools. Trim fondant neatly around base of cake; reserve scraps.

4 Use remaining fondant to cover large cake the same way as small cake; reserve scraps. Dry cakes overnight.

5 Push trimmed skewers into center of large cake to support the top tier. Secure small cake on top of large cake (page 212).

6 Reserve 1 heaped tablespoon of royal icing. Tint remaining royal icing pink to match cakes. Fill piping bag ¾ full with icing; pipe around base of each cake. Use fingertip to blend icing into any gaps where the cakes join the boards (page 212).
Dry cakes overnight.

7 Knead gum paste on surface dusted with cornstarch until it loses its stickiness. Roll out a little of the paste to ¹/₁₆-inch thick. Cut several

blossoms from paste using all cutters. Cover the paste with the vinyl mat to prevent it from drying out.

8 Working quickly, place a blossom in palm of hand dusted with a little cornstarch. Using small end of ball tool, gently press tool into blossom =to round the petals and center of blossom. Place blossoms on parchment-paper-lined tray to dry overnight. Repeat with more paste. You need about 35 small, 35 medium and 10 large blossoms.

9 Using paint brush, dust center of blossoms with equal quantities of combined cornstarch and petal dust.

10 Cut stamens to about ½-inch long. Fill piping bag ½ full with reserved white royal icing; pipe a small dot of icing in center of 6 blossoms. Use tweezers to position a few stamens in the icing in each blossom before it sets; stand until dry. Repeat with remaining blossoms.

11 Color scraps of reserved ready-to-use fondant brown using a little black and brown coloring.

12 Roll brown fondant into thin strips of random thicknesses, lengths and shapes to resemble cherry blossom branches; brush a little water on backs of branches, secure to cakes while still soft and pliable.

13 Secure blossoms to branches with a little royal icing.

tip Flower blossoms can be made several weeks ahead. Store at room temperature in an airtight container.

SQUEEZE SOME OF THE FONDANT STRIPS FOR THE BRANCHES WITH YOUR FINGERTIPS TO MAKE THEM LOOK GNARLED AND TWISTED. SECURE THE BRANCHES TO THE CAKE BEFORE THEY DRY. POSITION ALL THE BRANCHES FIRST, FOLLOWED BY THE BLOSSOMS.

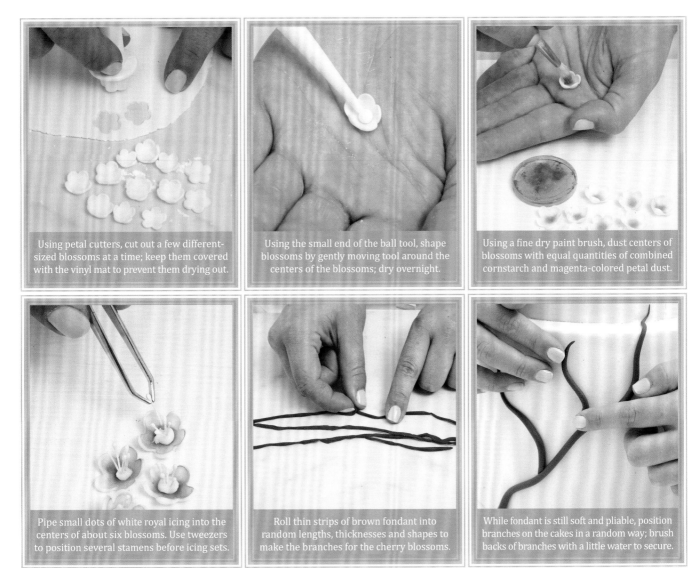

Using petal cutters, cut out a few different-sized blossoms at a time; keep them covered with the vinyl mat to prevent them drying out.

Using the small end of the ball tool, shape blossoms by gently moving tool around the centers of the blossoms; dry overnight.

Using a fine dry paint brush, dust centers of blossoms with equal quantities of combined cornstarch and magenta-colored petal dust.

Pipe small dots of white royal icing into the centers of about six blossoms. Use tweezers to position several stamens before icing sets.

Roll thin strips of brown fondant into random lengths, thicknesses and shapes to make the branches for the cherry blossoms.

While fondant is still soft and pliable, position branches on the cakes in a random way; brush backs of branches with a little water to secure.

LOLLIPOP
Flower Cake

LOLLIPOP
Flower Cake

THIS CAKE IS GOOD FOR A YOUNGER CHILD'S BIRTHDAY. USE ANY COLORS YOU LIKE.

EQUIPMENT
**13-inch square wooden cake board
(page 208)
7-inch square wooden cake board
(page 208)
smoothing tools
4 wooden skewers
paper piping bag (page 221)
tape measure
acrylic measure
pizza cutter
fine artist's paint brush
2-inch round cutter
1½-inch round cutter
¾-inch round cutter
vinyl mat
4 (12-hole) round-based, shallow
whoopie pie pans
ball tool
5 (8-inch) lengths 18-gauge floral
wire**
CAKE
**2 (deep 9-inch) square cakes of
choice (page 190)
deep 7-inch square cake of choice
(page 190)
shallow 7-inch square cake of
choice (page 190)
jam or ganache of choice (page 210)**
DECORATIONS
**5 pounds ready-to-use white
fondant
cornstarch
blue and yellow food colorings
1 quantity royal icing (page 220)
tylose powder**

1 Trim cakes (page 209). Secure
one 9-inch cake to largest board;
top with remaining 9-inch cake,
joining cakes with a little jam or
ganache (page 212). Secure deep
7-inch cake to smaller board; top
with remaining small cake, joining
cakes with jam or ganache. Prepare
cakes for covering with ready-to-use
fondant (page 209).
2 Knead ready-to-use fondant on
surface dusted with a little cornstarch

until fondant loses its stickiness. Tint
4½ pounds of the fondant pale blue.
Tint remaining fondant yellow;
enclose, separately, in plastic wrap.
3 Roll 2¼ pounds of the blue
fondant on cornstarched surface
until large enough to cover small
cake. Using rolling pin, lift fondant
onto cake; smooth with hands then
smoothing tools. Trim fondant neatly
around base.
4 Use fondant scraps and remaining
blue fondant to cover large cake in
the same way; reserve fondant
scraps. Dry cakes overnight.
5 Push trimmed skewers into center
of large cake to support top tier.
Secure small cake to large cake
(page 212).
6 Tint royal icing pale blue to match
cakes. Fill piping bag ¾ full with royal
icing; pipe around base of each cake.
Use fingertip to blend icing into any
gaps where cakes join the boards
(page 212). Dry overnight.
7 Measure around the base of each
cake. Roll half the yellow fondant on
cornstarched surface into ⅛-inch
thickness, long enough to wrap
around cakes. Using acrylic measure
and pizza cutter, cut a strip ¾-inch
wide and long enough to wrap around
the base of the top tier. Secure strip
to cake with a little water. Repeat for
bottom tier, joining strips if necessary;
reserve fondant scraps.
8 Knead a pinch of tylose powder
into remaining yellow fondant along
with any yellow fondant scraps. Roll
out on cornstarched surface until
about ⅛₃₂-inch thick. Using 2-inch
cutter, cut out 21 rounds; cover with
vinyl mat to prevent drying out.
9 Dust whoopie pie pan holes lightly
with cornstarch. Hold one 2-inch
round in the palm of a cornstarched

hand, using the large end of the ball
tool, smooth the edges of the round
until it starts to frill. Place in whoopie
pie pan to dry. Repeat with remaining
rounds.
10 Using ¾-inch cutter, cut 21
rounds from yellow fondant
(re-rolling scraps as necessary); frill
the edges in the same way as the
larger rounds. Place rounds in
whoopie pie pan (see tips). Reserve
fondant scraps.
11 Knead a pinch of tylose powder
into the reserved blue fondant. Roll
on cornstarched surface until about
⅛₃₂-inch thick. Using 1½-inch cutter,
cut 21 rounds and frill the edges in the
same way as for the yellow rounds.
Place rounds in whoopie pie pan.
12 Join fondant rounds in sets of three
with a little royal icing. Return flowers
to whoopie pie pan to dry overnight.
13 Roll scraps of yellow fondant
into thin rope shapes of different
lengths on surface dusted with
cornstarch to make flower stems;
stand on parchment-paper-lined tray
to dry overnight.
14 Cut wire into 5 different lengths,
secure to the back of 5 flowers with
a little royal icing; suspend wires
over a wooden spoon so wires dry
straight, leave to dry overnight. Push
wired flowers into the top of the cake.
15 Secure flower stems to sides of
cake with a little water (one on each
side of the top cake; three on each side
of the bottom cake). Secure flowers
into position with a little royal icing.

tips By the time you've made the
42 yellow petals they'll be firm enough
to remove from the whoopie pie pans
to make room for the blue petals.
Position the flowers in the top of the
cake on the day of serving.

THIS IS SUCH A CUTE CAKE, HOWEVER THERE ARE A COUPLE OF TECHNIQUES
TO MASTER, SUCH AS MAKING THE FLOWERS, AND WIRING THEM TO GIVE HEIGHT
AND DIMENSION. NO REAL PIPING SKILLS ARE NEEDED TO DECORATE THIS CAKE.

Measure around base of each cake. Using an acrylic measure and pizza cutter, cut a ribbon of fondant long enough to wrap around each cake.

Hold a round of fondant in cornstarched hand, use the large end of a ball tool to frill the rounds. Do this to all the rounds of fondant.

When set, join sets of three different-sized petals with a little royal icing. Leave to dry in whoopie pie pans dusted lightly with cornstarch.

Cut wire into 5 different lengths. Secure wire to back of 5 flowers with royal icing. Suspend wire so that it dries straight; dry overnight.

To make stems of flowers, roll scraps of yellow fondant on cornstarch-dusted surface into thin rope shapes of different lengths.

Secure fondant strips around cakes with a little water. Secure stems in the same way. Position flowers on cake using royal icing.

DIAMONDS ARE
Forever

EQUIPMENT
13-inch square wooden cake board
  (page 208)
7-inch square wooden cake board
  (page 208)
large plaque plunger cutter
smoothing tools
2-inch x 3½-inch diamond
  patchwork cutter
4 wooden skewers
paper piping bag (page 221)
fine pearl-headed pin
tweezers
white florist's tape
CAKE
2 (deep 9-inch) square cakes of
  choice (page 190)
deep 7-inch square cake of choice
  (page 190)
shallow 7-inch square cake of
  choice (page 190)
jam or ganache of choice (page 210)
DECORATIONS
3½ pounds ready-to-use white
  fondant
cornstarch
1 quantity royal icing (page 220)
2 yards narrow ribbon
72 x ⅛-inch clear edible diamonds
fresh organic flowers

1   Trim cakes (page 209). Secure one 9-inch cake to largest board; top with remaining 9-inch cake, joining cakes with a little jam or ganache (page 212). Secure deep 7-inch cake to smaller board; top with remaining small cake, joining cakes with jam or ganache. Prepare cakes for covering with ready-to-use fondant (page 209).
2   Knead 6 ounces of the ready-to-use fondant on cornstarched surface until fondant loses its stickiness. Roll fondant out on cornstarched surface into ⅛-inch thickness. Using plaque cutter, cut out 4 plaques from fondant. Place plaques on parchment-paper-lined tray to dry overnight.
3   Knead remaining fondant with any scraps on cornstarched surface until fondant loses its stickiness.
4   Roll 1½ pounds of the fondant on surface dusted with a little cornstarch until large enough to cover small cake. Using rolling pin, lift fondant onto cake; smooth with hands then smoothing tools. Trim fondant neatly around base of cake.
5   Use remaining fondant and scraps to cover the large cake in the same way.

6   While the fondant is still soft, press diamond patchwork cutter all around cake to make a quilted pattern. Dry cakes overnight.
7   Push trimmed skewers into center of large cake to support top tier. Secure small cake on large cake (page 212).
8   Fill piping bag ¾ full with royal icing; pipe around base of each cake. Use fingertip to blend icing into any gaps where cakes join the boards (page 212). Dry cakes overnight.
9   Wrap ribbon around base of each cake; secure with a little royal icing.
10 Secure a plaque to the center of the top cake with a little royal icing; repeat on all sides of cake, hold for a minute or so to make sure plaques are firmly attached.
11 Secure edible diamonds to joins in the pattern with a dab of royal icing.
12 Wrap stems of flowers with florist's tape; top cake with flowers.

tip Ask the florist to make you an appropriate arrangement for the top of the cake – they will tape the stems of the flowers for you. Prepare and place the flowers on the day of serving.

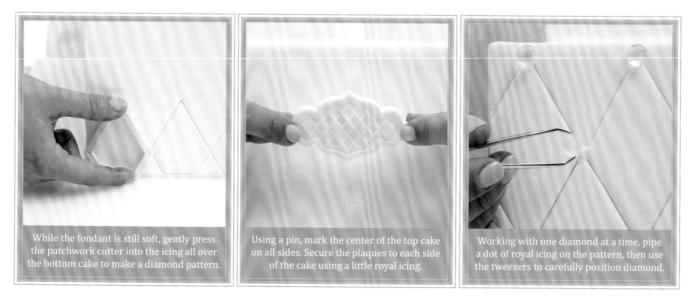

While the fondant is still soft, gently press the patchwork cutter into the icing all over the bottom cake to make a diamond pattern.

Using a pin, mark the center of the top cake on all sides. Secure the plaques to each side of the cake using a little royal icing.

Working with one diamond at a time, pipe a dot of royal icing on the pattern, then use the tweezers to carefully position diamond.

The edible diamonds are not fragile to handle, but they do lose their sparkle quickly, so attach the diamonds to the cake as late as possible (up to 3 hours is ideal). Use tweezers or cotton gloves when handling the diamonds, as the natural oils in your fingertips can make the surface of the diamonds dull.

SHIMMERING
Wedding Crystals

SHIMMERING
Wedding Crystals

THE SHIMMER ON THE CAKE AND THE CRYSTALS ON THE STAND CAPTURE
THE LIGHT, GIVING THIS STUNNING CAKE AN EYE-CATCHING SPARKLE.

EQUIPMENT
12-inch round wooden cake board (page 208)
8-inch round wooden cake board (page 208)
6-inch round wooden cake board (page 208)
smoothing tools
6 wooden skewers
large new make-up brush
2 paper piping bags (page 221)
large and small stencils
fine pearl-headed pins
small offset metal spatula
straight-sided metal scraper
craft glue
6½-inch cake stand
CAKE
deep 10-inch round cake of choice (page 190)
shallow 10-inch round cake of choice (page 190)
deep 8-inch round cake of choice (page 190)
deep 6-inch round cake of choice (page 190)
shallow 6-inch round cake of choice (page 190)
jam or ganache of choice (page 210)
DECORATIONS
3½ pounds ready-to-use white fondant
cornstarch
ivory, brown and black food colorings
shimmer powder
1 quantity royal icing (page 220)
1½ yards ribbon
medium-sized crystal-style brooch
1 yard crystal trimming

1 Trim cakes (page 209). Secure deep 10-inch cake on largest board (page 209); top with remaining large cake, joining cakes with a little jam or ganache (page 212). Stack and secure the two 6-inch cakes to same-sized board in the same way. Secure 8-inch cake to same-sized board. Prepare cakes for covering with ready-to-use fondant (page 209).

2 Knead ready-to-use fondant on surface dusted with a little cornstarch until fondant loses its stickiness. Tint 1 pound of fondant ivory; enclose in plastic wrap. Tint remaining fondant using brown coloring and a touch of black coloring.

3 Roll 12 ounces of the brown icing on cornstarched surface until large enough to cover 6-inch cake. Using rolling pin, lift fondant onto cake; smooth with hands then smoothing tools. Trim fondant neatly around base.

4 Use 1½ pounds of brown fondant to cover large cake in the same way as small cake. Use ivory fondant to cover medium cake in the same way. Dry cakes overnight.

5 Push 3 trimmed skewers into center of large cake to support middle tier (page 212). Push 3 trimmed skewers into center of medium cake to support cake stand and top tier. Using the large make-up brush, brush the small and large cakes evenly with shimmer powder. Secure medium cake to larger cake (page 212).

6 Tint 1 tablespoon royal icing brown to match the cakes; tint remaining royal icing ivory to match cake. Fill piping bags ½ full with 1 tablespoon of royal icing to match the cakes; pipe around base of same-colored cakes. Use fingertip to blend icing into any gaps where cakes join the boards (page 212). Dry cakes overnight. Cover the surface of the remaining royal icing with plastic wrap to prevent it drying out.

7 Secure large stencil to side of large cake with pins. Use spatula to spread royal icing over stencil, remove excess icing with scraper; return to bowl. Gently remove pins and stencil; wash and dry stencil before using again. Repeat until stencil is completed around the large cake. Stand cake about 1 hour to dry.

8 Use the smaller stencil to make a lace pattern on opposite sides of the small cake in the same way.

9 Wrap ribbon around middle cake; secure with a little royal icing. Make a bow using some of the ribbon (page 226); secure the ends with a little glue. Attach brooch to bow; attach bow to ribbon with glue.

10 Secure crystal trim to edge of cake stand with glue; wrap trim around cake stand twice, if necessary, so crystals hang close together. Secure small cake on cake stand with a little royal icing. Secure stand to middle cake with royal icing when assembling.

tips The cake stand needs to have a flat base so it can be supported by the skewers in the middle tier. If the base of the stand is not flat, cut a piece of strong white cardboard to fit the base of the stand, glue in position. It's best to position and secure the cake stand (holding the top tier) when the cake is positioned at the event.

STENCILLING IS AN EASY YET EFFECTIVE WAY TO DECORATE A CAKE, ESPECIALLY IF THE COVERING IS NOT QUITE PERFECT. THE TRICKS TO USING THE STENCIL ARE TO USE THE ROYAL ICING SPARINGLY AND TO REMOVE THE STENCIL GENTLY. PRACTICE USING THE STENCIL ON A CAKE PAN BEFORE DECORATING THE CAKE.

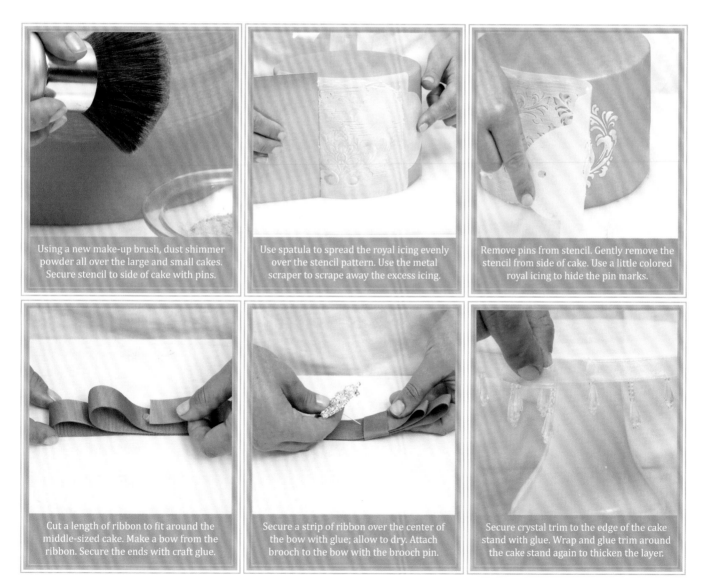

Using a new make-up brush, dust shimmer powder all over the large and small cakes. Secure stencil to side of cake with pins.

Use spatula to spread the royal icing evenly over the stencil pattern. Use the metal scraper to scrape away the excess icing.

Remove pins from stencil. Gently remove the stencil from side of cake. Use a little colored royal icing to hide the pin marks.

Cut a length of ribbon to fit around the middle-sized cake. Make a bow from the ribbon. Secure the ends with craft glue.

Secure a strip of ribbon over the center of the bow with glue; allow to dry. Attach brooch to the bow with the brooch pin.

Secure crystal trim to the edge of the cake stand with glue. Wrap and glue trim around the cake stand again to thicken the layer.

PLEATS & BOWS
Ribbon Cake

PLEATS & BOWS
Ribbon Cake

IT'S A LOVELY IDEA TO HAVE THE INITIALS OF A COUPLE ON THE TOP OF
AN ENGAGEMENT, COMMITMENT CEREMONY OR WEDDING CAKE.

EQUIPMENT
**14-inch round wooden cake board
(page 208)**
**8-inch round wooden cake board
(page 208)**
**6-inch round wooden cake board
(page 208)**
**4-inch round wooden cake board
(page 208)**
smoothing tools
19 wooden skewers
paper piping bag (page 221)
acrylic measure (1½-inch width)
fine artist's paint brush
tape measure
CAKE
**deep 10-inch round cake of choice
(page 190)**
**deep 8-inch round cake of choice
(page 190)**
**deep 6-inch round cake of choice
(page 190)**
**deep 4-inch round cake of choice
(page 190)**
DECORATIONS
**6 pounds (3kg) ready-made
white icing**
cornstarch
1 quantity royal icing (page 220)
4 yards narrow ribbon
acrylic cake topper initials

1 Trim cakes (page 209). Secure
10-inch cake to largest board; secure
remaining cakes to the same-sized
boards (page 209). Prepare cakes
for covering with ready-to-use
fondant (page 209).

2 Knead ready-to-use fondant on
surface dusted with a little cornstarch
until fondant loses its stickiness. Roll
9½ ounces of fondant on cornstarched
surface until large enough to cover
4-inch cake. Using rolling pin, lift
fondant onto cake; smooth with hands
then smoothing tools. Trim fondant
neatly around base of cake. (Reserve
and re-use all fondant scraps from
each cake for the next cake.)

3 Roll fondant on surface dusted
with a little cornstarch; use 12½
ounces of fondant to cover 6-inch cake;
1¼ pounds to cover 8-inch cake; and
1½ pounds to cover 10-inch cake, in
the same way as the 4-inch cake. Dry
cakes overnight.

4 Push 3 trimmed skewers into
centers of all cakes except the
smallest cake to support the next
tier (page 212).

5 Assemble cakes, securing each
tier to the tier below (page 212).

6 Fill piping bag ¾ full with royal
icing; pipe around base of each cake.
Use fingertip to blend icing into any
gaps where cakes join the boards
(page 212). Dry cakes overnight.

7 To make pleated strips: Divide the
remaining fondant into 5 balls;
working one at a time roll on
cornstarched surface into two strips
⅛-inch thick. Using the acrylic
measure, cut strips of fondant 1½
inches wide and 12 inches long.

8 Position 5 of the wooden skewers
parallel to the edge of the work
surface, about ½ inch apart. Lift the
strips of fondant over the top of the
skewers. Place 5 remaining skewers
on top of the fondant, in between
the first skewers. Gently push the
skewers closer together to pleat the
fondant. Carefully remove skewers,
and reposition them under and on
top of the next section of the fondant
strip. Continue until the strips are
pleated.

9 Use paint brush to brush bottom
1¼-inch of cake sparingly with water.
Carefully lift pleated strip and secure
into position around cake; cutting
strip to fit cake. Continue this process
all around the base of the cake,
joining, trimming and slightly
overlapping the ends of the strips.
Repeat with remaining fondant on
remaining cake tiers. Stand cake
overnight until pleats dry.

10 Measure around base of cake; trim
ribbon to fit around cake, securing to
pleats with tiny dots of royal icing.
Make small bows (page 226) to cover
seams in ribbon; secure bows with
royal icing. Secure acrylic initials
to cake with a little royal icing.

tips It's important to allow time for
the fondant on the assembled cakes
to dry before positioning the strips;
use the thick wooden skewers to
gently press the pleats into position
on the dampened fondant.

THE PLEATED STRIPS NEED TO BE SLIGHTLY FIRM, BUT STILL PLIABLE ENOUGH TO WRAP AROUND THE CAKES WITHOUT CRACKING OR BREAKING. YOU MAY NEED TO JOIN 2 STRIPS FOR THE LARGER CAKES; OVERLAP THE NEXT PLEATED STRIP TO MAKE NEAT SEAMS. WHILE WE USED BLACK ACRYLIC INITIALS ON THIS CAKE, THERE ARE MANY DIFFERENT TYPES, SHAPES AND SIZES OF TOPPERS AVAILABLE. THIS IS QUITE AN EASY CAKE TO MAKE, AND LOOKS CHIC AND LOVELY ALL AT THE SAME TIME.

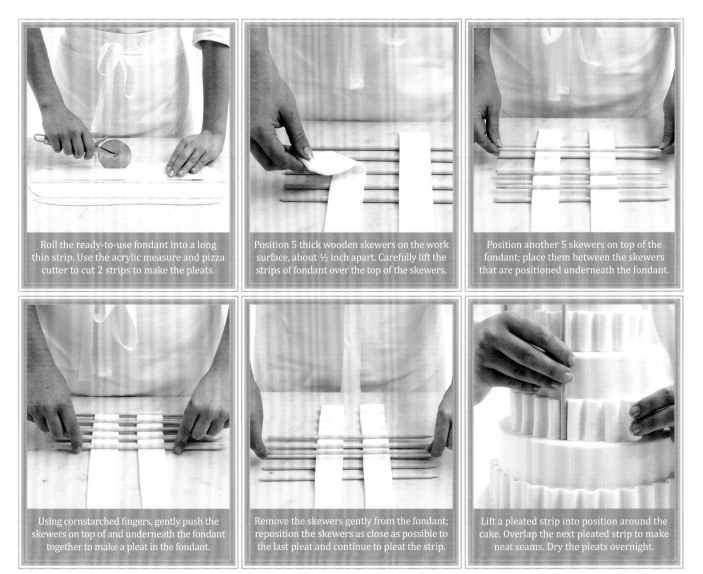

Roll the ready-to-use fondant into a long thin strip. Use the acrylic measure and pizza cutter to cut 2 strips to make the pleats.

Position 5 thick wooden skewers on the work surface, about ½ inch apart. Carefully lift the strips of fondant over the top of the skewers.

Position another 5 skewers on top of the fondant; place them between the skewers that are positioned underneath the fondant.

Using cornstarched fingers, gently push the skewers on top of and underneath the fondant together to make a pleat in the fondant.

Remove the skewers gently from the fondant; reposition the skewers as close as possible to the last pleat and continue to pleat the strip.

Lift a pleated strip into position around the cake. Overlap the next pleated strip to make neat seams. Dry the pleats overnight.

21ST
Celebration Cake

21ST
Celebration Cake

COVERED IN PASTEL HUES, THIS VERY SIMPLE, THOUGH ELEGANT, CAKE WOULD ALSO
SUIT A BABY'S FIRST BIRTHDAY – ANOTHER VERY IMPORTANT MILESTONE OF LIFE.

EQUIPMENT
12-inch round wooden cake board
(page 208)
6-inch round wooden cake board
(page 208)
smoothing tools
4 wooden skewers
2 paper piping bags (page 221)
number 1 and 2 cutters
2 (4-inch) pieces 18-gauge floral
wire
fine artist's paint brush
pasta machine (see tips)
½-inch plain piping tube
CAKE
deep 8-inch round cake of choice
(page 190)
deep 6-inch round cake of choice
(page 190)

DECORATIONS
3 pounds ready-to-use white
fondant
cornstarch
blue, pink, yellow and orange food
colorings
1 quantity royal icing (page 220)
3 teaspoons tylose powder

1 Trim cakes (page 209). Secure large cake to largest board; secure small cake to remaining board (page 209). Prepare cakes for covering with ready-to-use fondant (page 209).

2 Knead 2 pounds of the ready-to-use fondant on surface dusted with a little cornstarch until fondant loses its stickiness. Tint with blue coloring. Roll 2 ounces of the blue fondant on cornstarched surface until large enough to cover small cake. Using rolling pin, lift fondant onto cake; smooth with hands then smoothing tools. Trim fondant neatly around base. Use remaining fondant to cover large cake in the same way. Dry cakes overnight. Reserve fondant scraps, enclose in plastic wrap.

3 Push 3 trimmed skewers into center of large cake to support top tier. Secure small cake on top of large cake (page 212).

4 Tint royal icing blue to match cakes. Fill piping bag ½ full with royal icing; pipe around base of each cake. Use fingertip to blend icing into any gaps where cakes join the boards (page 212). Dry overnight. Cover the surface of the remaining royal icing with plastic wrap to prevent it drying out.

5 Knead reserved fondant scraps with three-quarters of the remaining white fondant on cornstarched surface; tint fondant to a darker blue color.

6 Knead 1 teaspoon of the tylose powder into half of the dark blue

fondant; roll out to ¼-inch thickness on surface dusted with cornstarch. Use cutters to cut out numbers. Dip one end of both pieces of wire about ¾-inch into water. Push wet end of wires into the bases of both numbers. Place numbers on parchment-paper-covered trays to dry overnight.

7 Roll remaining dark blue fondant into ¼-inch-thick rope shapes. Brush lightly around base of cakes with a little water, gently position fondant ropes around cakes. Carefully join ends.

8 Divide remaining white fondant into 4 portions. Tint with pink, yellow and orange colorings. Leave remaining portion white. Cover with plastic wrap.

9 To make strips: Knead ½ teaspoon tylose into one portion of fondant. Roll out on cornstarched surface into ⅛-inch thickness; roll through a pasta machine until ¹/₁₆-inch thick. Cut ½-inch x 4-inch strips from fondant. Coil strips around remaining skewer; carefully remove skewer.

Use the tip of piping tube to cut dots from leftover scraps of icing. Stand strips and dots on parchment-paper-lined tray for about 30 minutes or until barely firm. Repeat with remaining fondant.

10 Push wired numbers into cake. Fill piping bag ¾ full with royal icing. Decorate cake with "confetti" and "ribbons," securing to the cake with tiny dots of royal icing.

THERE ARE NO SPECIAL CAKE DECORATING SKILLS REQUIRED FOR THIS CELEBRATORY CAKE. WHILE THE DECORATIONS CAN BE MADE BY ROLLING THE FONDANT OUT THINLY TO $^1/_{16}$ INCH, ROLLING THE FONDANT THROUGH A PASTA MACHINE GIVES GREAT RESULTS. THE NUMBERS SHOULD BE POSITIONED IN THE CAKE ON THE DAY OF SERVING.

Knead a teaspoon of tylose powder into one-third of the fondant. Roll fondant out on cornstarched surface to cut out numbers.

Dip ends of both wires into water about ¾ inch. Push wet ends of wire about half-way into the number shapes. Dry overnight.

Roll fondant into rope shape long enough to wrap around cakes. Brush a little water around cake bases and carefully position fondant ropes.

To make decorations, feed fondant through a pasta machine set on the thickest setting. Or, roll out fondant to about $^1/_{16}$-inch thickness.

Coil strips of fondant around a thick wooden skewer, place on parchment-paper-lined tray to dry for about 3 hours or overnight.

Use tip of piping tube to cut out dots from different colored fondant. Dry for 3 hours or overnight on a parchment-paper-lined tray.

CASCADE OF *Butterflies*

EQUIPMENT
14-inch round wooden cake board (page 208)
8-inch round wooden cake board (page 208)
6-inch round wooden cake board (page 208)
smoothing tools
6 wooden skewers
tape measure
acrylic measure
pizza cutter
fine artist's paint brush
small non-stick rolling pin
3 (12-inch) cardboard squares
small, medium and large butterfly plunger cutter set
paper piping bag (page 221)
CAKE
deep 10-inch round cake of choice (page 190)
deep 8-inch round cake of choice (page 190)
deep 6-inch round cake of choice (page 190)
DECORATIONS
5 pounds ready-to-use white fondant
cornstarch
sky and royal blue food colorings
tylose powder
1 quantity royal icing (page 220)

1 Trim cakes (page 209). Secure 14-inch cake to largest board; secure remaining cakes to same-sized boards (page 209). Prepare cakes for covering with ready-to-use fondant (page 209).

2 Knead ready-to-use fondant on surface dusted with a little cornstarch until fondant loses its stickiness. Using both colorings, tint 6 ounces of the fondant very pale blue. Enclose in plastic wrap. Tint remaining fondant pale blue.

3 Roll 10 ounces of the pale blue fondant on cornstarched surface until large enough to cover small cake. Using rolling pin, lift fondant onto cake; smooth with hands then smoothing tools. Trim fondant neatly around base of cake. Reserve scraps.

4 Roll 1 pound of the pale blue fondant on cornstarched surface until large enough to cover medium cake in the same way as the small cake; roll 1¼ pounds fondant until large enough to cover the large cake in the same way. Reserve fondant scraps. Dry overnight.

5 Push 3 trimmed skewers into center of medium and large cakes to support the next tier (page 212).

6 Assemble cakes, securing each tier to the tier below (page 212). Dry cakes overnight.

7 To make the fondant ribbon: Knead the remaining pale blue fondant and scraps together, divide into thirds. Reserve two-thirds for the butterflies, enclose in plastic wrap. Tint remaining third of fondant a slightly darker blue than the covering on the cakes.

8 Use tape measure to measure around the bottom tier of cake. Roll out half the darker fondant into a strip about ⅛-inch thick and long enough to wrap around the cake. Use the acrylic ruler and pizza cutter to cut a straight edge down one long side of the strip. Use the paint brush to brush bottom ¾-inch of cake sparingly with water. Roll icing strip onto small rolling pin with cut edge at bottom of rolling pin; position rolling pin so that the cut edge is flush with the bottom and side of the cake. Unroll fondant onto side of cake; trim ends, reserve scraps.

9 Use acrylic measure and a small sharp knife to trim strip into a 1-inch wide ribbon. Be careful not to cut through the fondant underneath.

10 Use scraps and remaining fondant to make and secure ribbon for the remaining two cakes in the same way; reserve scraps.

11 To make the butterflies: Knead darker blue fondant scraps together with a pinch of tylose; enclose in plastic wrap. Knead a pinch of tylose into the reserved pale blue and very pale blue fondant. Enclose in plastic wrap. Fold each cardboard evenly into three to make an accordion shape.

12 Roll out one portion of the reserved fondant at a time on cornstarched surface into ⅛-inch thickness. Working quickly, use all the cutters to cut out random numbers of butterflies. Place butterflies onto the folded cardboard so that the wings fold upwards; leave the butterfly shapes in the cardboard overnight to dry completely.

13 Tint royal icing the same color as the cake. Fill piping bag ½ full with icing, pipe small dots of royal icing onto each butterfly; secure to cake.

tips The butterflies can be made months ahead; store in an airtight container at room temperature. Tylose powder is a hardening agent, it helps the butterflies maintain their wings in an upward position.

CASCADING BUTTERFLIES OF JUST ABOUT ANY COLOR WILL LOOK SPLENDID
ON A TIERED CAKE LIKE THIS. KEEP THE COLOR OF THE CAKES PALE, SO THAT
THE FLYING SWARM OF BUTTERFLIES BECOMES THE FEATURE.

To make the fondant ribbon, roll fondant into a long thin strip. Use the ruler and pizza cutter to cut the ribbon to fit around the cake.

Roll ribbon around a small rolling pin with the cut side at the bottom of the pin. Roll fondant into position so it's flush with the base.

Using a flat acrylic ruler, and a sharp knife, trim around top edge of ribbon so it's 1-inch wide. Don't cut through the icing underneath.

Using a clean piece of cardboard, fold it firmly and evenly into three to give an accordion shape for drying the butterflies.

Roll out one colored fondant at a time. Using all the different-sized cutters, cut out as many butterflies as possible from the three colors.

Position the butterflies into the wedge of the cardboard – leave butterflies in cardboard overnight so they dry out completely.

BRODERIE ANGLAISE
Lace Cake

BRODERIE ANGLAISE, FRENCH FOR "ENGLISH EMBROIDERY," IS CHARACTERIZED BY CUTWORK, LACE AND SMALL EYELET PATTERNS, JUST LIKE WE'VE USED IN THIS CAKE.

EQUIPMENT
10-inch square wooden cake board (page 208)
6-inch square wooden cake board (page 208)
smoothing tools
4 wooden skewers
medium artist's paint brush
tape measure & plastic ruler
scalloped-edge frill cutter
set of eyelet cutters
⅝ & ¾ inch flower cutters
fine pearl-headed pin
small piping bag
small (number 2) plain piping tube
tweezers
8¾-inch 20-gauge floral wire

CAKE
deep 8-inch square cake of choice (page 190)
deep 6-inch square cake of choice (page 190)

DECORATIONS
3¼ pounds ready-to-use white fondant
cornstarch
1 quantity royal icing (page 220)
pink food coloring
silver dragées

1 Trim cakes (page 209). Secure 8-inch cake to largest board; secure small cake to remaining board (page 209). Prepare cakes for covering with ready-to-use fondant (page 209).

2 Knead ready-to-use fondant on surface dusted with a little cornstarch until icing loses its stickiness. Roll 12 ounces of fondant on cornstarched surface until large enough to cover small cake. Using rolling pin, lift fondant onto cake; smooth with hands then smoothing tools. Trim fondant neatly around base of cake.

3 Use 1 pound of the fondant to cover large cake in the same way. Dry cakes overnight.

4 Push trimmed skewers into center of large cake to support the top tier (page 212). Secure small cake to large cake. Dry cakes overnight.

5 Use paint brush to lightly brush water around sides of cakes to cover where the pink bands of fondant will be positioned.

6 Tint remaining fondant pink, reserve one-third of the fondant in plastic wrap.

7 Measure around large cake. Roll fondant into a strip long enough to wrap around cake and wide enough to almost cover sides of cake. Using a ruler and knife, or pizza cutter, cut fondant into a neat strip, almost as wide as the side of the cake. Lift into position around cake. Repeat with small cake.

8 Gently press frill cutter, at an angle, into top of pink fondant to scallop edge; remove excess fondant. Using eyelet and flower cutters, and picture as a guide, cut out or mark random shapes on the cakes. Use a pin to remove some of the cut pieces.

9 Tint royal icing pink. Fit piping bag with tube. Fill bag ½ full with icing; pipe around scallop edges and some of the cut outs.

10 Using tweezers, attach dragées to cakes with a little royal icing.

11 Re-roll scraps of pink fondant, cut out several flower shapes; insert pieces of floral wire into shapes, stand on parchment-paper-covered tray to dry overnight. Position wired flowers on day of serving.

Carefully press the scalloped-edged frill cutter against the top edge of the fondant strip on both cakes; gently remove excess fondant.

Using a fine pin, remove some cut-out pieces of fondant; leave some pieces intact. Stick some flower cut-outs to the cake with royal icing.

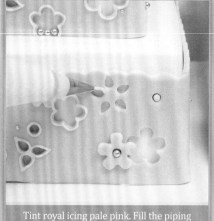

Tint royal icing pale pink. Fill the piping bag ½ full with icing, and pipe around the scalloped edges and some of the cut-outs.

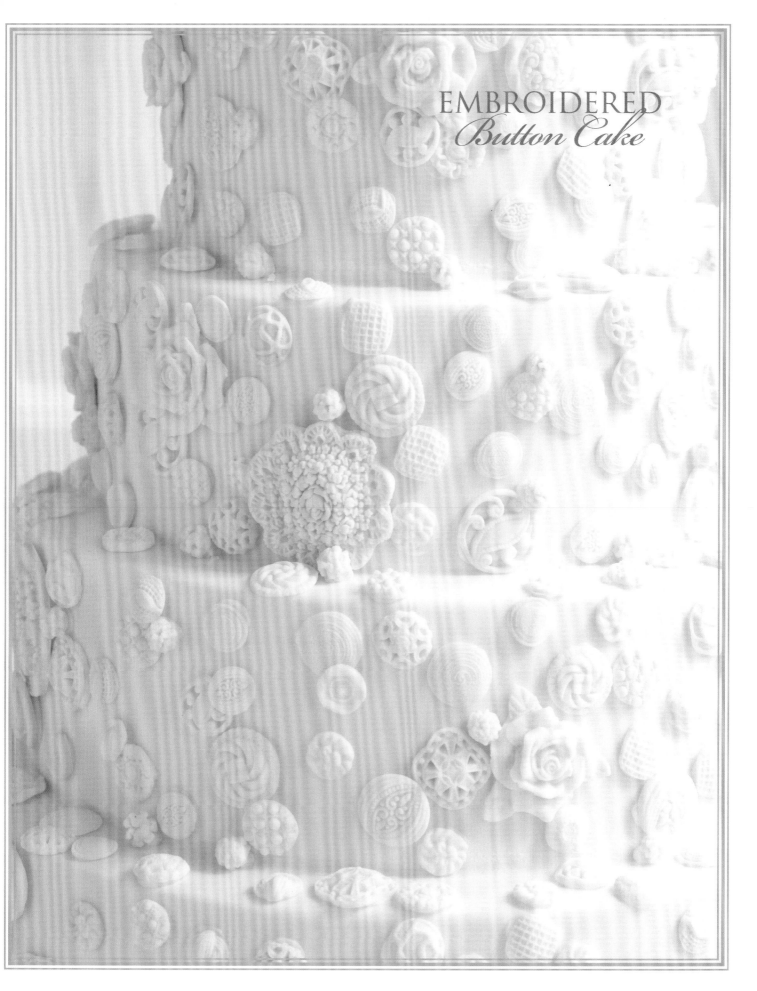

EMBROIDERED
Button Cake

EMBROIDERED
Button Cake

THE BUTTONS ON THIS CAKE CREATE A LOOK THAT'S REMINISCENT OF THE FLOUNCY WEDDING DRESSES OF YESTERYEAR. THE CAKE WOULD ALSO LOOK BEAUTIFUL COVERED IN A PLAIN WHITE ICING.

EQUIPMENT

18-inch round wooden cake board (page 208)

12-inch round wooden cake board (page 208)

10-inch round wooden cake board (page 208)

8-inch round wooden cake board (page 208)

6-inch round wooden cake board (page 208)

4-inch round wooden cake board (page 208)

smoothing tools

15 wooden skewers

paper piping bag (page 221)

silicone button-shaped molds

cooking-oil spray

small offset metal spatula

CAKE

deep 14-inch round cake of choice (page 190)

deep 12-inch round cake of choice (page 190)

deep 10-inch round cake of choice (page 190)

deep 8-inch round cake of choice (page 190)

deep 6-inch round cake of choice (page 190)

deep 4-inch round cake of choice (page 190)

DECORATIONS

11 pounds ready-to-use ivory fondant

cornstarch

1 quantity royal icing (page 220)

ivory food coloring

1 Trim cakes (page 209). Secure 14-inch cake to largest board; secure remaining cakes to the same-sized boards (page 209). Prepare cakes for covering with ready-to-use fondant (page 209).

2 Working with 4 pounds of the ready-to-use fondant, knead on surface dusted with a little cornstarch until fondant loses its stickiness. Roll 8 ounces of fondant on cornstarched surface until large enough to cover 4-inch cake. Using rolling pin, lift fondant onto cake; smooth with hands then smoothing tools. Trim fondant neatly around base of cake; reserve scraps.

3 Use 12 ounces of fondant to cover 6-inch cake; 1¼ pounds fondant to cover 8-inch cake and 1½ pounds fondant to cover 10-inch cake in the same way as step 2; reserve fondant scraps.

4 Knead another 4 pounds fondant with scraps on cornstarched surface until fondant loses its stickiness. Roll 2 pounds on cornstarched surface to cover 12-inch cake; roll remaining fondant to cover 14-inch cake in the same way as step 2. Reserve fondant scraps. Dry cakes overnight.

5 Push 3 trimmed skewers into centers of all cakes except smallest cake to support the next tier (page 212).

6 Assemble cakes, securing each tier to the tier below (page 212).

7 Tint royal icing to match cakes. Fill piping bag ¾ full with royal icing; pipe around base of each cake. Use fingertip to blend icing into any gaps where cakes join the boards (page 212). Dry cakes overnight. Reserve royal icing.

8 Knead remaining ready-to-use fondant with scraps on cornstarched surface until fondant loses its stickiness. Lightly spray molds with cooking oil. Working with a handful of fondant, push small amounts of fondant firmly into molds. Use spatula to scrape excess fondant from backs of shapes so fondant is flush with the mold.

9 When mold is full, bend slightly and lift out shapes; place, flat-side down, onto parchment-paper-lined trays to dry out completely for 2 days.

10 Using a few buttons at a time, pipe a little royal icing onto backs of buttons; secure all over cake in a random pattern.

tips You'll need to make around 400 buttons. This can be done months ahead. Store shapes in an airtight container. The fondant will keep well so the buttons can be made over a long period of time. If shapes don't come out of the molds easily, freeze them for 2 minutes, then release the shapes.

THERE ARE NO PIPING SKILLS REQUIRED FOR THIS CAKE – THE RICH EMBROIDERED EFFECT COMES FROM USING BUTTON MOLDS OF DIFFERENT SHAPES AND SIZES. THERE ARE LOTS OF DIFFERENT MOLDS AVAILABLE IN CAKE DECORATING SHOPS; TAKE THE TIME TO MIX AND MATCH THEM TO MAKE THIS CAKE A SUCCESS.

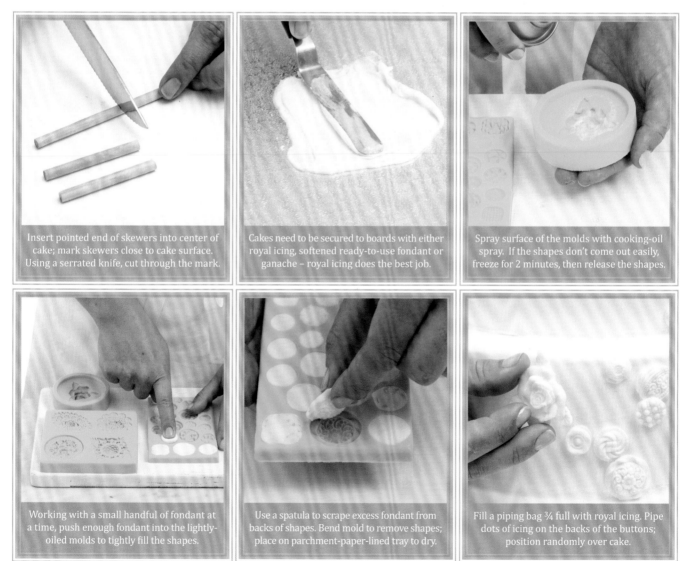

Insert pointed end of skewers into center of cake; mark skewers close to cake surface. Using a serrated knife, cut through the mark.

Cakes need to be secured to boards with either royal icing, softened ready-to-use fondant or ganache – royal icing does the best job.

Spray surface of the molds with cooking-oil spray. If the shapes don't come out easily, freeze for 2 minutes, then release the shapes.

Working with a small handful of fondant at a time, push enough fondant into the lightly-oiled molds to tightly fill the shapes.

Use a spatula to scrape excess fondant from backs of shapes. Bend mold to remove shapes; place on parchment-paper-lined tray to dry.

Fill a piping bag ¾ full with royal icing. Pipe dots of icing on the backs of the buttons; position randomly over cake.

BITE-SIZED
Stencilled Squares

ALMOST LIKE PETIT FOURS, THESE LITTLE CAKES WOULD BE GREAT AS PART OF A MENU FOR A STYLISH HIGH TEA. CHANGE THE COLORS TO SUIT YOUR THEME.

EQUIPMENT
2-inch square cutter
4 paper piping bags (page 221)
small stencils (see tips)
small offset metal spatula
16 plain colored paper liners
12-inch square wooden cake board
(page 208)
CAKE
shallow 9-inch square cake of
choice (page 190)
DECORATIONS
8 ounces ready-to-use white
fondant
cornstarch
yellow, blue, orange and pink food
colorings
1 quantity royal icing (page 220)
1 quantity butter cream (page 218)

1 Knead ready-to-use fondant on surface dusted with a little cornstarch until fondant loses its stickiness. Divide fondant into four equal portions: tint yellow, blue, orange and pink. Wrap separately in plastic wrap.

2 Roll each portion, separately, on cornstarched surface into a 1/8-inch thickness. Using cutter, cut out four squares from each colored fondant, place on parchment-paper-lined tray to dry, about 3 hours or overnight.
3 Divide royal icing evenly into four small bowls, tint using all four colorings. Cover surface of icings with plastic wrap to keep airtight.
4 Using one icing at a time, drop a teaspoon of icing into piping bag. Using corresponding color, pipe a dot of icing in the corners of the icing squares to anchor stencil in position.
5 Use spatula to spread royal icing thinly but evenly over stencil; scrape away excess icing, gently remove stencil. Wash and dry stencil before using again. Repeat with remaining squares and royal icing. Stand squares about 1 hour or until dry. Carefully remove the anchoring dots from the icing squares after the icing has dried.

6 Trim top of cake so it will sit flat when upside down (page 209). Turn cake upside down, trim sides to make a 8-inch square cake. Cut cake into 16 (2-inch) squares. Spread butter cream over cake tops; position fondant squares on cakes.
7 Place cake squares into paper liners. Secure cakes to board with a little royal icing or butter cream, to stop them sliding off the board.

tips Square paper liners are available in specialty food or kitchen shops, but we found round liners will change shape to accommodate the square cakes. The stencilled fondant squares can be made several weeks ahead; store in an airtight container at room temperature. The cake will become stale within a day of cutting. We used stencils used for dusting cappuccinos; they can be found online and at specialty markets.

Pipe a tiny dot of royal icing in two opposing corners of each square of fondant to anchor the stencil in place, if necessary.

Using a spatula, spread royal icing thinly and as evenly as possible over stencil (only cover the one shape). Scrape away excess icing.

Gently and slowly lift the stencil from the fondant square. Stand icing 1 hour to dry. Wash and dry stencil before using again.

ALMONDY WEDDING
Cookie Stacks

ALMONDY WEDDING
Cookie Stacks

THESE DELICATE COOKIES CAN BE COLORED TO SUIT YOUR THEME; THEY LOOK LOVELY IN ONE COLOR, OR LAYERED USING DIFFERENT COLORS, HOWEVER, IT IS QUICKER AND EASIER TO ICE THE COOKIES IN THE SAME COLOR.

EQUIPMENT
2½-inch round cutter
2-inch round cutter
1¼-inch round cutter
6 paper piping bags (page 221)
tweezers
ALMOND BISCUITS
2 sticks (1 cup) butter
2 teaspoons finely grated
    orange rind
½ cup superfine sugar
2 egg yolks
2 cups all-purpose flour
⅓ cup self-rising flour
½ cup cornstarch
1 cup ground almonds
DECORATIONS
2 quantities royal icing (page 220)
pink, blue and yellow food
    colorings
1 tablespoon strained lemon juice
1½ ounce package pearlized blush
    sugar pearls

1 Have butter at room temperature.
2 To make almond cookies: Beat chopped butter, rind, sugar and egg yolks in small bowl with electric mixer until light and fluffy. Transfer mixture to large bowl. Stir in sifted flours, cornstarch and ground almonds in two batches.

3 Knead dough on lightly floured surface until smooth; divide in half. Roll both pieces of dough, separately, between sheets of parchment paper into ⅛-inch thickness; refrigerate 30 minutes.
4 Preheat oven to 350°F. Line baking trays with parchment paper.
5 Using the largest cutter, cut 18 rounds from dough; place on baking trays. Using both medium and small cutters, cut 12 rounds of each from dough, re-rolling scraps as necessary; place on oven trays. Bake cookies about 15 minutes or until browned lightly. Cool on trays.
6 Divide royal icing equally between three small bowls; tint pale pink, blue and lemon. Cover surface of icing with plastic wrap to keep airtight.
7 Decide how many cookies are needed of the same color. Spread cookies out on a flat surface ready for piping.
8 Use one color of royal icing at a time: Fill one of the piping bags ½ full with icing. Pipe an unbroken border of icing around outside edge of the cookies; stand until set. Wrap piping bag in plastic wrap to keep airtight. Repeat with remaining colors.
9 Using one color at a time, add a drop or two of lemon juice to the remaining icing in bowl – the icing

should be the consistency of cream. Spoon icing into another paper piping bag; snip the tip from the bag. Pipe icing inside the same-colored border to "flood" the tops of the cookies. Stand overnight to set. Repeat with remaining batches of royal icing and cookies.
10 To assemble the wedding cakes: Stack 3 large cookies on top of each other, followed by 2 medium and 2 small cookies, joining each cookie with a dab of royal icing.
11 Use the reserved icing in piping bags (the normal royal icing, not the runny icing) to decorate the wedding cake stacks with loops (see tips), one layer at a time. Using tweezers, position pearls before the icing sets.

makes 6

tips To ensure the loops are evenly spaced, pipe small dots of royal icing around the cookies as a guide, if you like. The cookies can be finished a week ahead; store them in a single layer, covered, at room temperature. They're not hard to make, but they do require a good dose of patience. The cookies look pretty stacked on a tiered stemmed cake plate or cupcake stand. The "pearlized blush sugar pearls" are small edible pearls, and are available from cake decorating suppliers.

THESE COOKIES USE A TECHNIQUE KNOWN AS "FLOODING" OR "RUNOUT": THIS IS WHEN AN OUTLINE IS FILLED WITH RUNNY ICING. HERE THE COOKIES ARE OUTLINED WITH ROYAL ICING AND, WHEN THAT IS DRY, THEY'RE "FLOODED" WITH THINNED ROYAL ICING, WHICH BECOMES SMOOTH AND SHINY WHEN SET. THE COOKIES ARE QUITE FRAGILE ONCE THEY'VE BEEN DECORATED WITH THE ROYAL ICING LOOPS AND PEARLS, SO TREAT THEM GENTLY.

Lay cookies out on a flat surface ready for piping. Divide royal icing between 3 small bowls. Tint icing pink, blue and lemon.

Using one color at a time, pipe a border of royal icing in an unbroken line around the outside edge of the cookies; allow to dry.

Stir a drop or two of lemon juice into the royal icing to make it the consistency of cream. Place into the piping bag.

Using sharp scissors, snip the tip from the piping bag. Flood the icing into the center of the cookies within the piped border.

Stack 3 large, 2 medium, then 2 small cookies on top of each other, joining each layer with a little royal icing to secure.

Working with one stack of cookies at a time; pipe loops around cookies. Using tweezers, position pearls on icing before it sets.

MINT & PINK
Pearl Cake

PALE MINTY GREEN AND SOFT DUSTY PINK BLEND TOGETHER FOR A SWEET OLD-FASHIONED EFFECT. THIS IS DEFINITELY A GIRLY CAKE FOR OLD AND YOUNG ALIKE.

EQUIPMENT
12-inch round wooden cake board (page 208)
6-inch round wooden cake board (page 208)
smoothing tools
1¼-inch x 1½-inch scalloped cutter
3 wooden skewers
2 paper piping bags (page 221)
tape measure
fine artist's paint brush
acrylic measure (1-inch width)
tweezers
CAKE
deep 8-inch round cake of choice (page 190)
deep 6-inch round cake of choice (page 190)
DECORATIONS
2 pounds ready-to-use white fondant
cornstarch
pink and green food colorings
1 quantity royal icing (page 220)
1 (3½-ounce) package pearlized blush sugar pearls

1 Trim cakes (page 209). Secure large cake to largest board; secure small cake to remaining board (page 209). Prepare cakes for covering with ready-to-use fondant (page 209).

2 Knead ready-to-use fondant on surface dusted with cornstarch until fondant loses its stickiness. Tint 4 ounces of the fondant pink, enclose in plastic wrap. Tint the remaining fondant green.

3 Roll 12 ounces of green fondant on cornstarched surface until large enough to cover small cake. Using rolling pin, lift fondant onto cake; smooth with hands then smoothing tools. Trim fondant neatly around base of cake. Use remaining green fondant plus any scraps to cover large cake in the same way as the small cake.

4 Carefully press scallop cutter around side and over the top edge of large cake while the fondant is still soft. Dry cakes overnight.

5 Push trimmed skewers into center of large cake to support top tier. Secure small cake to large cake (page 212).

6 Color half the royal icing the same green as the cakes. Fill a piping bag ¾ full with icing. Pipe green icing around base of each cake. Use fingertip to blend icing into any gaps where cakes join the boards (page 212). Dry cakes overnight.

7 Measure around base of top tier. Roll pink fondant on cornstarched surface into ¹⁄₁₆-inch thickness, and long enough to wrap around cake. Cut a straight edge down one long side. Brush bottom ¾-inch of small cake sparingly with water; secure fondant strip around base, trim ends neatly. Use an acrylic measure and a small sharp knife to trim strip into a 1-inch-wide ribbon; don't cut into fondant underneath.

8 Re-roll pink fondant scraps to ⅛-inch thick. Using scallop cutter, cut a scallop from the fondant; secure to side of small cake with a little water.

9 Tint remaining royal icing pale pink. Half-fill piping bag with icing; pipe decorations onto cake. Pipe a 2-inch line of pink icing around base of small cake, position pearls on icing before it sets. Repeat all around cake.

As soon as the cake has been covered with fondant, gently press the cutter into the fondant starting from the bottom of the cake.

Use the acrylic measure and a sharp knife to trim the ribbon into a 1-inch width. Be careful not to cut through the fondant underneath.

Pipe a line about 2 inches long, position pearls with tweezers on icing before it sets. Repeat with icing and pearls all around the cake.

Mark the pattern on the fondant before it sets – do it carefully and slowly and you'll be pleased with the outcome. The cake would be suitable for birthdays, christenings, and baby showers. The "pearlized blush sugar pearls" are small edible pearls, and are available from cake decorating suppliers. The cutter we used came from a kit of patchwork cutters.

CHRISTMAS
Snowflakes

WE LOVE THE SNOWFLAKES ON THIS PRETTY CHRISTMAS CAKE. TRADITIONALLY, WE WOULD USE A RICH FRUIT CAKE, BUT A CHOCOLATE CAKE WOULD DO JUST AS WELL.

EQUIPMENT
10-inch round wooden cake board (page 208)
smoothing tools
set of 3 snowflake plunger cutters (small, medium, large)
fine artist's paint brush
paper piping bag (page 221)
CAKE
deep 8-inch round cake of choice (page 190)
DECORATIONS
1½ pounds ready-to-use white fondant
cornstarch
blue food coloring
1 teaspoon tylose powder
1 egg white, lightly beaten
½ cup white sanding sugar
1 quantity royal icing (page 220)
6 ounces small persian confetti

1 Trim cake (page 209). Secure cake to board (page 209). Prepare for covering with ready-to-use fondant (page 209).
2 Knead ready-to-use fondant on surface dusted with a little cornstarch until fondant loses its stickiness. Tint three-quarters of the fondant blue with coloring.
3 Roll out blue fondant on cornstarched surface into ⅛-inch thickness. Using rolling pin, lift fondant over cake; smooth with hands then smoothing tools. Trim fondant neatly around base of cake.
4 Knead remaining white ready-to-use fondant with tylose powder on surface dusted with cornstarch until smooth. Roll out on surface dusted with cornstarch into ⅛-inch thickness. Use cutters to cut out different-sized snowflakes. Place snowflakes on parchment-paper-lined tray to dry overnight.

5 Brush a very thin layer of egg white onto tips and around the centers of snowflake shapes; sprinkle sanding sugar over egg white. Stand the snowflakes for about 1 hour to dry.
6 Meanwhile, Fill piping bag ¾ full with royal icing. Pipe a line of icing all the way around base of cake. Position persian confetti on icing before it dries.
7 Secure snowflakes to cake with royal icing; leave to dry for about 1 hour.

tips The sanding sugar gives the snowflakes a lovely texture, however, if you can't find it, don't worry, the snowflakes look lovely without it. Snowflakes can be made months ahead; store them in an airtight container at room temperature. Persian confetti is sometimes sold as "snowfall." A fine dusting of sifted icing sugar added at the last minute adds to the snowy look.

Using a fine artist's paint brush, brush a very thin layer of egg white onto the tips and around the centers of all the snowflakes.

Sprinkle the centers and tips of the snowflakes with the sanding sugar; stand the snowflakes for about 1 hour or until they are dry.

Pipe royal icing on the back of a snowflake, position on cake; hold large snowflakes for about 5 seconds until they grip the cake.

PINK ON WHITE *Flower Cake*

EQUIPMENT
14-inch round wooden cake board (page 208)
8-inch round wooden cake board (page 208)
6-inch round wooden cake board (page 208)
smoothing tools
6 wooden skewers
fine long wooden skewer
silicone flower mold
small metal spatula
4 small piping bags
small (number 2) plain piping tube
CAKE
deep 10-inch round cake of choice (page 190)
deep 8-inch round cake of choice (page 190)
deep 6-inch round cake of choice (page 190)
DECORATIONS
4 pounds ready-to-use white fondant
cornstarch
tylose powder
pink food coloring
1 quantity royal icing (page 220)

1 Knead ready-to-use fondant on surface dusted with a little cornstarch until fondant loses its stickiness. Reserve 6 ounces of fondant for flowers.

2 Trim cakes (page 209). Secure 10-inch cake to largest board; secure remaining cakes to same-sized boards (page 209). Prepare cakes for covering with ready-to-use fondant (page 209).

3 Roll 12 ounces of the fondant on surface dusted with cornstarch until large enough to cover small cake. Using rolling pin, lift fondant onto cake; smooth with hands then smoothing tools. Trim fondant neatly around base of cake.

4 Use 1¼ pounds of the fondant to cover medium cake in the same way as small cake. Use remaining fondant to cover large cake. Reserve fondant scraps.

5 Use the fine wooden skewer to mark the fondant in random lengths all around cakes before the fondant sets. Dry cakes overnight.

6 Push 3 trimmed skewers into centers of large and medium cakes to support top tiers (page 212). Assemble cakes, securing each tier to the tier below (page 212).

7 Knead ½ teaspoon tylose powder into reserved fondant and scraps. Divide fondant into four portions; color three portions different shades of pink. Leave remaining portion white. Press small amounts of each colored fondant into flower molds; using spatula, scrape

excess fondant from backs of flowers so the shapes are flush with the mold. Bend mold gently to release flowers. Place the flowers, top-side up, on parchment-paper-lined tray to dry overnight.

8 Fit piping bag with tube. Fill bag ½ full with royal icing. Pipe snail trail (page 224) around base of each cake. Pipe white vertical lines in some of the grooves on the cakes. Wash and dry piping tube; place in clean piping bag.

9 Mix leftover icing in piping bag with remaining royal icing; divide between three small bowls. Color each batch a different shade of pink; cover surface with plastic wrap to keep airtight. Working with one color at a time, pipe vertical lines in some of the grooves on the cakes. Repeat with remaining icings leaving some grooves plain. Wash and dry piping tube after each color.

10 Using a few flowers at a time, pipe a little royal icing onto back of flowers; secure over cake in a random pattern.

tips Silicone molds come in myriad shapes and sizes. The mold we used gave us three different-sized flowers. The "snail trail" edging (page 224) around the cake bases requires a little practice before you start on the cakes.

Using the fine wooden skewer, mark grooves of random lengths around the sides of all the cakes. Do this before the fondant sets.

Press small amounts of fondant into mold. Scrape away excess fondant. Remove flowers from mold and allow to dry overnight.

Pipe vertical lines of royal icing into the grooves using white and three shades of pink icing. Leave some grooves without icing.

MINTY FLOCKED
Wedding Cake

SQUARE CAKES HAVE TO BE NEAR-PERFECT TO GIVE CRISP CLEAN LINES.

EQUIPMENT
**16-inch square wooden cake board
(page 208)**
**10-inch square wooden cake board
(page 208)**
**8-inch square wooden cake board
(page 208)**
**6-inch square wooden cake board
(page 208)**
smoothing tools
12 wooden skewers
large stencil
fine pearl-headed pins
small offset metal spatula
straight-sided metal scraper
2 paper piping bags (page 221)
craft glue
CAKE
**2 (deep 12-inch) square cakes of
choice (page 190)**
**deep 10-inch square cake of choice
(page 190)**
**shallow 10-inch square cake of
choice (page 190)**
**shallow 8-inch square cake of
choice (page 190)**
**deep 6-inch square cake of choice
(page 190)**
**shallow 6-inch square cake of
choice (page 190)**
jam or ganache of choice (page 210)
DECORATIONS
**7 pounds ready-to-use white
fondant**
cornstarch
green and blue food coloring
2 quantities royal icing (page 220)
2½ yards wide ribbon

1 Trim cakes (page 209). Secure one 12-inch cake to largest board (page 209); top with remaining 12-inch cake, joining cakes with a little jam or ganache (page 212). Stack and secure the two 10-inch and the two 6-inch cakes to same-sized boards in the same way. Secure 8-inch cake to same-sized board. Prepare cakes for covering with ready-to-use fondant (page 209).

2 Knead ready-to-use fondant on surface dusted with a little cornstarch until fondant loses its stickiness. Tint fondant pale green with coloring. Roll 3¼ pounds of fondant on cornstarched surface until large enough to cover the 12-inch cake. Using rolling pin, lift fondant onto cake; smooth with hands then smoothing tools. Trim fondant neatly around base of cake.

3 Use 1 pound of the fondant to cover the 6-inch cake and 12½ ounces of the fondant to cover the 8-inch cake in the same way.

4 Use blue coloring to color the remaining fondant and fondant scraps a shade of blue-green to tone with the green; use to cover the 10-inch cake in the same way as the large cake. Dry cakes overnight.

5 Push 4 trimmed skewers into centers of all cakes except the smallest cake to support the next tier (page 212).

6 To stencil the 12-inch cake: Working on one side of the cake at a time, use a wad of damp paper towel to lightly dampen the side of the cake to help hold the stencil in position. Hold stencil against side of cake; secure corners of stencil with pins,

if necessary. Use spatula to spread royal icing over entire stencil; remove excess icing back into bowl with metal scraper, gently remove stencil and pins. Wash and dry stencil before using again. Repeat on all sides of the cake. Stand about 1 hour or until dry.

7 Reserve 2 tablespoons of the royal icing. Tint remaining royal icing the same color as the 8-inch cake. Stencil sides in the same way as the large cake.

8 Assemble cakes, securing each tier to the tier below (page 212).

9 Tint the reserved royal icing a blue-green color to match the 10-inch cake. Fill piping bags ½ full with royal icing to match the cakes; pipe around bases of same-colored cakes. Use fingertip to blend icing into any gaps where cakes join the boards (page 212). Dry cakes overnight.

10 Trim ribbon to fit around the base of the top tier and the blue-green tier. Secure ends of ribbon with glue. Make small tailored bows (page 226) from ribbon. Glue bows into position over ribbon seams.

tips Covering the large cakes with the soft fondant can be a little difficult. Ask someone to help by supporting the fondant with their hands as it drapes down the sides of the cake. We used the same stencil on the small cake as we did on the large cake. When stencilling the small cake, rest it on a smaller cake pan to give it a bit of height off the countertop. This makes it easier to place the large stencil around the cake before applying the icing.

THE READY-TO-USE FONDANT COVERING THE CAKES SHOULD BE DONE AT LEAST A DAY AHEAD AND ALLOWED TO DRY BEFORE APPLYING THE STENCIL. USING A STENCIL ON A CAKE NEEDS A LITTLE PRACTICE; DO THIS ON THE SIDE OF A CAKE PAN TO GET THE FEEL OF JUST HOW MUCH ROYAL ICING TO USE AND HOW TO REMOVE THE STENCIL WITH CONFIDENCE. IF YOU MAKE A MISTAKE USING THE STENCIL, QUICKLY SCRAPE THE ICING OFF THE CAKE BEFORE IT SETS, THEN REPEAT THE STENCILLING.

Working on one side of the cake at time, gently blot the side of the cake with damp paper towel to lightly moisten the fondant.

Position the stencil on the side of the cake. If necessary, secure the stencil to the cake using fine pins at the corners of the stencil.

Using a small offset metal spatula, carefully spread the royal icing as evenly as possible over the stencil along one side of the cake.

Using the metal scraper, scrape excess icing from the stencil and return to the bowl. Press firmly, but not too heavily, against the stencil.

Starting from the end of the stencil, remove the pins, then carefully remove the stencil from the cake by pulling back along the cake.

Secure the ribbon around the cake, then make a small flat bow and glue in position to cover where the ends of the ribbon meet.

WEDDING CAKE *Wonder*

ELEGANCE AND SIMPLICITY IS WHAT THIS STUNNING CAKE IS ALL ABOUT. THE STYROFOAM DISCS ARE USED TO SUPPORT THE FLOWERS BETWEEN EACH LAYER.

EQUIPMENT
drill
½ inch (12mm) drill bit with centering tip (see tips)
14-inch round wooden cake board (page 208)
12-inch round wooden cake board (page 208)
10-inch round wooden cake board (page 208)
8-inch round wooden cake board (page 208)
6-inch round wooden cake board (page 208)
3¾-inch x 8-inch diameter styrofoam disc
3¾-inch x 6-inch diameter styrofoam disc
3¾-inch x 4-inch diameter styrofoam disc
craft glue (or glue gun)
½-inch x 24-inch wooden dowel
smoothing tools
pastry brush
plastic ruler
pizza cutter
pencil
fine pearl-headed pins
small piping bag
small (number 2) plain piping tube
7 wooden skewers

CAKE
deep 10-inch round cake of choice (page 190)
shallow 10-inch round cake of choice (page 190)
deep 8-inch round cake of choice (page 190)
shallow 8-inch round cake of choice (page 190)
deep 6-inch round cake of choice (page 190)
shallow 6-inch round cake of choice (page 190)
jam or ganache of choice (page 210)

DECORATIONS
5 pounds ready-to-use ivory fondant
cornstarch
1 quantity sugar syrup (page 217)
1 quantity royal icing (page 220)
pink food coloring
fresh large organic flowers

1 Knead 1 pound ready-to-use fondant on surface dusted with a little cornstarch until fondant loses its stickiness. Brush 14-inch board with sugar syrup. Roll fondant large enough to cover board. Using rolling pin, lift fondant onto board; smooth with hands then smoothing tools. Trim fondant neatly around base (page 208); use cornstarched fingertip to smooth edge. Stand overnight to dry.

2 Mark the center of each cake board and styrofoam disc. Except for the 12-inch wooden board, drill a ½-inch hole through the center of each disc and each board. Glue the 14-inch board on top of the 12-inch board (this gives clearance under the board so you can pick it up off the counter). Squeeze glue into hole in the 14-inch board; position dowel in the hole. Stand until dry.

3 Trim cakes (page 209). Secure deep 10-inch cake to largest board. Secure remaining deep cakes to same-sized boards (page 209). Join same-sized cakes together with jam or ganache (page 212). Prepare cakes for covering with ready-to-use fondant (page 209).

4 Knead fondant on surface dusted with a little cornstarch until fondant loses its stickiness. Roll 12 ounces of fondant on cornstarched surface until large enough to cover small cake. Using rolling pin, lift fondant onto cake; smooth with hands then smoothing tools. Trim fondant neatly around base.

5 Use 1¼ pounds of fondant to cover medium cake and use 1½ pounds of fondant to cover large cake in the same way as small cake. Dry cakes overnight.

6 Using one styrofoam disc at a time, brush syrup sparingly around sides of discs. Roll 2½ ounces fondant on cornstarched surface until long enough to wrap around side of smallest disc; using ruler and pizza cutter, trim to fit. Cover side of styrofoam; reserve scraps. Trim away any excess fondant on top and bottom of disc. Knead scraps and remaining fondant together; cover sides of remaining discs in the same way.

7 Using picture as a guide, draw 'stitch' pattern onto a strip of parchment paper large enough to wrap around large cake; attach to cake, marked-side out, using pins. Using a fine pin, mark pattern onto each cake, reducing the length of the paper to fit around the middle cake, then the small cake.

8 Tint royal icing pale pink. Fit piping bag with tube. Fill bag ¾ full with royal icing; pipe pattern onto cakes using pin marks as a guide; leave to dry for at least 1 hour.

9 To assemble the cake: Position the largest styrofoam disc onto the dowel, secure to board with a little royal icing. Next, firmly push the large cake down over the dowel; secure to the disc below with royal icing. Push 3 trimmed skewers into top of large cake. Top with the medium disc then medium cake in the same way; push 3 trimmed skewers into medium cake. Top with the small disc then small cake.

10 Use remaining skewer to pierce holes into side of styrofoam discs; push stems into holes to fill the gaps between the cakes with flowers. Lay more flowers on top of cake. Position flowers on the day of serving.

tips The drill bit should be suitable for drilling wood. Discuss the type of flowers to be used with a florist to make sure they'll stay fresh. Use artificial flowers, if you prefer.

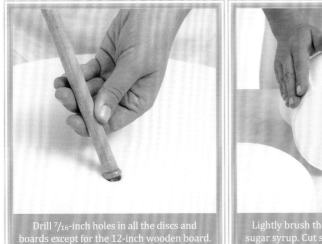

Drill $^{7}/_{16}$-inch holes in all the discs and boards except for the 12-inch wooden board. Use glue to secure the dowel into position.

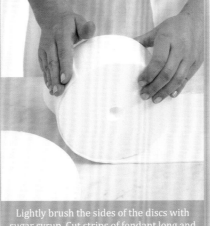

Lightly brush the sides of the discs with sugar syrup. Cut strips of fondant long and wide enough to wrap around sides of discs.

Use a sharp knife to cut away any excess fondant from the top and bottom of each disc. Be careful not to cut into the disc.

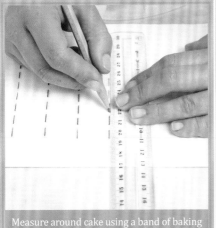

Measure around cake using a band of baking paper; using pencil and ruler, draw 'stitch' markings of varying lengths onto the paper.

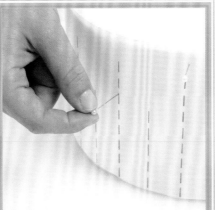

Secure the band of parchment paper (marked-side outwards) around the cake with fine pins. Mark the pattern onto the cake with pins.

Remove parchment paper. Fit piping bag with tube and, following the pin markings, pipe the pattern onto the cakes. Leave to dry.

Position the largest disc on the dowel; secure to board with royal icing. Spread more royal icing on top of the disc.

Push the large cake onto the dowel to meet the disc. Push the trimmed skewers into the cake to support the next disc.

Push a wooden skewer into the disc; wriggle it around to make holes large enough to hold the flower stems firmly in position.

DIVINE WHITE SILK
Rose Cake

THIS CAKE IS TOPPED WITH A FABULOUS SILK CABBAGE ROSE. IF YOU PREFER, BUY
FRESH ORGANIC FLOWERS TO DECORATE THE CAKE ON THE DAY OF SERVING.

EQUIPMENT

**12-inch round wooden cake board
(page 208)**

**6-inch round wooden cake board
(page 208)**

smoothing tools

number 3 strip cutter ¼-inch wide

3 wooden skewers

2 paper piping bags (page 221)

white florist's tape

CAKE

**deep 8-inch round cake of choice
(page 190)**

**2 (deep 6-inch) round cakes of
choice (page 190)**

jam or ganache of choice (page 210)

DECORATIONS

**2 pounds ready-to-use white
fondant**

cornstarch

green food coloring

1 quantity royal icing (page 220)

1 yard wide ribbon

1 yard narrow ribbon

**white silk cabbage rose or
fresh organic flowers**

1 Trim cakes (page 209). Secure large cake to largest board. Secure small deep cake to remaining board (page 209); top with shallow cake, joining with a little jam or ganache (page 212). Prepare cakes for covering with ready-to-use fondant (pages 209).

2 Knead ready-to-use fondant on surface dusted with a little cornstarch until fondant loses its stickiness. Tint half the fondant pale green.

3 Roll fondant on cornstarched surface until large enough to cover 8-inch cake. Using rolling pin, lift fondant onto cake; smooth with hands then smoothing tools. Trim fondant neatly around base.

4 Use white fondant to cover 6-inch cake in the same way. While fondant is still soft, use strip cutter to mark grooves into the fondant on the top tier. Dry cakes overnight.

5 Push trimmed skewers into center of large cake to support the top tier. Secure small cake on top of large cake (page 212).

6 Tint half the royal icing green to match the bottom tier. Fill a piping bag ¾ full with icing; pipe around base of cake. Use fingertip to blend icing into any gaps where cake joins the board (page 212). Repeat process using white royal icing for top tier. Dry cakes overnight.

7 Wrap ribbons around base of bottom cake; cut to fit. Secure ends with a little white royal icing.

8 Trim silk flower to fit top of cake. Wrap stem in white florist's tape. Gently pry open flower petals; lay flower on top of cake.

tips The strip cutter, used for marking the fondant on the top tier of this cake, is very useful if the fondant is not quite perfect. It's important to mark the grooves on the fondant before it begins to develop a crust and becomes firm. Position the flower on the day of serving.

Using the strip cutter, gently, but evenly, press it onto the soft fondant before the fondant begins to dry and develop a crust.

Measure around the base of the bottom tier; cut ribbons to fit. Position and secure ribbons to cake with tiny dabs of royal icing.

Trim the stem, leaves and buds of the silk rose to fit the cake; tape stems with florist's tape. Gently pry open the flower petals.

PEACHES & CREAM
Frilled Cake

PEACHES & CREAM
Frilled Cake

WHILE THIS FRILLY LITTLE CAKE IS IDEAL FOR A BABY SHOWER OR CHRISTENING, IT WOULD ALSO DELIGHT ANY BUDDING PRIMA BALLERINA IN THE FAMILY. USE SHADES OF PINK TO RESEMBLE A TUTU, AND TOP WITH A PAIR OF BALLET SLIPPERS.

EQUIPMENT
8-inch square wooden cake board (page 208)
smoothing tools
6-inch scalloped edge frill cutter
vinyl mat
frilling tool
medium artist's paint brush
CAKE
deep 6-inch square cake of choice (page 190)
DECORATIONS
1 pound ready-to-use ivory fondant
cornstarch
peach food coloring

1 Trim cake (page 209). Secure cake to board (page 209). Prepare cake for covering with ready-to-use fondant (page 209).

2 Knead three-quarters of the ready-to-use fondant on surface dusted with a little cornstarch until fondant loses its stickiness. Roll fondant on cornstarched surface into ⅛-inch thickness. Using rolling pin, lift fondant over cake, smooth with hands then smoothing tools. Trim fondant neatly around base. Dry cake overnight.

3 Divide remaining fondant into 5 equal portions. Working with cornstarched hands, tint 4 portions with peach coloring so that each portion is a slightly darker shade than the last. Leave remaining portion ivory. Wrap portions, separately, in plastic wrap.

4 Roll out darkest shade of fondant into ⅛-inch thickness on surface dusted with cornstarch. Using frill cutter, cut out 4 scalloped shapes; cover with vinyl mat.

5 Working with one shape at a time on a surface dusted with cornstarch, frill the scalloped edge of the shape by rolling the frilling tool backwards and forwards over the edge of the shape. Repeat with remaining shapes.

6 Brush a tiny amount of water ¾ inch up from the base of the cake. Position the straight edge of the frilled shape onto the damp area of the cake. (Brush only where the top of the frill is to sit, not the frill itself.) Continue this process around the cake, using one frilled shape for each side.

7 Repeat using remaining portions of fondant, ending with the ivory-colored frill, and overlapping frilled layers slightly, until the sides are completely covered with frills.

tips The frilled strips of fondant should still be slightly soft when positioned on the cake. The fondant strips will stretch a little to cover the sides of the cake. If you prefer to color this cake a different color, you will need to use white ready-to-use fondant, not ivory colored.

THE CHARM OF THIS DAINTY LITTLE CAKE IS IN THE DELICATE SHADES OF ITS COLOR ALONG WITH ITS PEACHY FRILLS. THE FRILLS ARE QUITE EASY TO MAKE, HOWEVER, THEY ARE FRAGILE AND MUST BE HANDLED WITH CARE OTHERWISE THEY MAY STRETCH OR TEAR WHEN BEING POSITIONED AROUND THE CAKE.

Divide the fondant into 5 equal portions. Using tiny amounts of coloring, tint 4 portions varying shades of peach; leave 1 portion ivory.

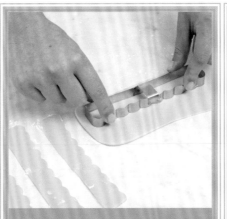

Roll out darkest shade of fondant on a surface dusted with cornstarch into a ⅛-inch thickness, cut out 4 strips using scalloped frill cutter.

Cover 3 strips with vinyl mat. Using frilling tool, roll the tool backwards and forwards over the edge of the remaining strip.

Continue rolling the frilling tool backwards and forwards over one edge of the fondant strip until the frill covers the whole edge.

Brush water sparingly about ¾-inch up from the base of the cake. Only brush where the top of the frill is to sit, not the frill part itself.

Position frill on cake. Continue to make frills in the various shades; position each layer on the cake, with the frill showing beneath.

A POSY
of Daisies

THIS CAKE IS SO PRETTY IT REMINDS US OF YOUTH AND SPRING. IT
WOULD MAKE A DELIGHTFUL ENGAGEMENT OR 21ST BIRTHDAY CAKE.

EQUIPMENT
1-inch flower cutter
¾-inch flower cutter
vinyl mat
flower mat
small ball tool
metal skewer
4-inch styrofoam ball
½-inch x 8-inch wooden dowel
craft glue
small styrofoam block
12-inch round wooden cake board
    (page 208)
6-inch round wooden cake board
    (page 208)
smoothing tools
3 wooden skewers
paper piping bag (page 221)
pastry brush
CAKE
deep 8-inch round cake of choice
    (page 190)
deep 6-inch round cake of choice
    (page 190)
1 quantity sugar syrup (page 217)
DECORATIONS
4 ounces modeling paste
cornstarch
1 yard narrow white ribbon
2 pounds ready-to-use white
    fondant
yellow food coloring
1 quantity royal icing (page 220)

1 Knead gum paste on surface
dusted with a little cornstarch until
paste loses its stickiness. Roll paste out
on cornstarched surface into 1/32-inch
thickness. Using both cutters, cut out
5 flowers of each size at a time. Cover
paste with vinyl mat to prevent it
drying out.
2 Place 5 flowers on the flower mat;
using the ball tool, press into the center
of each flower, in a circular motion, until
the flower has thinned out and curled
into a cup shape. Place the flowers on
a fine wire rack or a parchment-paper-
lined tray to dry. Repeat process until
all the paste is used.
3 Push the metal skewer halfway
into the styrofoam ball and wriggle it
around to create a hole large enough
to push the dowel into. Place a little
glue around one end of the dowel,
push dowel into hole in the ball. Stand
1 hour to dry. Spread a little glue
along the back of the ribbon. Starting
at the top of the dowel, wrap ribbon
around the dowel. Allow to dry; stand
ball upright in the styrofoam block to
support it.
4 Trim cakes (page 209). Secure large
cake to largest board; secure small
cake to remaining board (page 209).
Prepare cakes for covering with
ready-to-use fondant (page 209).
5 Knead ready-to-use fondant on
surface dusted with a little cornstarch
until fondant loses its stickiness. Tint
fondant pale yellow.
6 Roll 9 ounces of the fondant on
cornstarched surface until large
enough to cover small cake. Using

rolling pin, lift fondant onto cake;
smooth with hands then smoothing
tools. Trim fondant neatly around base.
7 Using 1 pound of the fondant,
cover large cake in the same way. Dry
cakes overnight.
8 Push trimmed skewers into center
of large cake to support the top tier
(page 212). Secure small cake to
large cake (page 212).
9 Tint royal icing yellow to match
cakes. Fill piping bag ¾ full with royal
icing; pipe around base of each cake.
Use fingertip to blend icing into any
gaps where cakes join the boards
(page 212). Dry overnight.
10 Pipe yellow centers into each of
the flowers with royal icing; stand
3 hours or overnight to dry.
11 Brush styrofoam ball lightly
with sugar syrup. Roll out remaining
yellow fondant until large enough to
cover the ball. Using rolling pin, lift
fondant onto ball; smooth with hands
then smoothing tools. Trim fondant
neatly around base of the ball.
12 Push dowel through the center
of the top cake until it reaches the
board below. Using small and large
flowers, pipe a dot of royal icing onto
the back of a flower, position on the
ball. Continue positioning flowers to
cover the ball. Leave assembled cake
to dry overnight.
13 Using picture as a guide, use
flowers to decorate both cakes.

tips Gum paste is also sold as "petal
paste," "flower molding paste" and
"modeling paste".

THERE ARE NO SPECIAL PIPING SKILLS REQUIRED FOR THIS CAKE, BUT COVERING THE
BALL CAN BE A LITTLE TRICKY. DRAPE THE ROLLED READY-TO-USE FONDANT OVER
THE BALL – IT WILL HANG WITH LOOSE FOLDS. GENTLY, WITHOUT STRETCHING,
EASE THE FOLDS OUT OF THE FONDANT AS YOU PRESS THE FONDANT ONTO AND
AROUND THE BALL. TRIM OFF EXCESS FONDANT AT THE BASE OF THE BALL. THERE
SHOULD BE NO CREASES IN THE FONDANT IF DONE CORRECTLY.

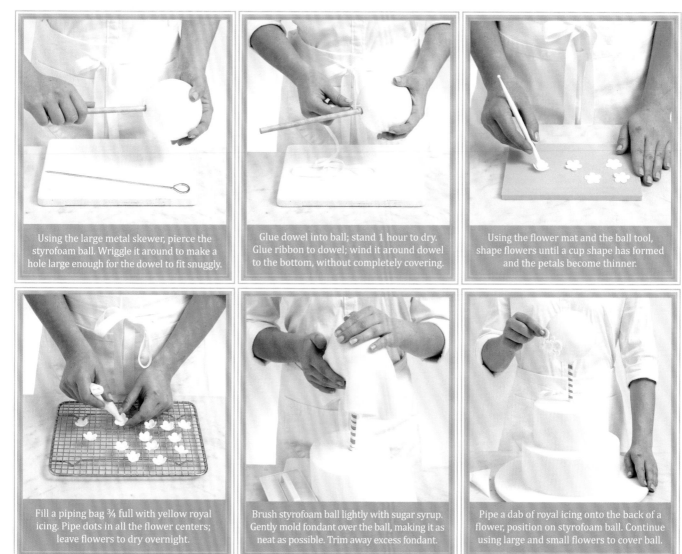

Using the large metal skewer, pierce the styrofoam ball. Wriggle it around to make a hole large enough for the dowel to fit snuggly.

Glue dowel into ball; stand 1 hour to dry. Glue ribbon to dowel; wind it around dowel to the bottom, without completely covering.

Using the flower mat and the ball tool, shape flowers until a cup shape has formed and the petals become thinner.

Fill a piping bag ¾ full with yellow royal icing. Pipe dots in all the flower centers; leave flowers to dry overnight.

Brush styrofoam ball lightly with sugar syrup. Gently mold fondant over the ball, making it as neat as possible. Trim away excess fondant.

Pipe a dab of royal icing onto the back of a flower, position on styrofoam ball. Continue using large and small flowers to cover ball.

Latte Lace CAKE

EQUIPMENT
16-inch square wooden cake board (page 208)
10-inch square wooden cake board (page 208)
8-inch square wooden cake board (page 208)
6-inch square wooden cake board (page 208)
4-inch square wooden cake board (page 208)
smoothing tools
16 wooden skewers
3 paper piping bags (page 221)
lace patterns (page 228)
CAKE
2 (deep 12-inch) square cakes of choice (page 190)
deep 10-inch square cake of choice (page 190)
deep 8-inch square cake of choice (page 190)
shallow 8-inch square cake of choice (page 190)
shallow 6-inch square cake of choice (page 190)
deep 4-inch square cake of choice (page 190)
shallow 4-inch square cake of choice (page 190)
jam or ganache of choice (page 210)
DECORATIONS
7 pounds ready-to-use ivory fondant
cornstarch

brown food coloring
1 quantity royal icing (page 220)
9ounces white chocolate Melts
1½ yards wide ribbon

1   Trim cakes (page 209). Secure one 12-inch cake to largest board (page 209); top with remaining 12-inch cake, joining cakes with a little jam or ganache (page 212). Join the two 8-inch cakes and the two 4-inch cakes in the same way, securing cakes to same-sized boards (page 209). Secure 10-inch and 6-inch cakes to same-sized boards. Prepare cakes for covering with ready-to-use fondant (page 209).

2   Knead 2 pounds ready-to-use fondant on surface dusted with a little cornstarch until fondant loses its stickiness. Tint light brown with coloring.

3   Knead one-third of the fondant on cornstarched surface. Roll fondant until large enough to cover the 6-inch cake. Using rolling pin, lift fondant onto cake; smooth with hands then smoothing tools. Trim fondant neatly around base of cake. Use remaining fondant and scraps to cover the 10-inch cake.

4   Knead remaining ivory fondant on surface dusted with cornstarch; tint a darker shade of brown than the previous cakes. Use 11 ounces of the fondant to cover the 4-inch cake; use 1½ pounds to cover the 8-inch cake; use the remaining fondant, plus scraps, to cover the 12-inch cake. Dry cakes overnight.

5   Push 4 trimmed skewers into center of all cakes except the top cake to support the next tier (page 212).

6   Assemble cakes, securing each tier to the tier below (page 212).

7   Tint royal icing to match the two colors of the cakes. Fill two piping bags ¾ full with each of the colored royal icings; pipe around base of each cake to match the icing. Use fingertip to blend icing into any gaps where cakes join the boards. Dry cakes overnight.

8   Trace lace patterns onto parchment paper; turn paper over. Melt chocolate (page 222). Fill piping bag ½ full with chocolate, snip tip off bag. Carefully pipe pattern onto parchment paper; stand until set.

9   Pipe small dots of chocolate onto backs of chocolate lace; carefully secure lace to cake. Wrap ribbon around base of large cake; secure with royal icing.

Carefully trace the lace patterns for the cakes onto sheets of parchment paper; turn paper over so tracings are on the other side.

Fill a paper piping bag ½ full with melted chocolate; pipe chocolate over patterns, then stand about 5 minutes or until set.

Pipe dots of chocolate onto the back of one piece of lace; position on cake. Repeat process to cover cake with lace pattern.

If you prefer, draw patterns of your own to suit the purpose of the cake. You will need to pipe extra chocolate lace in case of breakages. The chocolate will set quite quickly so, if you break any of the piped patterns, simply re-melt the chocolate and pipe the pattern again.

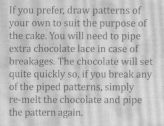

SOME OF THE CAKES IN THIS CHAPTER
are easy until you get to the
HAND-MADE FLOWERS – THESE NEED
practice, skill and patience –
YOU CAN USE SILK OR FRESH FLOWERS
in their place. Think of
READY-TO-USE FONDANT AND GUM
paste as play dough and let
YOUR IMAGINATION RUN LOOSE.

CHAPTER THREE
EXPERT

BOWTIE
Mini Cakes

BOWTIE
Mini Cakes

INVITATION ONLY – THESE ARE JUST THE TICKET FOR A FORMAL OR BLACK-TIE EVENT.

EQUIPMENT
2¾-inch round cutter
9 x 2¾-inch round cardboard cake boards (page 208)
2-inch round cutter
tape measure
plastic ruler
pizza cutter
vinyl mat
fine artist's paint brush
plaque plunger cutter
CAKE
2 (shallow 8-inch) square cakes of choice (page 190)
1 quantity ganache of choice (page 210)
1 quantity sugar syrup (page 217)
DECORATIONS
4 pounds ready-to-use white fondant
tylose powder
cornstarch
ivory, black and pink food coloring

1 Trim tops of cakes so they sit flat when upside-down (page 209). Turn cakes upside-down. Using 2¾-inch cutter, cut nine rounds from each cake. Secure nine cakes to cardboards (page 209) with a little ganache (see tips). Spread tops of cakes with more ganache; top with remaining nine cakes. Spread cakes lightly, but evenly, all over with remaining ganache. Stand overnight at a cool room temperature.
2 Knead 12 ounces of the ready-to-use fondant with ½ teaspoon tylose on cornstarched surface until smooth. Roll fondant on cornstarched surface into ⅛-inch thickness. Using 2¾-inch cutter, cut nine rounds from the fondant. Reserve fondant scraps. Place rounds on parchment-paper-lined trays; stand 2 hours or until dry.

3 Color 9 ounces of the ready-to-use fondant ivory with a little coloring. Knead fondant with ½ teaspoon tylose on lightly cornstarched surface until smooth. Roll fondant on cornstarched surface into ⅛-inch thickness. Using 2-inch cutter, cut nine rounds from fondant. Place rounds on parchment-paper-lined trays; stand 2 hours or until dry.
4 Brush cakes lightly all over with sugar syrup. Knead remaining white fondant on cornstarched surface until fondant loses its stickiness.
5 Measure and note height and circumference of cake. Roll fondant into ⅛-inch thickness on cornstarched surface until large enough to cover sides of all cakes; using ruler and pizza cutter, cut nine rectangles of required size to cover cakes, re-rolling icing as necessary. Cover eight rectangles with vinyl mat. Cover cake with fondant rectangle, as pictured; trim end neatly, join ends with a little water. The fondant should cover the edge of the cardboard. Repeat with remaining cakes and icing. Reserve icing scraps.
6 Brush the backs of the ivory rounds with a little water; position on top of the white rounds.
7 Combine reserved fondant scraps with another 3 ounces of icing; color black. Knead in a pinch of tylose on cornstarched surface. Roll out about one-third of the fondant on cornstarched surface into ⅛-inch thickness. Using pizza cutter and plastic ruler; cut out nine ¼-inch x 2-inch strips of fondant. Brush a little water on the backs of the strips, position on top and over sides of ivory rounds.

8 To make bows: Knead black fondant scraps together on cornstarched surface; roll into ⅛-inch thickness. Using pizza cutter and plastic ruler cut nine ¼-inch x 3¼-inch strips of fondant; secure to center of black strips on rounds with a little water. Brush a little water over center of strip, bring each end in to meet in the middle to make loops of bows. Cover seams with small strips of black fondant secured across the center of the bow with a little water. Secure rounds to cakes.
9 Roll remaining white fondant into ⅛-inch thickness on cornstarched surface. Using plaque cutter, cut out nine plaques. Brush backs with a little water, secure on cakes.
10 Color white fondant scraps pink, roll out on cornstarched surface into ⅛-inch thickness; cut out heart shapes (see tips).
11 Roll remaining black fondant with scraps on cornstarched surface into ⅛-inch thickness, cut out letters about ½-inch high (see tips).
12 Position and secure letters and hearts to plaque with a little water.

makes 9

tips If necessary, cut the cake boards to the same size as the base of the cakes. The boards should be invisible after the ready-to-use fondant is wrapped around the cakes. Make templates for your chosen letters and a small heart shape for the cakes, or buy small alphabet and heart-shaped cutters from cake decorating suppliers.

YOU'LL NEED A FAIRLY SOLID CAKE, SUCH AS A FRUIT OR CHOCOLATE CAKE, TO SUPPORT THE WEIGHT OF THE ICING. IF USING FRUIT OR CHOCOLATE CAKES, THEY CAN BE COMPLETED AT LEAST A MONTH AHEAD; STORE IN AN AIRTIGHT CONTAINER AT ROOM TEMPERATURE.

Using 2¾-inch cutter, cut out 9 rounds from each cake. Join rounds with a little ganache. Secure cylinders to boards with ganache.

Knead ½ teaspoon tylose into white fondant, roll out on lightly cornstarched surface. Cut out 9 (2⁹/₁₆-inch) rounds from fondant.

Spread cakes all over with ganache; stand overnight. Brush sugar syrup lightly over cakes, then cover with a length of fondant.

Join ivory rounds to white rounds with a little water. Secure black fondant ribbon to rounds. Brush center of ribbon with water.

Cut a narrow strip of black fondant, long enough to make both loops of bow. Join ends to center of ribbon to make loops with a little water.

Cut a short strip of black fondant just long enough to cover the seams of the bows. Secure into position with a little water.

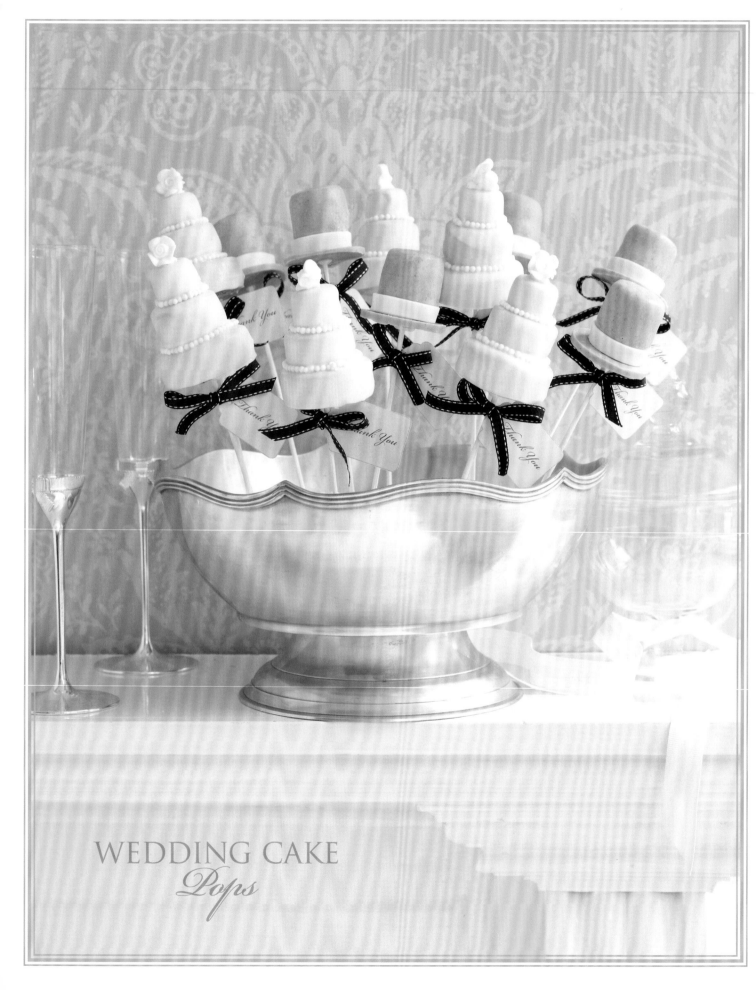

WEDDING CAKE
Pops

WEDDING CAKE
Pops

EQUIPMENT
8-inch x 12-inch rectangular cake
    pan
8-inch styrofoam block
1-inch round cutter
1¼-inch round cutter
1½-inch round cutter
2-inch round cutter
18 long thin toothpicks
18 (12-inch) cake pop sticks
paper piping bag (page 221)
tweezers
metal skewer
ruler
CAKE
5 cups firmly packed butter cake
    crumbs
½ quantity butter cream (page 218)
DECORATIONS
3 (12-ounce) packages white
    chocolate Melts
golden yellow and black food
    colorings
1 quantity royal icing (page 220)
1 packet (¹/₁₆-inch) white sugar
    pearls
9 white sugar flowers
1½ ounces ready-to-use white
    fondant
cornstarch
4 yards narrow ribbon

1 Grease and line rectangular pan
with parchment paper. Combine cake
crumbs and butter cream in medium
bowl. Press mixture evenly into pan;
cover, freeze 1 hour or refrigerate
overnight until firm.
2 Stir two-thirds of the chocolate
in medium heatproof bowl over
medium saucepan of simmering
water until smooth (don't let water
touch base of bowl). Transfer to tall
narrow heatproof glass or bowl.
3 Meanwhile, use a sharp pointed
knife to make 18 small holes, about 2
inches apart, in styrofoam.
4 To make all cake pops: For the
hats, use 1¼-inch cutter to cut 18

rounds from the cake crumb mixture.
For the wedding cakes, cut 9 (1-inch)
rounds, 9 (1½-inch) rounds and 9
(2-inch) rounds.
5 To make wedding cake pops: Dip
the end of a toothpick into melted
white chocolate; push about halfway
into the middle of a 1-inch round.
Repeat with remaining toothpicks and
remaining 1-inch and 1½-inch rounds.
Freeze cakes about 5 minutes.
6 Dip the end of a cake pop stick into
white chocolate; push stick all the
way through 2-inch round, extending
about 1¾-inch past the top of the
cake. Repeat with remaining cake pop
sticks and remaining 2-inch rounds.
Freeze cakes about 5 minutes.
7 Dip wedding cake rounds in melted
chocolate to coat; rock back and forth,
don't twist or cakes will break (re-melt
chocolate as necessary). Stand upright
in styrofoam, refrigerate until set.
8 To assemble wedding cakes; scrape
away any excess visible chocolate
from the toothpicks or cake pop sticks
to prevent damaging any of the tiers.
Remove 1½-inch rounds from
toothpicks, carefully push onto cake
pop sticks on top of the 2-inch
rounds. Repeat with 1-inch rounds.
Use a little re-melted white chocolate
to join tiers together.
9 Use a tiny bit of yellow coloring to
tint the royal icing the same color as
the chocolate on the wedding cakes
(see tips). Fill paper piping bag ½ full
with icing, use to fill any gaps between
tiers of cakes; smooth with fingertip.
10 Pipe tiny dots around base of
1-inch and 1½-inch tiers, about 2
inches at a time; using tweezers,
position pearls in wet icing. Repeat all
the way around cakes. Secure flowers
to cakes with a little royal icing.
11 To make top hats: Melt remaining
chocolate; use black coloring to tint

chocolate grey. Transfer chocolate to
tall narrow heatproof glass or bowl.
Dip end of cake pop stick into
chocolate; push stick through 2
(1¼-inch) rounds about halfway into
the top round. Join rounds with a
little melted chocolate; freeze cakes
about 5 minutes. Dip hats in melted
grey chocolate to coat (re-melt
chocolate, if necessary); stand upright
in styrofoam, refrigerate until set.
12 To make brims for hats: re-melt
grey chocolate as necessary, spread
onto a sheet of parchment paper
about ¹/₁₆-inch thick. Stand about
10 minutes or until almost set.
13 Use 2-inch-round cutter to cut
9 rounds from chocolate. Use a metal
skewer to pierce a hole through the
center of the rounds (heat skewer if
the chocolate has become too hard);
thread onto cake pop sticks. Secure
with chocolate. Return cake pop sticks
to styrofoam, refrigerate until set.
14 Knead ready-to-use fondant on
surface dusted with cornstarch until
fondant loses its stickiness. Roll fondant
on surface dusted with cornstarch until
¹/₁₆-inch thick. Cut fondant into 9 strips,
measuring ½-inch x 3¼-inches (they
should be long enough to wrap around
the hat). Secure bands to hats with a
little royal icing.
15 Tie small bows (page 226)
around cake pop sticks.

tips Cut out cake rounds as close as
possible. Squash and press remaining
cake mixture together, freeze and
cut out more shapes, if necessary.
Because the royal icing is very white,
and the white chocolate is a creamy
color, it is necessary to tint the icing
with a tiny bit of yellow coloring to
give it a creamy color so it blends
with the white chocolate. Re-melt
chocolate as necessary (page 222).

STORE THE WEDDING CAKE POPS AT A COOL ROOM TEMPERATURE, STANDING UP IN STYROFOAM, COVERED, TO PROTECT THEM FROM DUST. OR, STORE THEM FLAT IN AIRTIGHT CONTAINERS. THE CAKE POPS REQUIRE PATIENCE TO MAKE, BUT ARE WELL WORTH THE EFFORT. WE USED LITTLE SUGAR ROSES, BOUGHT FROM THE SUPERMARKET, TO DECORATE THE TOP OF THE WEDDING CAKES.

The cake crumb mixture must be frozen or very firm before cutting out rounds for the wedding cake and top hat cake pops.

Dip ends of the cake pop sticks in chocolate; push sticks through large rounds, extending about 1¾ inches past the top of the cake.

Dip all the tiers for the wedding cake in melted chocolate. Let excess chocolate drip off, then level under each tier with a knife.

Push the medium and small tiers onto the extended cake pop stick; secure the tiers together with a little melted chocolate.

Push two of the cake rounds for the top hats onto a cake pop stick to form the hats. Join rounds with a little melted chocolate.

Push a round of chocolate onto cake pop stick to make the brim of the hat. Secure brim to hat with a little melted chocolate.

DUSKY ROSE *Cake*

EQUIPMENT
12 lengths 18-gauge floral wire
long-nosed pliers
flower glue (page 227)
styrofoam block
vinyl mat
1-inch, 1½-inch, 2¾-inch round
    cutters
flower mat
ball tool
fine artist's paint brush
small non-stick rolling pin
12-hole round-based, shallow
    whoopie pie pan
stamens
¾-inch 4-petal blossom cutter
florist's tape
18-inch round wooden cake board
    (page 208)
6-inch round wooden cake board
    (page 208)
smoothing tools
3 wooden skewers
paper piping bag (page 221)

CAKE
deep 9-inch round cake of choice
    (page 190)
deep 7-inch round cake of choice
    (page 190)

DECORATIONS
2 quantities gum paste (page 227)
pink and purple food coloring
cornstarch
4 pounds ready-to-use white
    fondant
1 quantity royal icing (page 220)

1 To make roses: Cut two lengths of wire into 3 (4¾-inch) lengths each. Make small hook at one end of each piece of wire using pliers.

2 Reserve 3 ounces of gum paste for blossoms. Color one-third of the remaining paste dark pink, use to make 6 centers for 4 roses and 2 buds: Roll a marble-sized piece of paste into a rounded cone shape; dip hooked end of wire into flower glue, push halfway into broad end of cone. Push wire into styrofoam; dry overnight. Make 5 more centers in the same way.

3 When working with petals and blossoms, work with one at a time, and keep the remaining petals and blossoms covered with a vinyl mat.

4 Roll remaining dark pink paste on a cornstarched surface into ⅛-inch thickness; using the 1-inch cutter, cut out 3 petals, place on flower mat. Use ball tool to thin top of petal. Brush bottom third of petal lightly with flower glue; wrap around a bud. Secure and wrap remaining 2 petals around bud in the same way. Stand in styrofoam to dry overnight. Make 5 more buds in the same way. Reserve paste scraps.

5 Knead paste scraps into one-third of the remaining paste; use coloring to tint to a shade slightly lighter than the buds, if necessary. Roll paste on cornstarched surface until ⅛-inch thick; cut out 3 (1½-inch) petals.

6 Use rolling pin to thin top half of petal; place petal on flower mat, use ball tool to curl edge of petal. Secure around rose bud with flower glue. Repeat with the remaining 2 petals, overlapping each petal; dry overnight. Make 5 more buds in the same way.

7 Knead paste scraps into remaining paste; use coloring to tint to a paler shade than previous layer of petals.

8 To make the rose: Roll and cut out 5 petals using the 2¾-inch cutter. Use rolling pin to thin top half of petals; place petals on flower mat, use ball tool to curl edge. Place petals in cornstarched whoopie pie pan until edges of petals begin to firm. Glue in position around previous petals, overlapping each petal. Make 3 more roses the same way.

9 Make cup shapes from foil so the outside petals are supported by foil. Place rose in foil cup, poke wire through foil. Suspend a wire cake rack above the counter so the rose wire can sit in rack unimpeded while the rose is drying.

10 To make blossoms: Cut 10 pieces of wire into 6 equal lengths each. Cut 30 of the stamens in half. Roll half the reserved paste into a ⅛-inch thickness; using ¾-inch cutter, cut out 30 blossoms.

11 Place 5 blossoms on flower mat (keep remainder under vinyl mat); shape petals with ball tool. Dab a dot of flower glue in center of blossom; poke a stamen through the glue. Repeat with remaining blossoms. Roll out remaining paste and make another 30 blossoms. Dry blossoms overnight.

12 Gather five blossoms together, position a piece of wire close to the bottom of the blossom, secure stamens to wire with florist's tape.

13 Trim cakes (page 209). Secure large cake to large board; secure small cake to small board. Prepare for covering with ready-to-use fondant (page 209).

14 Tint ready-to-use fondant light purple with purple coloring. Knead fondant on cornstarched surface until fondant loses its stickiness. Roll one-quarter of the fondant on cornstarched surface until large enough to cover small cake. Use rolling pin to lift fondant onto cake; smooth with hands then smoothing tools. Trim fondant neatly around base; reserve scraps.

15 Use half the remaining fondant to cover large cake in the same way as the small cake; dry cakes overnight.

16 Push trimmed skewers into center of large cake to support top tier (page 212). Secure small cake on top of large cake (page 212).

17 Tint royal icing light purple to match cakes. Fill piping bag ¾ full with icing; pipe around base of each cake. Use fingertip to blend icing into any gaps where cakes join the board (page 212). Dry cakes overnight.

18 Knead reserved purple fondant and fondant scraps on cornstarched surface. Roll fondant large enough to make a 6 inch x 12 inch rectangle. Gently fold fondant into three pleats. Gather and pinch ends together and, using picture as a guide, position and secure draped fondant to cake with a little water; stand overnight to dry.

19 Position roses and blossoms, by gently pushing wires into cake.

Cut 2 lengths of wire into 3 (4¾ inch) lengths. Using pliers, bend each piece of wire into a loop at one end to make a small hook.

Roll a small piece of gum paste into a cone shape. Dip hooked end of wire into flower glue, push into cone; dry overnight.

For each rose, cut out 3 (1-inch) petals. Roll out the top half of each petal thinly, frill with a ball tool, then glue around the 'bud'.

Cut out 3 (1½-inch) petals for each rose, roll and frill the tops of each petal thinly. Position and secure on rose with flower glue.

Using the blossom cutter, cut 30 blossoms from gum paste. Place 5 blossoms on flower mat; shape using the ball tool.

Dab a tiny dot of flower glue in the center of a blossom; pull end of stamen through blossom to secure the tip on the glue.

Gather five of the blossoms together, secure the stamens to a piece of wire by firmly wrapping with a single layer of florist's tape.

Roll purple fondant on a cornstarched surface into a 6-inch x 12-inch rectangle; gently fold the fondant into three large pleats.

Gently drape the fondant over the cake. Gather the ends together and secure the ends of the fondant to the cake with a little water.

TRADITIONAL
Wedding Cake

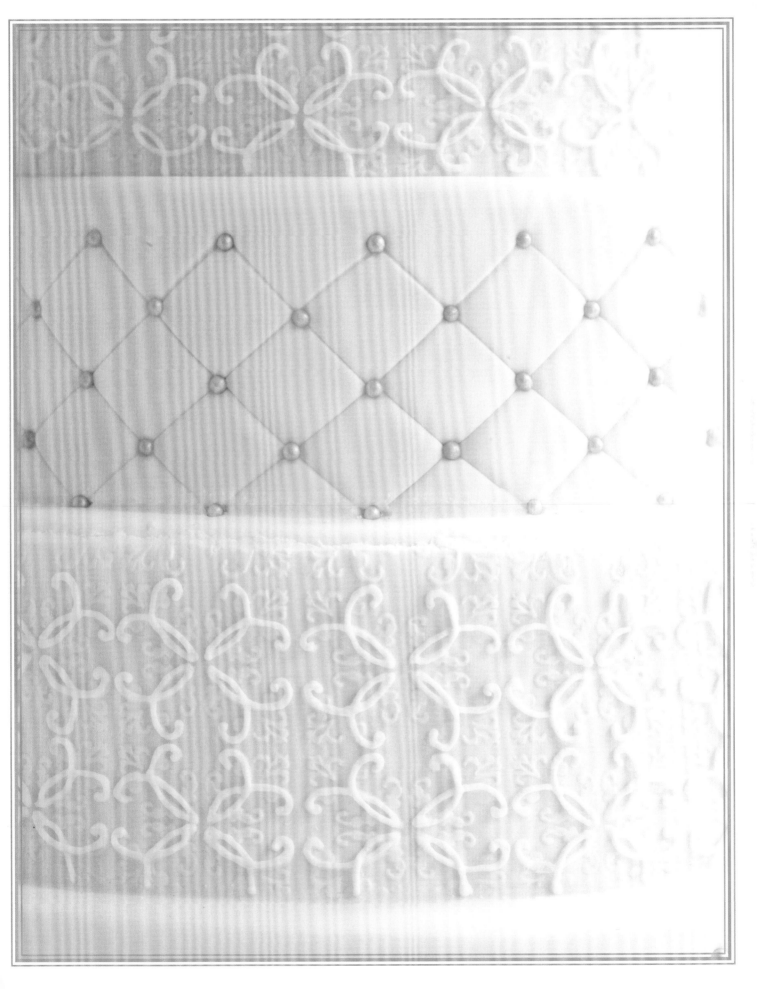

TRADITIONAL
Wedding Cake

EQUIPMENT

18-inch round wooden cake board (page 208)
12-inch round wooden cake board (page 208)
10-inch round wooden cake board (page 208)
8-inch round wooden cake board (page 208)
6-inch round wooden cake board (page 208)
smoothing tools
quilting tool
tape measure
embossed rolling pin
plastic ruler
pizza cutter
small non-stick rolling pin
12 wooden skewers
paper piping bag (page 221)
small piping bag
small (number 2) plain piping tube
tweezers
craft glue

CAKE

deep 14-inch round cake of choice (page 190)
deep 12-inch round cake of choice (page 190)
deep 10-inch round cake of choice (page 190)
deep 8-inch round cake of choice (page 190)
deep 6-inch round cake of choice (page 190)

DECORATIONS

9½ pounds ready-to-use white fondant
cornstarch
2 quantities royal icing (page 220)
2 tablespoons pearlized blush sugar pearls
1 yard narrow ribbon

1 Trim cakes (page 209). Secure 14-inch cake to largest board; secure remaining cakes to the same-sized boards (page 209). Prepare cakes for covering with ready-to-use fondant (page 209).

2 Knead ready-to-use fondant on surface dusted with a little cornstarch until fondant loses its stickiness.

3 Roll 2½ pounds of fondant on cornstarched surface until large enough to cover the 14-inch cake. Using rolling pin, lift fondant onto cake; smooth with hands then smoothing tools. Trim fondant neatly around base. Use quilting tool to mark pattern on side of cake.

4 Use 1¼ pounds of fondant to cover the 10-inch cake in the same way. Use quilting tool to mark pattern on cake, the same way as the 14-inch cake.

5 Use 1½ pounds of fondant to cover the 12-inch cake; 1 pound of fondant to cover the 8-inch cake; and 9 ounces of fondant to cover the 6-inch cake in the same way. Dry cakes overnight.

6 Use the tape measure to measure the circumference of the 12-inch cake. Roll 1 pound of the remaining fondant into a strip about 3¼ inches wide, and long enough to wrap around the cake. Use the embossed rolling pin to mark a pattern onto the strip of fondant. Use the ruler and the pizza cutter to cut a straight edge down one long side of the strip.

7 Lightly blot dried fondant around the side of the 12-inch cake with damp kitchen paper to hold the strip of fondant in place. Carefully roll the fondant strip, embossed-side in, around the small rolling pin. Position the rolling pin so that the straight edge of the fondant is flush with the

bottom and side of the cake. Unroll fondant onto side of cake.

8 Use a sharp knife to trim the excess fondant flush with the top edge of the cake. Use fingertip to gently blend the soft fondant edge with the firm fondant on the top of the cake. Leave to dry 3 hours or overnight.

9 Use remaining 12 ounces of fondant to make embossed strip to cover side of the 8-inch cake in the same way.

10 Push 3 trimmed skewers into the centers of all the cakes except the smallest cake to support the next tier (page 212). Assemble cakes, securing each tier to the tier below (page 212). Fill paper piping bag ½ full with royal icing; pipe around base of each cake. Use fingertip to blend icing into any gaps where cakes join the boards. Dry cakes overnight.

11 Fit piping bag with piping tube. Fill bag ½ full with royal icing. Pipe dots onto six corners at time on the quilting pattern; use tweezers to position pearls on dots. Continue this way on the 14-inch and 10-inch quilted cakes.

12 Pipe over some of the embossed pattern on the 8-inch and 12-inch cakes. Leave all cakes to dry overnight.

13 Wrap and secure ribbon to top cake tier with a little royal icing. Use ribbon to make bow (page 226); secure bow to ribbon with a little craft glue.

tips Keep in a cool dark dust-free place. This cake is extremely heavy to lift and move, especially if the cakes are fruit cakes. You will need two people to lift the cake. The "pearlized blush sugar pearls" are small edible pearls, and are available from cake decorating suppliers.

HERE WE HAVE A BEAUTIFUL TRADITIONAL FIVE-TIER WEDDING CAKE.
THE PIPING TECHNIQUES USED FOR THIS CAKE ARE RELATIVELY SIMPLE, BUT
THE PIPING NEEDS TO BE REALLY GOOD FOR THE CAKE TO LOOK WONDERFUL.

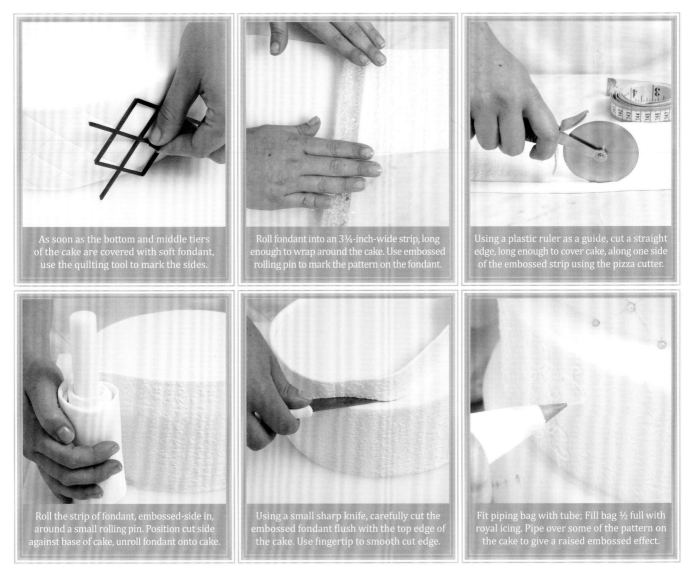

As soon as the bottom and middle tiers of the cake are covered with soft fondant, use the quilting tool to mark the sides.

Roll fondant into an 3¼-inch-wide strip, long enough to wrap around the cake. Use embossed rolling pin to mark the pattern on the fondant.

Using a plastic ruler as a guide, cut a straight edge, long enough to cover cake, along one side of the embossed strip using the pizza cutter.

Roll the strip of fondant, embossed-side in, around a small rolling pin. Position cut side against base of cake, unroll fondant onto cake.

Using a small sharp knife, carefully cut the embossed fondant flush with the top edge of the cake. Use fingertip to smooth cut edge.

Fit piping bag with tube; Fill bag ½ full with royal icing. Pipe over some of the pattern on the cake to give a raised embossed effect.

The croquembouche can be completed up to 12 hours ahead and kept in a refrigerated cool room (most catering venues have these). Don't make the croquembouche in humid weather as the humidity will affect the spun sugar, the toffee, and the crispness of the puffs. We used a huge mold for this impressive croquembouche, but there are smaller molds available to buy or hire.

CROQUEMBOUCHE

CROQUEMBOUCHE

EQUIPMENT
**24-inch deep croquembouche mold
(diameter 12¾ inches/32cm)
large piping bag
¼-inch plain piping tube
candy or digital thermometer
16-inch round wooden cake board
(page 208)
masking tape
2 wooden spoons
modified wire whisk (see page 155)**
PASTRY PUFFS (1 QUANTITY)
**½ cup water
½ stick (¼ cup) butter
1 tablespoon superfine sugar
½ cup baker's flour
3 eggs**
PASTRY CREAM (1 QUANTITY)
**1 cup milk
⅓ cup superfine sugar
1 teaspoon vanilla extract
2 tablespoons cornstarch
3 egg yolks**
TOFFEE (1 QUANTITY)
**2 cups granulated sugar
1 cup water**
DECORATIONS
fresh organic or sugar flowers

1 Make pastry puffs and pastry cream.
2 Grease and line croquembouche mold with strips of parchment paper as neatly as possible.
3 Fit piping bag with tube, spoon pastry cream into bag; pipe into pastry puffs.
4 Make one batch of toffee. Use a fork to hold filled pastry puffs, dip quickly into hot toffee; place into mold (do not leave any large gaps between puffs). Repeat to completely fill mold with pastry puffs; stand about 1 hour or until set.
5 Gently turn croquembouche onto board. Make another batch of toffee. Drizzle toffee as evenly as possible over croquembouche.

6 Using masking tape, secure two wooden spoons about 2 feet apart on counter top, placing spoons so that the handles overhang the edge. Place newspaper on floor under handles to catch any toffee drips. Make another batch of toffee; cool for about 3 minutes or until toffee is slightly thickened. Dip ends of modified whisk into hot toffee and wave the whisk back and forth over the spoon handles to make spun toffee threads.
7 Carefully lift spun toffee onto croquembouche; position flowers.

pastry puffs Preheat oven to 400°F. Grease and line baking trays with parchment paper. Combine the water, finely chopped butter and superfine sugar in medium saucepan; bring to the boil. Add flour, beat with a wooden spoon over heat until mixture comes away from base and side of pan and forms a smooth ball. Transfer mixture to medium bowl; continue beating with wooden spoon until mixture cools slightly. Beat in two of the eggs, one at a time. Lightly beat the third egg in a cup, gradually beat in egg, a bit at a time, until the mixture becomes glossy and gently folds over when the wooden spoon is lifted out of the mixture (you may not need to use all the egg). Drop level tablespoons of mixture onto trays about 2 inches apart. Bake 10 minutes. Reduce oven temperature to 350°F; bake a further 15 minutes. Cut a small opening in the base of each pastry puff; bake a further 10 minutes or until puffs are dry and crisp. Cool on trays. You need to make 20 quantities of the pastry puff recipe to fill this sized croquembouche mold.

pastry cream Combine milk, sugar and extract in small saucepan; bring to the boil. Meanwhile, whisk cornstarch with egg yolks in medium heatproof bowl; gradually whisk in hot milk mixture. Return mixture to pan; stir over medium-high heat until mixture boils and thickens. Cover surface of mixture with plastic wrap; refrigerate 2 hours. You will need to make 20 quantities to fill the pastry puffs.

toffee Combine sugar and the water in large saucepan; stir over high heat without boiling until sugar dissolves. Bring to the boil; boil, without stirring, until toffee reaches a temperature of 300°F on a candy or digital thermometer, or becomes a light golden brown in color. Remove from heat, allow bubbles to subside before using. You need about 5 quantities of toffee for the croquembouche; make each batch as you need it.

tips When handling toffee, exercise great care and make sure to wear long sleeves and a heavy apron to minimize the risk of accidental burns. If burned, immediately plunge fingers into cold water. The pastry puffs can be made well in advance. You need about 400 to fill the mold we used – make sure they've completely dried out in the oven then cooled before storing. Unfilled puffs can be stored in an airtight container for up to 4 weeks, or can be frozen for up to 3 months. It's best to make the toffee, one batch at a time, as you need it. Digital thermometers are easier to read and quicker to use than candy thermometers (see page 219).

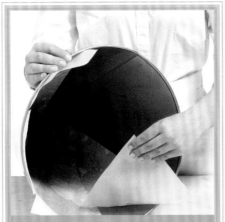

Line well-greased croquembouche mold as neatly as possible with long strips of parchment paper. Cut the paper to fit the mould.

Fit the piping bag with the tube then fill the bag ½ way with pastry cream. Fill the puffs through the hole in the bottom.

Using a fork to hold each filled puff, carefully and quickly dip puff into the toffee, hold until toffee drips subside.

Place puff into mold immediately after dipping it; pack puffs as evenly as possible without squashing them.

Turn croquembouche onto board, remove mold and paper. Drizzle more toffee as evenly as possible over croquembouche.

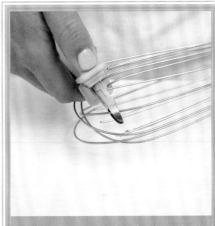

Modifying a wire whisk will make it easier to make the spun toffee: just snip off the rounded ends of the wire using wire cutters.

Secure 2 wooden spoons on edge of counter. Dip ends of whisk into toffee, wave whisk over spoon handles to make spun toffee.

Carefully gather spun toffee and gently wrap around the croquembouche. Make as much toffee as is needed to wrap around the tower.

Position flowers on spun toffee. If using sugar flowers, position them with a little of the warmed toffee leftover from coating the puffs.

YELLOW PEONY
Rose Cake

While making the cake is easy – making the peony rose is not, it is an advanced technique. Once the petals are made, it's a matter of carefully assembling them. It would be wise to buy all the bits and pieces listed, to make the challenge easier.

YELLOW PEONY
Rose Cake

EQUIPMENT
4¾-inch length 18-gauge floral wire
long-nosed pliers
white florist's tape
pasta machine (see tips)
vinyl mat
small, medium, large and
    extra large peony cutters
wire cutters
7 lengths x 26-gauge floral wire
flower glue (page 227)
2 (12-hole) round-based, shallow
    whoopie pie pans
peony petal veiner
flower mat
ball tool
fine artist's paint brush
14-inch square wooden cake board
    (page 208)
8-inch square wooden cake board
    (page 208)
6-inch square wooden cake board
    (page 208)
smoothing tools
8 wooden skewers
3 paper piping bags (page 221)
craft glue

CAKE
deep 10-inch square cake of choice
    (page 190)
deep 8-inch square cake of choice
    (page 190)
deep 6-inch square cake of choice
    (page 190)

DECORATIONS
1 bundle small white stamens
3 ounces gum paste
ivory and yellow food coloring
cornstarch
yellow petal dust
4 pounds ready-to-use white
    fondant
1 quantity royal icing (page 220)
4 yards wide ribbon

1 To make peony: Make a small hook in one end of the 18-gauge wire using pliers, don't fully close it. Fold the bunch of stamens in half, pull the center of the stamens into the hook; close the hook by twisting the wire together with pliers. Secure stamens to wire with florist's tape.

2 Tint gum paste ivory. Knead paste on surface dusted with a little cornstarch until smooth. Roll paste on cornstarched surface until thin enough to be rolled through a pasta machine set on the thickest setting (see tips). Cover paste with vinyl mat.

3 Using petal cutters, cut 3 small, 5 medium, 5 large and 7 extra large petals from paste; cover with vinyl mat.

4 Using wire cutters, cut each piece of 26-gauge wire into 3 even lengths. Work with one petal at a time, keeping remaining petals covered with vinyl mat. Thread one petal onto one piece of wire by dipping one end of wire into flower glue and gently pushing wire into pointed end of petal, one-third of the way into petal.

5 Dust whoopie pie pans lightly with cornstarch. Dust petal veiner with cornstarch; press wired petal in petal veiner. Place petal onto flower mat; frill edge of petal by gently rolling ball tool over edge of petal. Place petal into whoopie pie pan to dry overnight. Repeat with remaining petals.

6 To color petals, combine a pinch of petal dust with a pinch of cornstarch. Using paint brush, brush dust into centers of petals and stamens.

7 To assemble peony: Gently bend wire on a small petal to a 45 degree angle, hold against base of prepared flower center (with stamens), secure by wrapping florist's tape once around wires. Repeat with remaining small petals, spacing evenly around center of peony.

8 Continue wiring the petals in the same way using medium, then large, then extra large petals; placing each layer of petals evenly around flower center slightly below the previous layer of petals.

9 Trim cakes (page 209). Secure 10-inch cake to largest board; secure remaining cakes to same-sized boards (page 209). Prepare cakes for covering with ready-to-use fondant (page 209).

10 Knead ready-to-use fondant on cornstarched surface until fondant loses its stickiness. Tint 1 pound fondant very pale yellow, 1½ pounds a slightly darker yellow shade, and the remaining fondant a darker shade again. Enclose, separately, in plastic wrap.

11 Roll pale yellow fondant on surface dusted with cornstarch until large enough to cover small cake. Using rolling pin, lift fondant onto cake; smooth with hands then smoothing tools. Trim fondant neatly around base of cake.

12 Knead pale yellow fondant scraps into medium-yellow fondant; use to cover medium cake in the same way as small cake. Knead fondant scraps into darkest yellow icing and use to cover the large cake in the same way. Dry cakes overnight.

13 Push 4 trimmed skewers into centers of large and medium cakes to support the next tier (page 212).

14 Assemble cakes, securing each tier to the tier below (page 212).

15 Divide royal icing into 3 bowls; tint each to match color of the cakes. Fill piping bags ½ full to match cakes; pipe around bases of same-colored cakes. Use fingertip to blend icing into any gaps where cakes join the boards (page 212). Dry overnight.

16 Trim ribbon to fit around bases of all tiers. Secure ends neatly with glue.

17 Gently push stem of peony into top of cake just before serving.

tips The petals can be made by rolling the paste out thinly to ¹⁄₁₆-inch, rather than rolling through the pasta machine, however, the machine gives great results. The flower can be made months ahead; keep it in an airtight container at a cool room temperature.

Using pliers, make a small hook on the end of the piece of 18-gauge wire. It should be barely large enough to hold the bunch of stamens.

Fold the stamens in half and pull the center of the stamens into the hook. Twist wire with pliers to hold the stamens securely in place.

Firmly wrap the florist's tape around the stamens to secure them to the wire. Only wrap the base of the stamens to the wire.

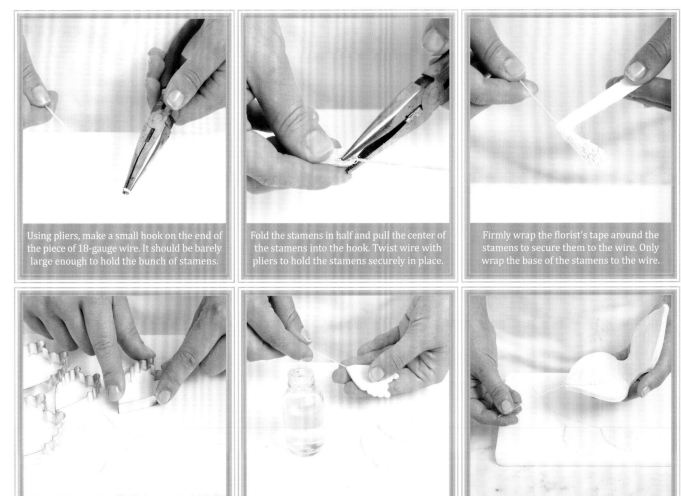

Roll the gum paste through the pasta machine. Cut out 3 small, 5 medium, 5 large and 7 extra large petals from the paste.

Using a piece of 26-gauge wire, dip end of the wire into flower glue, push wire a third of the way into the pointy end of the petal.

Dust the petal-veiner with cornstarch; working with one petal at a time, press the wired petal in petal-veiner to create veins in paste.

Place petal on the flower mat, frill the edge of the petal using the ball tool. Place petal in cornstarched whoopie pie pan to dry overnight.

Use equal amounts of combined petal dust and cornstarch, and brush lightly onto petals, graduating the color from dark to light.

Bend wire on a small petal to 45 degrees, tape onto wire holding the stamens. Wire all petals in the same way, from small to extra large.

SILHOUETTE
Spectacular

BLACK AND WHITE MAY BE CONSIDERED NEUTRAL COLORS, BUT THEY BRING A BOLD LOOK TO THIS CAKE. THE COLORS COMPLEMENT EACH OTHER, GIVING THIS CAKE CLEAN CLASSIC LINES THAT HAVE PLENTY OF 'WOW' FACTOR.

EQUIPMENT
12-inch round wooden cake board (page 208)
pastry brush
1 quantity sugar syrup (page 217)
smoothing tools
stencil
medium offset metal spatula
6 wooden skewers
2 (7-inch) round wooden cake boards (page 208)
fine pearl-headed pins
straight-sided metal scraper
paper piping bag (page 221)
small shallow bowls
3 lengths 18-gauge floral wire
wire cutters
CAKE
2 (deep 7-inch) round cakes of choice (page 190)
1 shallow 7-inch round cake of choice (page 190)
jam or ganache of choice (page 210)
DECORATIONS
5 pounds ready-to-use white fondant
cornstarch
1 quantity royal icing (page 220)
black food coloring
tylose powder
1 yard narrow ribbon

1 Knead 1 pound ready-to-use fondant on surface dusted with a little cornstarch until fondant loses its stickiness. Brush the large wooden board with sugar syrup. Roll fondant large enough to cover board. Using rolling pin, lift fondant onto board; smooth with hands then smoothing tools. Trim fondant neatly around base of board (page 208); then smooth edge with cornstarched fingertip. Stand overnight to dry.

2 Reserve half the royal icing; cover surface to keep airtight. Use a damp paper towel to dampen the fondant on board (this helps hold the stencil in position). Hold stencil against fondant on board, use spatula to spread royal icing over entire stencil, scrape away excess, return to bowl; gently remove stencil. Wash and dry stencil before reusing. Repeat until board is stencilled all over. Stand 1 hour or until dry. Cover surface of leftover royal icing in bowl.

3 Trim cakes (page 209). Secure one deep cake to stencilled board (page 209); push 3 trimmed skewers into center of cake (page 212).

4 Secure remaining cakes to smaller boards; push 3 trimmed skewers into center of deep cake and secure to top of cake on stencilled board. Secure the shallow cake on top of the cake stack. Prepare cake for covering with ready-to-use fondant (page 209).

5 Knead 3 pounds ready-to-use fondant on surface dusted with a little cornstarch until fondant loses its stickiness. Roll fondant on cornstarched surface until large enough to cover cake. Using rolling pin, lift fondant onto cake; smooth with hands then smoothing tools. Trim fondant neatly around base of cake. Dry overnight.

6 Secure stencil around lower third of cake with pins. Use spatula to spread royal icing over stencil, remove excess icing with scraper; return to bowl. Gently remove pins and stencil; wash and dry stencil before using again. Repeat until stencil is completed around the lower third of the cake. Stand about 1 hour to dry.

7 Fill piping bag ½ full with royal icing; pipe around base of cake. Use fingertip to blend icing into any gaps where cake joins the board (page 212). Dry cake overnight.

8 Tint any leftover royal icing black; cover surface to keep airtight.

9 Lightly dust shallow bowls with cornstarch.

10 Knead remaining ready-to-use fondant with a pinch of tylose on cornstarched surface until fondant loses its stickiness. Roll fondant on cornstarched surface into 1/16-inch thickness. Roll fondant into a rectangle about 10-inch x 14-inch. Use damp paper towel to dampen the fondant to help hold the stencil in position. Place stencil over fondant, spread evenly with black royal icing, scrape away excess icing, return to bowl; gently remove stencil. Wash and dry stencil before reusing to stencil over another area.

11 Use a sharp pointed knife to cut fondant into 6 random-sized elliptical shapes before the royal icing dries. Drape shapes in shallow bowls; stand overnight to dry.

12 Cut wire into 7¼-inch lengths, then bend in half. Secure wire to backs of shapes with royal icing. Place on parchment-paper-lined tray to dry overnight.

13 Push wired shapes into top of cake on day of serving (keep in an airtight container until ready to use). Wrap ribbon around base of cake; secure ends with a dab of royal icing.

As with the "posy of daisies" cake (page 130), this cake can be a little tricky to cover. Drape the rolled ready-to-use fondant over the cake – it will hang with loose folds. Gently, without stretching, ease the folds out of the fondant as you press the fondant around the cake. Trim off excess fondant at the base of the cake. There should be no pleats or creases in the fondant if done correctly. If you use the same recipe for all three cakes, you can simply join the cakes with jam or ganache, and not use the cake boards between the layers. However, if you want to use different cakes for the layers – use the cake boards under each cake to make serving the cakes easier.

Use spatula to spread royal icing over the ready-to-use fondant on board; remove stencil. Repeat until board is stencilled all over.

Roll out a strip of ready-to-use fondant; dampen with a paper towel to hold the stencil in place. Spread stencil evenly with black royal icing.

Carefully remove the stencil from fondant. Wash and dry the stencil before using again. Stencil all over the rectangle of fondant.

Using a sharp pointed knife, cut out 6 random-sized elliptical shapes. Do this quickly and evenly before the royal icing sets.

Drape the shapes in and over the sides of the lightly cornstarched shallow bowls (stencilled-side up). Stand the shapes overnight to dry.

Bend the wire in half and secure to the backs of the dried shapes with royal icing. When dry, position the shapes in the top of the cake.

GIFT BOX
for Baby

BABY

GIFT BOX
for Baby

ALTHOUGH THIS CAKE IS A LABOR OF LOVE, IT'S WORTH EVERY BIT OF EFFORT.

EQUIPMENT
14-inch square wooden cake board (page 208)
smoothing tools
pasta machine (see tips)
acrylic measures (¾-inch and 1¾-inch widths)
vinyl mat
fine artist's paint brush
stitching tool
alphabet cutters
paper piping bag (page 221)
CAKE
2 (deep 8-inch) square cakes of choice (page 190)
jam or ganache of choice (page 210)
DECORATIONS
4 pounds ready-to-use white fondant
cornstarch
green food coloring
1 quantity royal icing (page 220)
tylose powder

1 Trim cakes (page 209). Secure one cake to wooden board (page 209); top with remaining cake, joining cakes with a little jam or ganache (page 212). Prepare cake for covering with ready-to-use fondant (page 209).
2 Knead ready-to-use fondant on surface dusted with a little cornstarch until fondant loses its stickiness. Tint three-quarters of the fondant pale green.
3 Roll 2 pounds of the green fondant on cornstarched surface until large enough to cover cake. Using rolling pin, lift fondant onto cake; smooth with hands then smoothing tools. Trim fondant neatly around base of cake. Dry cake overnight. Knead green fondant scraps into remaining green fondant.

4 Using apricot-sized pieces of both the green and white fondant, roll out each fondant, separately, into a rectangle the width of the pasta machine. Feed pieces through the pasta machine set on the thickest setting (see tips).
5 Using the ¾-inch acrylic measure as a guide, cut 6-inch lengths of green and white fondant, each ¾-inch wide. You need 7 strips of each colored fondant for each side of the cake. Cover fondant strips with vinyl mat to prevent drying out. Roll any fondant scraps into same-colored fondant; cover, separately, with plastic wrap.
6 Brush a little water onto the sides of the cake, secure fondant strips to all sides of the cake, alternating colors.
7 Before the icing strips dry, Use ¾-inch acrylic measure to mark sides of cake for lid. Dry cake overnight.
8 To make the lid: Brush a little water onto the area where the box lid will sit. Roll out remaining white fondant on cornstarched surface until large enough to cover top of cake and extend over the sides to cover marked area for lid. Using rolling pin, lift fondant onto cake; smooth with hands then smoothing tools. Use ¾-inch measure to mark the sides of the fondant. Cut off excess fondant with a sharp knife. Reserve fondant scraps. Use stitching tool to mark pattern around bottom edge of lid. Dry cake overnight.
9 To make the plaque: Roll scraps of white fondant on surface dusted with cornstarch into 2½-inch x 6½-inch rectangle. Use stitching tool to mark edges. Roll half the remaining green fondant into a ⅛-inch thickness; use

alphabet cutters to cut out letters. Outline letters with stitching tool. Fill piping bag ½ full with royal icing; secure letters to plaque with icing. Leave to dry overnight.
10 To make bow: Knead ¼ teaspoon tylose into remaining green fondant. Roll out half the fondant on surface dusted with cornstarch into ⅛-inch thickness. Using 1¾-inch acrylic ruler, cut 5 strips of fondant 1¾- inches wide and 8-inches long. Run stitching tool along both edges of all strips. Fold strips in half to make loops, secure ends with a little water. Cut end into "V" shapes, turn loops on their side on a parchment-paper-lined tray to dry overnight.
11 Roll out remaining green fondant, cut 4 strips of icing 1¾-inches x 8-inches. Run the stitching tool along both edges of all strips. Using picture as a guide, secure the fondant strips to four sides of the cake with a little water. Roll scraps of fondant long enough to make 2 tails for the bows; cut "V" shapes into ends, secure to top of cake with a little royal icing. Position dried loops on cake to finish the bow; secure with royal icing.

tips The strips of fondant can be made by rolling the fondant out thinly to ⅛-inch, however, rolling the fondant through a pasta machine results in the fondant being an even thickness all over. To make this cake look really good, it has to look very square. Measure all the strips precisely.

Set pasta machine to thickest setting. Roll a piece of fondant into a rectangle the same width as the machine, feed through the machine.

Cut strips of green and white fondant long enough to cover each side of the cake. Secure alternate colored strips to cake with water.

Use an acrylic measure to mark fondant around the sides of the box where the lid will sit. Brush a little water over this area of the box.

Roll fondant out until it covers the top and sides of the cake. Use measure to mark the sides of the lid. Cut off excess fondant with a sharp knife.

Make the plaque from scraps of white fondant. Cut out letters from green fondant. Use the stitching tool to mark the plaque and letters.

Secure the letters to the plaque with a little royal icing. Stand the plaque on a parchment-paper-lined tray to dry overnight.

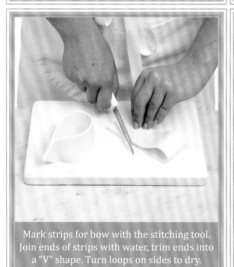

Mark strips for bow with the stitching tool. Join ends of strips with water, trim ends into a "V" shape. Turn loops on sides to dry.

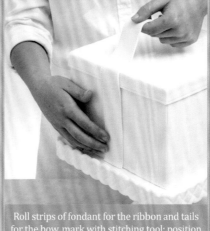

Roll strips of fondant for the ribbon and tails for the bow, mark with stitching tool; position and secure to the cake with a little water.

Fill a paper piping bag ½ full with royal icing. Pipe dots of icing onto the ribbon to secure the loops of the bow on the cake.

BRIDAL
Mosaic Squares

TO ACHIEVE THEIR CRISP, CLEAN LOOK, THE FONDANT SQUARES MUST BE PERFECTLY SQUARE AND THE PIPING NEAT AND TIDY. PRACTICE PIPING ON A FLAT SURFACE TO LEARN HOW TO CONTROL THE PRESSURE ON THE PIPING BAG FOR BEST RESULTS.

EQUIPMENT
patchwork cutter trellis
star template (page 229)
fine pearl-headed pin
small piping bag
small (number 2) plain piping tube
paper piping bag (page 221)
small metal spatula
11-inch square wooden cake board
   (page 208)
CAKE
deep 10-inch square cake of choice
   (page 190)
DECORATIONS
11 ounces ready-to-use ivory
   fondant
cornstarch
1 quantity royal icing (page 220)
1 package small pearlized blush
   sugar pearls
1 tablespoon strained lemon juice
1 quantity white chocolate
   ganache (page 210)

1 Knead ready-to-use fondant on surface dusted with a little cornstarch until icing loses its stickiness; roll out on surface dusted with cornstarch into ⅛-inch thickness. Cut 9 x 3-inch squares from fondant. Use the patchwork cutter to mark pattern on icing while fondant is still soft. Place squares on parchment-paper-lined tray to dry overnight.

2 Cut around star template, place on top of dried fondant square. Scratch outline into fondant with a fine pin.

3 Fit piping bag with tube; fill bag ½ full with royal icing. Using picture as a guide, pipe patterns onto fondant squares; pipe over patchwork outline. Position pearls, if using, on royal icing before it dries. Stand overnight to dry.

4 For star shape, add a drop or two of lemon juice to the remaining royal icing – icing should be the consistency of cream. Spoon icing into paper piping bag; snip tip from bag. Pipe the icing inside the star points to "flood" the star. Flood icing into any other shape as required. Stand overnight to set.

5 Trim cake top so it sits flat when turned upside down. Turn cake upside down, cut into 9 (3-inch) squares.

6 Spread cakes evenly all over with ganache; freeze 10 minutes. Smooth ganache with a hot dry metal spatula.

7 Position cakes on board, top cakes with fondant squares.

tips The fondant squares can be made months ahead. Store them in a single layer (to protect the delicate piping) in airtight containers. Trim and cut the cakes a day ahead. Cover the cakes evenly with ganache to keep them as fresh as possible. Store them at a cool room temperature. The patchwork cutter is also known as a "quilting embosser." The "pearlized blush sugar pearls" are small edible pearls, and are available from cake decorating suppliers.

Hold the piping bag at a 45 degree angle. Squeeze the bag firmly with an even pressure. Pipe a tiny dot of icing at the starting point.

Continue to keep a firm pressure on the piping bag, lift the line of icing about ¼-inch from the surface of the fondant square.

Keeping the pressure even, touch down with the tip of the piping tube on the end of the fondant square. Repeat to cover the square.

BUCKLE UP
Baby Cakes

THESE LITTLE BUCKLES ARE SO TRENDY YOUR BABY WILL MAKE THE FASHION PAGES. THE BUCKLES CAN BE A LITTLE TRICKY TO MAKE AND, BECAUSE THEY'RE QUITE DELICATE, IT'S BEST TO MAKE A FEW MORE JUST IN CASE ANY BREAKAGES OCCUR.

EQUIPMENT
2-inch square cutter
buckle template (page 229)
4 paper piping bags (page 221)
16 plain yellow paper liners
CAKE
shallow 9-inch square cake of choice (page 190)
DECORATIONS
2 pounds ready-to-use white fondant
cornstarch
1 quantity royal icing (page 220)
yellow food coloring
1 tablespoon strained lemon juice
2 egg whites
3 yards (¾ inch) wide ribbon

1 Knead a quarter of the ready-to-use fondant on surface dusted with a little cornstarch until fondant loses its stickiness. Roll 6 ounces of the icing on surface dusted with cornstarch until ⅛-inch thick. Using cutter, cut 16 (2-inch) squares from fondant. Transfer squares to parchment-paper-lined tray to dry. Reserve fondant scraps.

2 Using buckle template, trace 16 buckles onto parchment paper. Turn paper over, place on a flat surface.

3 Tint half the royal icing yellow. Fill piping bag ¾ full with yellow icing; snip tip off bag. Pipe around the inside and outside edges of 8 buckles in unbroken lines. Spoon white royal icing into another piping bag, repeat to make 8 white buckles. Allow buckles to dry.

4 Add a drop or two of lemon juice to the remaining white royal icing (icing should be the consistency of cream). Spoon icing into another paper piping bag; snip tip from bag. Using picture as a guide, pipe icing into the yellow buckles by piping into the space to flood the area. Repeat with the yellow royal icing and white buckles. Allow the buckles to dry overnight.

5 Trim cake into a 8-inch square; cut cake into 16 (2-inch) squares. Transfer cakes to wire rack; place rack over a baking tray. Secure fondant squares to tops of all cakes with a little royal icing.

6 Chop half the remaining ready-to-use fondant (including scraps) into medium heatproof bowl; add one lightly beaten egg white. Stir mixture over medium saucepan of simmering water (don't let water touch base of bowl). Gradually stir in about 1 tablespoon of warm water until the mixture becomes smooth and of a thick, slightly runny (but not too runny), coating consistency. Do not over-heat the mixture.

7 Carefully pour the mixture over eight of the cake squares, covering the tops and sides of the cakes completely. Repeat process with remaining fondant, egg white and water. Stand cakes about 1 hour or until the fondant feels firm.

8 Cut ribbon into lengths long enough to extend over sides of each cake. Thread through the buckles. Place each cake into a paper liner. Place a buckle on each cake, push the ribbon down the sides of the cakes. Push the paper liners against the fondant on the cakes to form a seal.

makes 16

tips The squares of fondant and the buckles can be made at least 2 weeks ahead. Make a few more buckles to allow for breakages. Square paper liners are available in specialty food or kitchen shops, but we found round paper liners happily change shape to accommodate the square cakes. You could also secure the fondant squares to the cakes using a little jam or lemon curd, if you prefer. The cakes can be completed up to 2 days ahead.

USE A MOIST CAKE, SUCH AS A WHITE CHOCOLATE CAKE, FOR THIS RECIPE.
MAKE SURE THAT THE CAKE IS COVERED WITH FONDANT AND THE PAPER
LINERS ARE PRESSED FIRMLY AROUND THE CAKES AS THIS WILL HELP TO
KEEP THEM FRESH FOR A DAY OR SO.

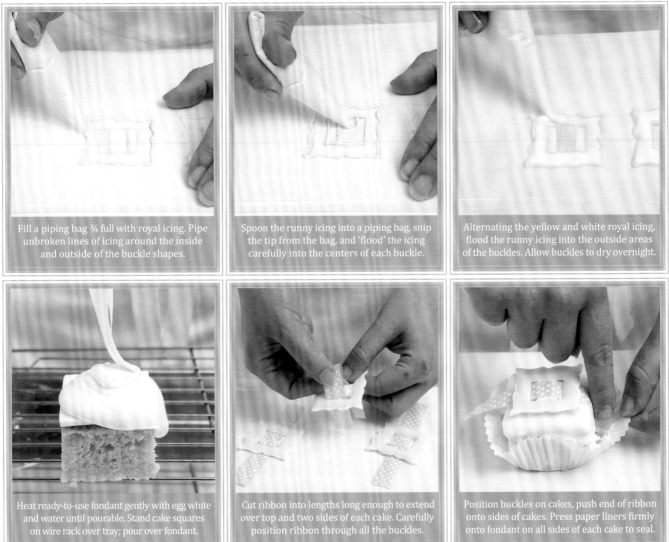

Fill a piping bag ¾ full with royal icing. Pipe unbroken lines of icing around the inside and outside of the buckle shapes.

Spoon the runny icing into a piping bag, snip the tip from the bag, and 'flood' the icing carefully into the centers of each buckle.

Alternating the yellow and white royal icing, flood the runny icing into the outside areas of the buckles. Allow buckles to dry overnight.

Heat ready-to-use fondant gently with egg white and water until pourable. Stand cake squares on wire rack over tray; pour over fondant.

Cut ribbon into lengths long enough to extend over top and two sides of each cake. Carefully position ribbon through all the buckles.

Position buckles on cakes, push end of ribbon onto sides of cakes. Press paper liners firmly onto fondant on all sides of each cake to seal.

PASTEL TEA
Cookies

PASTEL TEA
Cookies

THESE PRETTY TEACUPS AND TEAPOTS ARE VERSATILE LITTLE COOKIES – THEY'D BE PERFECT TO SERVE AT A FORMAL TEA, BUT WOULD ALSO BE GREAT AT A LITTLE GIRL'S FIRST TEA PARTY, OR AS A DELICIOUS GIFT TO TAKE TO A HOUSE-WARMING PARTY.

EQUIPMENT
baking trays
2½-inch x 3¾-inch teacup cutter
2¾-inch x 3-inch teapot cutter
pastry brush
small piping bag
small (number 2) plain piping tube
¾-inch blossom cutter
1-inch blossom cutter
tweezers
COOKIES
1 stick (½ cup) butter
2 eggs
1 teaspoon vanilla extract
⅔ cup superfine sugar
1⅓ cups self-rising flour
1 cup all-purpose flour
DECORATIONS
1 pound ready-to-use white
    fondant
cornstarch
purple, pink, blue, green and
    yellow food colorings
1 egg white, lightly beaten
1 quantity royal icing (page 220)
2 teaspoons pearlized blush sugar
    pearls

1 Have butter and eggs at room temperature.

2 To make cookies: Beat butter, extract and sugar in small bowl with electric mixer until combined. Beat in eggs, one at a time; beat only until combined. (Do not overbeat; mixture will curdle at this stage, but will come together later.) Transfer mixture to large bowl. Stir in sifted flours in two batches; mix to a soft dough. Knead dough on floured surface until smooth; cover, refrigerate 30 minutes.

3 Preheat oven to 350°F. Grease and line baking trays with parchment paper.

4 Roll dough between sheets of parchment paper until ¼-inch thick. Using teacup and teapot cutters, cut 10 of each shape from dough, re-rolling dough as necessary.

5 Place shapes, about 1-inch apart, on trays. Bake about 15 minutes or until cookies are firm and browned lightly. Stand cookies on trays for 5 minutes; lift onto wire racks to cool.

6 Knead ready-to-use fondant on surface dusted with a little cornstarch until fondant loses its stickiness. Divide fondant into 5 equal portions. Tint each portion with one of the colorings; enclose, separately, in plastic wrap.

7 Roll each fondant portion, separately, on cornstarched surface until ⅛-inch thick. Using cutters, cut 10 teacups and 10 teapots from fondant, re-rolling fondant as necessary. Reserve all fondant scraps, enclose, separately, in plastic wrap.

8 Working with 2 or 3 shapes at a time, lightly brush tops of cookies with egg white; position fondant shapes on cookies.

9 Fit piping bag with tube. Fill the bag ¾ full with royal icing; pipe outlines and lines on cookies, as pictured.

10 Re-roll fondant scraps on surface dusted with cornstarch until ¹⁄₃₂-inch thick; using blossom cutters, cut 20 small and 10 large blossoms from fondant. Secure the 10 small blossoms to large blossoms with a little royal icing; secure to teapot cookies. Secure remaining small blossoms to teacup cookies with a little royal icing.

11 Pipe a dot of royal icing in the center of each flower; using tweezers, position a pearl in flower center. Pipe dots around flowers on teapots; pipe dots in teapot lids.

makes 20
tips You could use a paper piping bag without a tube to pipe the decorations on the cookies. The "pearlized blush sugar pearls" are small edible pearls, and are available from cake decorating suppliers.

ONCE DECORATED AND DRIED, LAYER THE COOKIES CAREFULLY BETWEEN SHEETS OF PARCHMENT PAPER IN AN AIRTIGHT CONTAINER. THEY WILL KEEP FOR ABOUT 4 WEEKS AT ROOM TEMPERATURE. THE ONLY TRICKY PART TO MAKING THESE COOKIES IS THE PIPING; PRACTICE ON A FLAT SURFACE FIRST, BEFORE PIPING ONTO THE COOKIES.

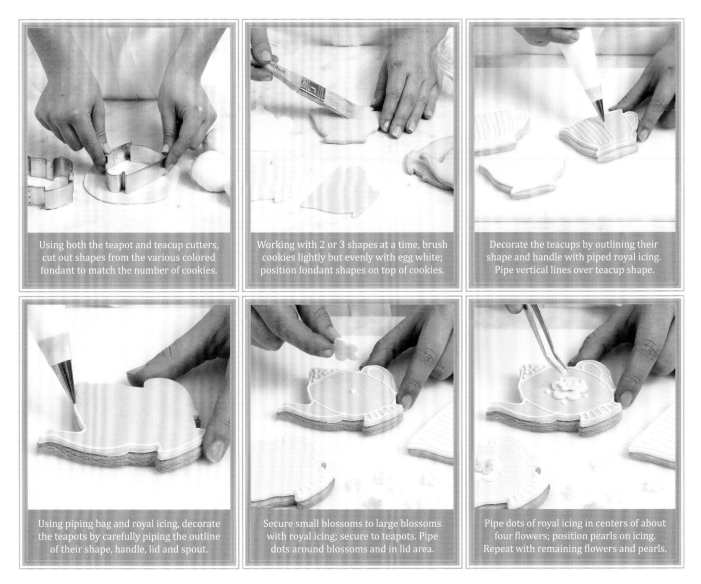

Using both the teapot and teacup cutters, cut out shapes from the various colored fondant to match the number of cookies.

Working with 2 or 3 shapes at a time, brush cookies lightly but evenly with egg white; position fondant shapes on top of cookies.

Decorate the teacups by outlining their shape and handle with piped royal icing. Pipe vertical lines over teacup shape.

Using piping bag and royal icing, decorate the teapots by carefully piping the outline of their shape, handle, lid and spout.

Secure small blossoms to large blossoms with royal icing; secure to teapots. Pipe dots around blossoms and in lid area.

Pipe dots of royal icing in centers of about four flowers; position pearls on icing. Repeat with remaining flowers and pearls.

BOOTIES
for Baby

We love this cake with its little boots on top, it's a perfect christening cake. The patterned roller and ball tool make the plaques very easy to make. Shaping the booties is a little harder, but well worth the effort. You can buy ready-made booties from some cake decorating suppliers.

BOOTIES
for Baby

EQUIPMENT
14-inch round wooden cake board (page 208)
5-inch round wooden cake board (page 208)
smoothing tools
3 wooden skewers
paper piping bag (page 221)
plastic ruler
ball tool
quilted pattern rolling pin
bootie pattern template (page 229)
vinyl mat
fine artist's paint brush
metal skewer
CAKE
deep 8-inch octagonal cake of choice (page 190)
deep 6-inch octagonal cake of choice (page 190)
DECORATIONS
3 pounds ready-to-use white fondant
cornstarch
teal food coloring
1 quantity royal icing (page 220)
3 ounces gum paste

1 Trim cakes (page 209). Secure large cake to largest board; secure small cake to remaining board (page 209). Prepare cakes for covering with ready-to-use fondant (page 209).

2 Knead ready-to-use fondant on surface dusted with a little cornstarch until fondant loses its stickiness. Tint 2½ pounds of the fondant pale teal with coloring.

3 Roll 1 pound of the pale teal fondant on cornstarched surface until large enough to cover small cake. Using rolling pin, lift fondant onto cake; smooth with hands then smoothing tools. Trim fondant neatly around base; reserve fondant scraps.

4 Use 1½ pounds of the pale teal fondant to cover large cake in the same way as the small cake. Dry cakes overnight. Reserve fondant scraps.

5 Push trimmed skewers into center of large cake to support the top tier. Secure small cake on top of large cake (page 212).

6 Tint royal icing pale teal to match cakes. Fill piping bag ¾ full with royal icing; pipe around base of each cake. Use fingertip to blend icing into any gaps where cakes join the boards (page 212). Dry overnight.

7 Knead half the remaining pale teal fondant with reserved fondant scraps on surface dusted with a little cornstarch. Roll fondant on cornstarched surface into ¼-inch thickness. Using ruler and sharp knife, cut out eight (2½-inch x 3¼-inch) rectangles from fondant. Using ball tool, gently rub edges of rectangles to make a frill. Place on parchment-paper-lined tray to dry overnight.

8 Firmly roll patterned rolling pin over remaining pale teal fondant (re-roll icing as necessary); cut out eight (1½-inch x 1¾-inch) rectangles from fondant. Place on parchment-paper-lined trays to dry overnight.

9 Roll remaining ready-to-use white fondant on cornstarched surface into ¼-inch thickness. Using ruler and sharp knife, cut out four (2¾-inch x 2¼-inch) rectangles from fondant. Using ball tool, gently rub edges of rectangles to make a frill. Place on parchment-paper-lined tray to dry overnight.

10 Firmly roll the patterned rolling pin over remaining white fondant (re-roll the fondant as necessary); cut out eight (1¾-inch x 2½-inch) rectangles from icing. Place on parchment-paper-lined tray; stand overnight to dry.

11 Using picture as a guide, join the plain rectangles to the frilled rectangles with a little royal icing contrasting the colors and matching the small and large rectangles.

12 Knead gum paste on surface dusted with cornstarch until it loses its stickiness. Tint half the paste the same teal color as the cake covering. Cover paste with plastic wrap when not using.

13 Make one bootie at a time: Roll teal modeling paste on surface dusted with cornstarch until ¹⁄₁₆-inch thick. Using template, carefully cut out one of each shape. Cover paste with vinyl mat to prevent drying out while making the bootie. Lightly brush a little water onto edge of sole of bootie, attach front of bootie to sole; carefully mold edges together into shape of a bootie.

14 Attach heel section to back of bootie with a little water. Using the skewer, make 4 holes for the shoelace (two on each side). Using tip of a fork, press around edge where booties and the sole join.

15 Roll ½ ounce of the white gum paste on cornstarched surface into an oval shape about ⅛-inch thick and slightly larger than the pattern for the sole. Attach to bottom of bootie with a little water. Place bootie on parchment-paper-lined tray to dry overnight. Repeat to make second bootie.

16 To make laces: Roll small pieces of white gum paste into thin bootlace lengths. Attach to booties with a little water.

17 Using a little royal icing, secure panels around sides of cakes and booties to top of cake.

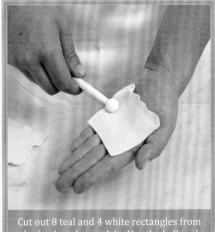

Cut out 8 teal and 4 white rectangles from the fondant; leave plain. Use the ball tool to frill the edges of the rectangles.

Roll teal fondant out on surface dusted with cornstarch into ⅛-inch thickness. Roll quilted rolling pin firmly over icing to create pattern.

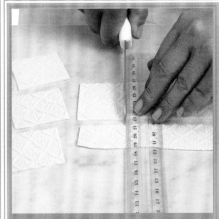

Using a plastic ruler and a sharp knife, cut out eight (1½ inch x 1¾ inch) patterned rectangles from the teal-colored fondant.

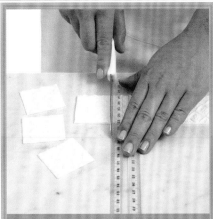

Roll quilted rolling pin firmly over white fondant to create pattern. Cut eight (2½ inch x 1¾) inch patterned rectangles from fondant.

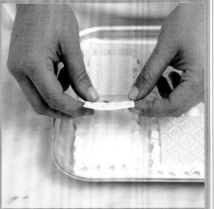

Join 4 patterned teal rectangles to 4 frilled white rectangles; join 8 patterned white rectangles to 8 frilled blue rectangles.

Tint gum paste and roll to ⅛-inch thick. Using pattern, cut out one of each shape. Cover with vinyl mat while making bootie.

Brush water sparingly over front edge of sole. Attach front of bootie to sole; gently mold edges together to make bootie shape.

Cut white gum paste into an oval shape slightly larger than the sole of the bootie; secure to base of bootie with a little water.

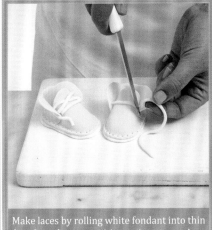

Make laces by rolling white fondant into thin bootlace shapes; position so it appears they are threaded through the holes for laces.

PRETTY PINK
Boxes & Bows

EQUIPMENT

12-inch square wooden cake board (page 208)
6-inch square wooden cake board (page 208)
4-inch square wooden cake board (page 208)
smoothing tools
acrylic measures in 1-inch, 1¼-inch and 1½-inch widths
fine artist's paint brush
stitching tool
8 wooden skewers
3 paper piping bags (page 221)
vinyl mat
tape measure
cotton wool

CAKE

deep 8-inch square cake of choice (page 190)
shallow 8-inch square cake of choice (page 190)
deep 6-inch square cake of choice (page 190)
deep 4-inch square cake of choice (page 190)
jam or ganache of choice (page 210)

DECORATIONS

6¾ pounds ready-to-use white fondant
cornstarch
pink food coloring
1 quantity royal icing (page 220)
tylose powder

1 Trim cakes (page 209). Secure deep 8-inch cake to largest board (page 209); top with remaining 8-inch cake, joining cakes with jam or ganache (page 212). Secure remaining cakes to same-sized boards. Prepare cakes for covering with ready-to-use fondant (page 209).

2 Reserve 1 pound of the ready-to-use fondant for bow. Knead 3 pounds of remaining fondant on surface dusted with a little cornstarch until fondant loses its stickiness. Tint pale pink with coloring. Reserve 1 pound for box lid.

3 Roll remaining pale pink fondant on cornstarched surface until large enough to cover largest cake. Using rolling pin, lift fondant onto cake; smooth with hands then smoothing tools. Trim fondant around base. Reserve fondant scraps. Use 1½-inch-width acrylic measure to mark sides of cake where lid will cover sides of box.

4 Tint 1 pound of the remaining white fondant medium pink. Reserve 7 ounces for box lid. Roll remaining medium pink fondant on surface dusted with a little cornstarch until large enough to cover small cake in the same way as the large cake. Reserve scraps. Use 1-inch-wide acrylic measure to mark sides of cake for lid.

5 Tint remaining fondant a darker pink. Reserve 9 ounces for box lid. Roll remaining fondant on cornstarched surface until large enough to cover medium cake in the same way as the large cake. Reserve scraps. Use 1¼-inch-wide acrylic measure to mark sides of cake for lid. Dry cakes overnight.

6 To make lids: Work with one cake at a time, using matching reserved fondant and scraps, and corresponding acrylic measure. Lightly brush a little water in marked area for lid. Roll fondant out on cornstarched surface until large enough to cover top of cake and extend over sides to cover marked area. Use acrylic measure and a sharp knife to cut away excess fondant. Reserve scraps. Smooth fondant with hands then smoothing tools.

7 Using the stitching tool, mark around the bottom edge of all lids.

8 Push 4 trimmed skewers into centers of large and medium cakes to support the next tier (page 212). Assemble cakes, securing each tier to the tier below (page 212).

9 Divide royal icing into three bowls, tint to match cakes. Fill each of the piping bags ½ full with royal icing; pipe around base of same-colored cake. Use fingertip to blend icing into any gaps where cakes join the boards (page 212). Dry cakes overnight.

10 To make ribbons: Take tiny pieces of the reserved fondant scraps, roll into tiny balls. Place balls under vinyl mat. Knead two-thirds of the white fondant on cornstarched surface until fondant loses its stickiness.

11 Measure height of stacked cakes, roll out fondant long enough to match height of cakes. Place dots randomly over fondant; gently roll over the dots to push them into the fondant. Cut a 1¼-inch-wide rectangle of the required length. Secure ribbon to cakes with a little royal icing. Repeat process to make three more ribbons.

12 To make bow: Make more tiny pink balls, place under vinyl mat. Knead ½ teaspoon tylose into the remaining white fondant on cornstarched surface. Roll fondant on cornstarched surface until large enough to cut out a 4-inch x 12-inch strip and a 1-inch x 8-inch strip. Roll balls into fondant the same way as the ribbon. Place large strip under vinyl mat. To make tails for bow, cut the small strip of fondant in half crossways; cut 'V's into ends. Secure tails to cake with royal icing. Pinch the blunt ends of the tails to make narrower.

13 Cut the large strip of fondant in half crossways. Place cotton wool on both rectangles of fondant, fold fondant over to enclose cotton wool, join edges with a little water. Gently pleat edges together. Stand each bow on one end almost touching; cover seam with a scrap of fondant, secure with a little water. Stand overnight to dry.

14 Remove cotton wool from bow when dry. Position bow on cake, secure with a little royal icing.

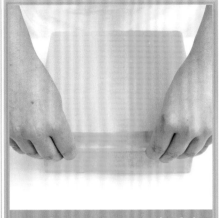

Use acrylic measure to measure sides of cakes for lids. Press the measure into the icing to mark the area before the fondant sets.

Brush marked areas on sides of cakes with a little water. Cover cakes with reserved fondant extending fondant over sides; trim excess fondant.

Smooth the fondant with the smoothing tools. Make the lids as square as possible, then use the stitching tool to mark pattern on lids.

Using reserved scraps of all the fondant, roll tiny balls of random sizes in palm of your hand. Keep the balls under the vinyl mat.

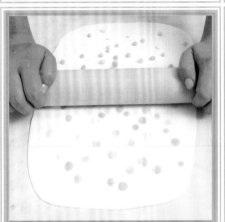

Place the colored fondant balls randomly over the white fondant. Gently roll over the balls with a rolling pin pressing the balls into the fondant.

Make the ribbons and tails for the bow; secure to cake stack with royal icing. Pinch blunt ends of tails to make them narrower.

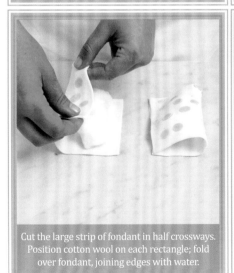

Cut the large strip of fondant in half crossways. Position cotton wool on each rectangle; fold over fondant, joining edges with water.

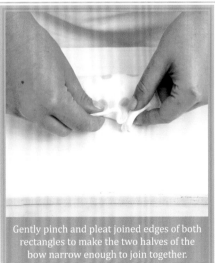

Gently pinch and pleat joined edges of both rectangles to make the two halves of the bow narrow enough to join together.

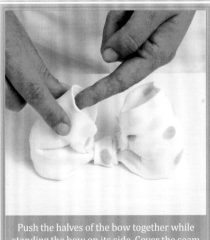

Push the halves of the bow together while standing the bow on its side. Cover the seam with a scrap of fondant. Push bow into shape.

MAGNOLIA *& Pearls*

EQUIPMENT

4¾-inch 18-gauge floral wire
long nose pliers; wire cutters
3 lengths 26-gauge floral wire
flower glue (page 227)
fine artist's paint brush
magnolia cutter set
vinyl mat
12-hole round-based, shallow
    whoopie pie pan
flower mat
ball tool
small non-stick rolling pin
white florist's tape
12-inch round wooden cake board
    (page 208)
smoothing tools
paper piping bag (page 221)
tweezers

CAKE

deep 8-inch round cake of choice
    (page 190)
shallow 8-inch round cake of
    choice (page 190)
jam or ganache of choice (page 210)

DECORATIONS

3 ounces gum paste
tylose powder
cornstarch
yellow and pink petal dust
1½ pounds ready-to-use ivory
    fondant
1 quantity royal icing (page 220)
ivory food coloring
½ ounce large ivory pearls
½ ounce small grey pearls

1 To make magnolia: Make a small hook in one end of the 18-gauge wire using pliers. Cut each 26-gauge wire into 3 even lengths.

2 Knead gum paste with a pinch of tylose on cornstarched surface until paste loses its stickiness.

3 To make flower center, roll a piece of paste into a ball the size of a large marble. Dip wire hook into flower glue; push into ball of paste. Use small scissors to snip the paste into small points; dry upright overnight. Dust center with yellow petal dust.

4 Roll paste ⅛-inch thick on cornstarched surface. Using cutters, cut 3 small and 5 large petals. Cover petals with vinyl mat. Dust pan with cornstarch.

5 Dip one end of a piece of wire into glue; gently push wire into pointed end of small petal. Working with one small petal at a time, place petal on flower mat, use ball tool to frill the edge. Dry petals overnight in pan. Combine a pinch each of cornstarch and pink petal dust; use to brush insides of petals.

6 To make large petals, insert wire one-third of the way through pointed end. Using small rolling pin, roll top two-thirds of petals to make larger. Frill edge of petals on flower mat using ball tool. Dry overnight in whoopie pie pan.

7 To assemble magnolia: See steps 7 and 8 of *Yellow Peony Rose Cake* (page 158) for full assembly instructions. Using tape, secure wired small petals, one at a time, to wired flower center. Attach large petals in the same way.

8 Trim cakes (page 209). Secure deep cake to wooden board (page 209); top with remaining cake, joining cakes with a little jam or ganache (page 212). Prepare cake for covering with ready-to-use fondant (page 209).

9 Knead ready-to-use fondant on cornstarched surface until fondant loses its stickiness. Roll fondant on cornstarched surface until large enough to cover cake. Using rolling pin, lift fondant onto cake; smooth with hands then smoothing tools. Trim fondant neatly around base of cake.

10 Tint royal icing ivory. Fill piping bag ½ full with icing; pipe around base of cake. Use fingertip to blend icing into any gap where cake joins the board (page 212). Dry overnight.

11 Pipe a line of icing round base of cake. Use tweezers to position large pearls on icing. Pipe small dots of icing, a few at a time, between first row of pearls; position small pearls. Repeat to make 5 rows of large pearls and 4 rows of small pearls. Position magnolia in cake.

Make a hook on the end of a piece of wire, push into large-marble sized ball of paste, snip with scissors to make flower center.

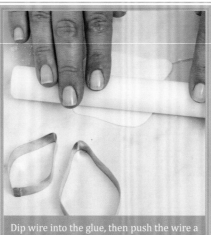

Dip wire into the glue, then push the wire a third of the way through petal from pointed end. Roll top two-thirds of the petal thinly.

Position 3 petals around center of magnolia. Position and secure one large petal at a time around center. Secure wire with florist's tape.

The magnolia is made in much
the same way as the peony on
page 158; check the finer details
there. The magnolia can be made
months ahead; store in an airtight
container. The pearls should be
positioned a day or two before
the cake is needed to preserve
their lustre. Position the magnolia
on the day of serving.

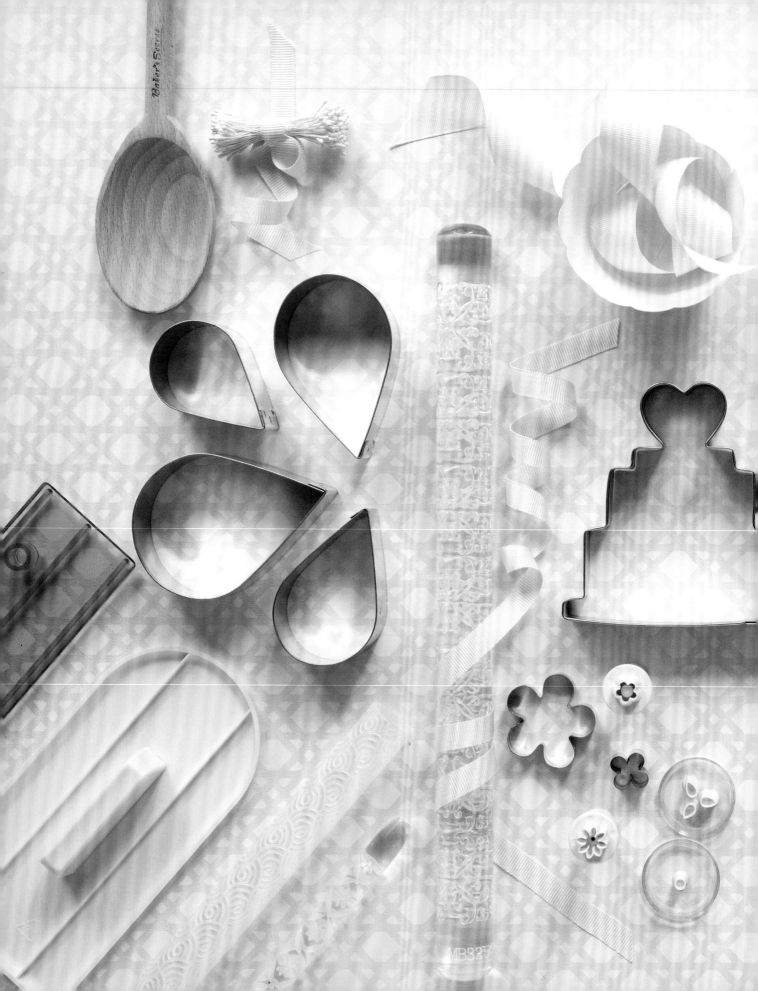

THE
MECHANICS

Butter Cake

INGREDIENTS	DEEP 4-INCH ROUND	DEEP 5-INCH ROUND	SHALLOW 6-INCH ROUND	DEEP 6-INCH ROUND	SHALLOW 7-INCH ROUND	DEEP 7-INCH ROUND	SHALLOW 8-INCH ROUND
BUTTER	3 tbsp	4 tbsp (½ stick)	4 tbsp (½ stick)	6 tbsp	5 tbsp	12 tbsp (1½ sticks)	8 tbsp (1 stick)
VANILLA EXTRACT	½ teaspoon	½ teaspoon	½ teaspoon	½ teaspoon	½ teaspoon	1½ teaspoons	1 teaspoon
SUPERFINE SUGAR	¼ cup	⅓ cup	⅓ cup	½ cup	⅓ cup	1 cup	¾ cup
EGGS (2oz)	1	1	1	1	1	3	2
SELF-RISING FLOUR	⅔ cup	¾ cup	¾ cup	1¼ cups	1 cup	2¼ cups	1½ cups
MILK	¼ cup	¼ cup	¼ cup	⅓ cup	⅓ cup	¾ cup	½ cup
BAKING TIME (approx)	30 minutes	40 minutes	40 minutes	50 minutes	35 minutes	1 hour	1 hour

INGREDIENTS	DEEP 8-INCH ROUND	DEEP 9-INCH ROUND	SHALLOW 10-INCH ROUND	DEEP 10-INCH ROUND	DEEP 12-INCH ROUND	DEEP 14-INCH ROUND
BUTTER	1½ sticks (¾ cup)	2 sticks (1 cup)	1½ sticks (¾ cup)	3 sticks (1½ cups)	5 sticks (2½ cups)	8 sticks (4 cups)
VANILLA EXTRACT	1½ teaspoons	2 teaspoons	1½ teaspoons	3 teaspoons	1 tablespoon	1 tablespoon
SUPERFINE SUGAR	1 cup	1½ cups	1¼ cups	2½ cups	3¾ cups	5 cups
EGGS (2oz)	3	4	3	6	10	14
SELF-RISING FLOUR	2¼ cups	3 cups	2¼ cups	4½ cups	7½ cups	12½ cups
MILK	¾ cup	1 cup	¾ cup	1½ cups	2½ cups	4 cups
BAKING TIME (approx)	1 hour	1¼ hours	45 minutes	1½ hours	1¾ hours	2 hours

INGREDIENTS	SHALLOW 4-INCH SQUARE	DEEP 4-INCH SQUARE	SHALLOW 6-INCH SQUARE	DEEP 6-INCH SQUARE	SHALLOW 7-INCH SQUARE	DEEP 7-INCH SQUARE	SHALLOW 8-INCH SQUARE
BUTTER	4 tbsp (½ stick)	5 tbsp	5 tbsp	1 stick (½ cup)	1 stick (½ cup)	1¾ sticks	1½ sticks (¾ cup)
VANILLA EXTRACT	½ teaspoon	½ teaspoon	½ teaspoon	1 teaspoon	1 teaspoon	1½ teaspoons	1½ teaspoons
SUPERFINE SUGAR	⅓ cup	⅓ cup	⅓ cup	¾ cup	¾ cup	1¼ cups	1 cup
EGGS (2oz)	1	1	1	2	2	4	3
SELF-RISING FLOUR	¾ cup	1 cup	1 cup	1½ cups	1½ cups	2¾ cups	2¼ cups
MILK	¼ cup	⅓ cup	⅓ cup	½ cup	½ cup	¾ cup	¾ cup
BAKING TIME (approx)	30 minutes	30 minutes	40 minutes	1 hour	1 hour	1 hour	50 minutes

INGREDIENTS	DEEP 8-INCH SQUARE	SHALLOW 9-INCH SQUARE	DEEP 9-INCH SQUARE	SHALLOW 10-INCH SQUARE	DEEP 10-INCH SQUARE	DEEP 12-INCH SQUARE
BUTTER	2 sticks (1 cup)	2 sticks (1 cup)	3 sticks (1½ cups)	3 sticks (1½ cups)	5 sticks (2½ cups)	6 sticks (3 cups)
VANILLA EXTRACT	2 teaspoons	2 teaspoons	3 teaspoons	3 teaspoons	1 tablespoon	1 tablespoon
SUPERFINE SUGAR	1½ cups	1½ cups	2½ cups	2½ cups	3¾ cups	4½ cups
EGGS (2oz)	4	4	6	6	10	12
SELF-RISING FLOUR	3 cups	3 cups	4½ cups	4½ cups	7½ cups	9 cups
MILK	1 cup	1 cup	1½ cups	1½ cups	2½ cups	3 cups
BAKING TIME (approx)	1¼ hours	1 hour	1½ hours	1¼ hours	1¾ hours	2 hours

INGREDIENTS	DEEP 7-INCH HEART SHAPED	DEEP 6-INCH OCTAGONAL	DEEP 8-INCH OCTAGONAL	12-HOLE MUFFIN PAN (⅓-CUP)
BUTTER	1 stick (½ cup)	1 stick (½ cup)	1½ sticks (¾ cup)	1½ sticks (¾ cup)
VANILLA EXTRACT	1 teaspoon	1 teaspoon	1½ teaspoons	1½ teaspoons
SUPERFINE SUGAR	¾ cup	¾ cup	1 cup	1 cup
EGGS (2oz)	2	2	3	3
SELF-RISING FLOUR	1½ cups	1½ cups	2¼ cups	2¼ cups
MILK	½ cup	½ cup	¾ cup	¾ cup
BAKING TIME (approx)	1 hour	1 hour	50 minutes	20 minutes

WE USED 3-INCH DEEP CAKE PANS WITH STRAIGHT SIDES. BUTTER, EGGS AND MILK SHOULD BE AT ROOM TEMPERATURE FOR BEST RESULTS.

1 Preheat oven to 350°F. Grease and line base and side(s) of cake pan with parchment paper, extending paper 2 inches above side(s).

2 Beat butter, extract and sugar in bowl with electric mixer until light and fluffy. Beat in eggs, one at a time. Transfer mixture to larger bowl; stir in sifted flour and milk, in two batches. Spread mixture into pan.

3 Bake cake for the time given in chart. Cover cake with foil halfway through baking if cake is over-browning, or lower the oven temperature by 10-20 degrees if cake is over 8 inches.

4 Test cake by inserting a skewer into center of cake; if cooked, skewer will be clean, if there is cake mixture on the skewer, bake cake 10 minutes longer before testing again.

5 Stand cake in the pan for 10 to 30 minutes, depending on the size of cake, before turning, top-side down, onto wire rack to cool.

tip The cake will keep well for 2 days in an airtight container, or can be frozen for 3 months.

Raspberry Hazelnut Cake

INGREDIENTS	DEEP 4-INCH ROUND	DEEP 5-INCH ROUND	SHALLOW 6-INCH ROUND	DEEP 6-INCH ROUND	SHALLOW 7-INCH ROUND	DEEP 7-INCH ROUND	SHALLOW 8-INCH ROUND
BUTTER	4 tbsp (½ stick)	6 tbsp	6 tbsp	1 stick (½ cup)	6 tbsp	10 tbsp	6 tbsp
SUPERFINE SUGAR	½ cup	¾ cup	¾ cup	1 cup	¾ cup	1¼ cups	1 cup
EGGS (2oz)	1	2	2	3	2	4	3
ALL-PURPOSE FLOUR	¼ cup	⅓ cup	⅓ cup	½ cup	⅓ cup	⅔ cup	½ cup
SELF-RISING FLOUR	1 tablespoon	1½ tablespoons	1½ tablespoons	¼ cup	1½ tablespoons	⅓ cup	¼ cup
GROUND HAZELNUTS	¼ cup	⅓ cup	⅓ cup	½ cup	⅓ cup	⅔ cup	½ cup
SOUR CREAM	2 tablespoons	¼ cup	¼ cup	⅓ cup	¼ cup	½ cup	⅓ cup
FRESH OR FROZEN RASPBERRIES	2½oz	3oz	3oz	4oz	3oz	6oz	4oz
BAKING TIME (approx)	1 hour	1¼ hours	1 hour	1¼ hours	1¼ hours	1½ hours	1 hour

INGREDIENTS	DEEP 8-INCH ROUND	DEEP 9-INCH ROUND	SHALLOW 10-INCH ROUND	DEEP 10-INCH ROUND	DEEP 12-INCH ROUND	DEEP 14-INCH ROUND
BUTTER	1¾ sticks	2 sticks (1 cup)	11 tbsp	2 sticks + 2 tbsp	4 sticks (2 cups)	6½ sticks (3 cups)
SUPERFINE SUGAR	1¾ cups	2 cups	⅓ cup	2½ cups	4¼ cups	6 cups
EGGS (2oz)	5	6	4	7	13	18
ALL-PURPOSE FLOUR	1 cup	1 cup	⅔ cup	1¼ cups	2 cups	3 cups
SELF-RISING FLOUR	½ cup	½ cup	⅓ cup	⅔ cup	1¼ cups	1½ cups
GROUND HAZELNUTS	1 cup	1 cup	⅔ cup	1¼ cups	2 cups	3 cups
SOUR CREAM	⅔ cup	⅔ cup	½ cup	¾ cup	1½ cups	1⅔ cups
FRESH OR FROZEN RASPBERRIES	8oz	9½oz	6oz	11oz	1¼lb	1¾lb
BAKING TIME (approx)	1¾ hours	1½ hours	1¼ hours	1¾ hours	1¾ hours	2½ hours

INGREDIENTS	SHALLOW 4-INCH SQUARE	DEEP 4-INCH SQUARE	SHALLOW 6-INCH SQUARE	DEEP 6-INCH SQUARE	SHALLOW 7-INCH SQUARE	DEEP 7-INCH SQUARE	SHALLOW 8-INCH SQUARE
BUTTER	3 tablespoons	6 tbsp	6 tbsp	1½ sticks (¾ cup)	1 stick (½ cup)	2 sticks (1 cup)	10 tbsp
SUPERFINE SUGAR	⅓ cup	¾ cup	¾ cup	1½ cups	1 cup	2 cups	1¼ cups
EGGS (2oz)	1	2	2	4	3	6	4
ALL-PURPOSE FLOUR	2 tablespoons	⅓ cup	⅓ cup	¾ cup	½ cup	1 cup	⅔ cup
SELF-RISING FLOUR	1 tablespoon	1½ tablespoons	1½ tablespoons	⅓ cup	¼ cup	½ cup	⅓ cup
GROUND HAZELNUTS	2 tablespoons	⅓ cup	⅓ cup	¾ cup	½ cup	1 cup	⅔ cup
SOUR CREAM	1½ tablespoons	¼ cup	¼ cup	½ cup	⅓ cup	⅔ cup	½ cup
FRESH OR FROZEN RASPBERRIES	2oz	3oz	3oz	7oz	4oz	9oz	6oz
BAKING TIME (approx)	1 hour	1¼ hours	1¼ hours	1½ hours	1 hour	1½ hours	1 hour

INGREDIENTS	DEEP 8-INCH SQUARE	SHALLOW 9-INCH SQUARE	DEEP 9-INCH SQUARE	SHALLOW 10-INCH SQUARE	DEEP 10-INCH SQUARE	DEEP 12-INCH SQUARE
BUTTER	2 sticks (1 cup)	1¾ sticks	2 sticks + 2 tbsp	2 sticks + 2 tbsp	4 sticks (2 cups)	5 sticks (2½ cups)
SUPERFINE SUGAR	2 cups	1¾ cups	2½ cups	2½ cups	4 cups	4¾ cups
EGGS (2oz)	6	5	7	7	12	14
ALL-PURPOSE FLOUR	1 cup	1 cup	1¼ cups	1¼ cups	2 cups	2⅓ cups
SELF-RISING FLOUR	½ cup	½ cup	⅔ cup	⅔ cup	1 cup	1¼ cups
GROUND HAZELNUTS	1 cup	1 cup	1¼ cups	1¼ cups	2 cups	2⅓ cups
SOUR CREAM	⅔ cup	¾ cup	¾ cup	¾ cup	1 cup	1⅔ cups
FRESH OR FROZEN RASPBERRIES	9oz	8oz	11oz	11oz	1¼lb	1½lb
BAKING TIME (approx)	1½ hours	1¼ hours	1¾ hours	2¼ hours	2¼ hours	2¼ hours

INGREDIENTS	DEEP 7-INCH HEART SHAPED	DEEP 6-INCH OCTAGONAL	DEEP 8-INCH OCTAGONAL	12-HOLE MUFFIN PAN (⅓ CUP)
BUTTER	2 sticks (1 cup)	10 tbsp	1¾ sticks	6 tbsp
SUPERFINE SUGAR	2 cups	1¼ cups	1¾ cups	¾ cup
EGGS (2oz)	6	4	5	2
ALL-PURPOSE FLOUR	1 cup	⅔ cup	1 cup	⅓ cup
SELF-RISING FLOUR	½ cup	⅓ cup	½ cup	1½ tablespoons
GROUND HAZELNUTS	1 cup	⅔ cup	1 cup	⅓ cup
SOUR CREAM	⅔ cup	½ cup	⅔ cup	¼ cup
FRESH OR FROZEN RASPBERRIES	9oz	6oz	8oz	3oz
BAKING TIME (approx)	2 hours	1½ hours	1¾ hours	30 minutes

WE USED 3-INCH DEEP CAKE PANS WITH STRAIGHT SIDES. THE BUTTER, EGGS AND SOUR CREAM SHOULD BE AT ROOM TEMPERATURE FOR BEST RESULTS.

1   Preheat oven to 325°F. Grease and line base and side(s) of cake pan with parchment paper, extending paper 2 inches above side(s).

2   Beat butter and sugar in bowl with electric mixer until light and fluffy. Beat in eggs, one at a time. (Mixture will curdle at this stage but will come together later.)

3   Transfer mixture to a larger bowl; stir in the sifted flours and ground hazelnuts, sour cream and berries. Spread mixture into pan.

4   Bake cake for the time given in chart. Cover cake with foil halfway through baking if cake is over-browning, or lower the oven temperature by 10-20 degrees if cake is over 8 inches.

5   Test cake by inserting a skewer into center of cake; if cooked, skewer will be clean, if there is cake mixture on the skewer, bake cake 10 minutes longer before testing again.

6   Stand cake in the pan for 10 to 30 minutes, depending on the size of the cake, before turning, top-side down, onto wire rack to cool.

tips   Make sure to measure berries by weight, not volume for this recipe; one dry pint typically weighs 12 ounces. If using frozen berries do not thaw them; frozen berries are less likely to "bleed" into the cake mixture. The cake will keep well for 3 days in an airtight container, or can be frozen for 3 months.

Devil's Food Chocolate Cake

INGREDIENTS	DEEP 4-INCH ROUND	DEEP 5-INCH ROUND	SHALLOW 6-INCH ROUND	DEEP 6-INCH ROUND	SHALLOW 7-INCH ROUND	DEEP 7-INCH ROUND	SHALLOW 8-INCH ROUND
DARK CHOCOLATE	1½oz	2oz	1½oz	3oz	3oz	3oz	3oz
COCOA POWDER	1 teaspoon	2 teaspoons	1 teaspoon	2 teaspoons	1½ tablespoons	3 teaspoons	2 teaspoons
WATER	½ cup	½ cup	½ cup	¾ cup	¾ cup	1 cup	¾ cup
BUTTER	4 tbsp (½ stick)	5 tbsp	4 tbsp (½ stick)	1 stick (½ cup)	1 stick (½ cup)	10 tbsp	1 stick (½ cup)
DARK BROWN SUGAR	½ cup	½ cup	½ cup	1 cup	¾ cup	1¼ cups	1 cup
EGGS (2oz)	1	1	1	2	2	3	2
VANILLA EXTRACT	¼ teaspoon	¼ teaspoon	¼ teaspoon	½ teaspoon	½ teaspoon	1 teaspoon	½ teaspoon
SOUR CREAM	¼ cup	¼ cup	¼ cup	⅓ cup	⅓ cup	½ cup	⅓ cup
ALL-PURPOSE FLOUR	¼ cup	⅓ cup	¼ cup	½ cup	½ cup	⅔ cup	½ cup
SELF-RISING FLOUR	¼ cup	⅓ cup	¼ cup	½ cup	½ cup	⅔ cup	½ cup
BAKING SODA	¼ teaspoon	½ teaspoon	¼ teaspoon	½ teaspoon	½ teaspoon	½ teaspoon	½ teaspoon
BAKING TIME (approx)	1 hour	1 hour	1 hour	1¼ hours	1 hour	1½ hours	1¼ hours

INGREDIENTS	DEEP 8-INCH ROUND	DEEP 9-INCH ROUND	SHALLOW 10-INCH ROUND	DEEP 10-INCH ROUND	DEEP 12-INCH ROUND	DEEP 14-INCH ROUND
DARK CHOCOLATE	4oz	5½oz	4oz	6oz	10½oz	14½oz
COCOA POWDER	1 tablespoon	¼ cup	1 tablespoon	⅓ cup	½ cup	¾ cup
WATER	1¼ cups	1½ cups	1¼ cups	1⅔ cups	3 cups	4 cups
BUTTER	11 tbsp	1 stick + 7 tbsp	11 tbsp	2 sticks (1 cup)	3 sticks + 7 tbsp	5 sticks (2½ cups)
DARK BROWN SUGAR	1⅓ cups	1¾ cups	1⅓ cups	2 cups	3½ cups	5 cups
EGGS (2oz)	3	4	3	4	7	10
VANILLA EXTRACT	1 teaspoon	1 teaspoon	1 teaspoon	1 teaspoon	2 teaspoons	2½ teaspoons
SOUR CREAM	½ cup	⅔ cup	½ cup	¾ cup	1⅓ cups	1¾ cups
ALL-PURPOSE FLOUR	¼ cup	¾ cup	¼ cup	1 cup	1¾ cups	2½ cups
SELF-RISING FLOUR	⅓ cup	¾ cup	⅓ cup	1 cup	1¾ cups	2½ cups
BAKING SODA	½ teaspoon	1 teaspoon	½ teaspoon	1 teaspoon	1½ teaspoons	2½ teaspoons
BAKING TIME (approx)	1½ hours	1¾ hours	1¼ hours	1¼ hours	2 hours	2½ hours

INGREDIENTS	SHALLOW 4-INCH SQUARE	DEEP 4-INCH SQUARE	SHALLOW 6-INCH SQUARE	DEEP 6-INCH SQUARE	SHALLOW 7-INCH SQUARE	DEEP 7-INCH SQUARE	SHALLOW 8-INCH SQUARE
DARK CHOCOLATE	1oz	1½oz	3oz	3½oz	3oz	4½oz	3½oz
COCOA POWDER	2 teaspoons	1 teaspoon	1½ tablespoons	3 teaspoons	2 teaspoons	¼ cup	3 teaspoons
WATER	¼ cup	⅓ cup	¾ cup	1 cup	¾ cup	1¼ cups	1 cup
BUTTER	3 tbsp	4 tbsp (½ stick)	1 stick (½ cup)	1 stick + 1 tbsp	1 stick (½ cup)	1½ sticks (¾ cup)	1 stick + 1 tbsp
DARK BROWN SUGAR	⅓ cup	½ cup	¾ cup	1 cup	1 cup	1½ cups	1 cup
EGGS (2oz)	1	1	2	2	2	3	2
VANILLA EXTRACT	¼ teaspoon	¼ teaspoon	½ teaspoon	½ teaspoon	½ teaspoon	¾ teaspoon	½ teaspoon
SOUR CREAM	1½ tablespoons	¼ cup	⅓ cup	⅓ cup	⅓ cup	1 cup	⅓ cup
ALL-PURPOSE FLOUR	2 tablespoons	¼ cup	½ cup	½ cup	½ cup	¾ cup	½ cup
SELF-RISING FLOUR	2 tablespoons	¼ cup	½ cup	½ cup	½ cup	¾ cup	½ cup
BAKING SODA	¼ teaspoon	¼ teaspoon	½ teaspoon	½ teaspoon	½ teaspoon	1 teaspoon	½ teaspoon
BAKING TIME (approx)	50 minutes	1 hour	1¼ hours	1¼ hours	1¼ hours	1¾ hours	1¼ hours

INGREDIENTS	DEEP 8-INCH SQUARE	SHALLOW 9-INCH SQUARE	DEEP 9-INCH SQUARE	SHALLOW 10-INCH SQUARE	DEEP 10-INCH SQUARE	DEEP 12-INCH SQUARE
DARK CHOCOLATE	5½oz	4oz	6oz	6oz	8½oz	12oz
COCOA POWDER	¼ cup	1 tablespoon	⅓ cup	⅓ cup	½ cup	⅔ cup
WATER	1½ cups	1¼ cups	1⅔ cups	1⅔ cups	2¼ cups	3⅓ cups
BUTTER	1 stick + 7 tbsp	11 tbsp	2 sticks (1 cup)	2 sticks (1 cup)	2 sticks + 6 tbsp	4 sticks (2 cups)
DARK BROWN SUGAR	1¾ cups	⅓ cup	2 cups	2 cups	3 cups	4 cups
EGGS (2oz)	4	3	4	4	6	8
VANILLA EXTRACT	1 teaspoon	1 teaspoon	1 teaspoon	1 teaspoon	1½ teaspoons	2 teaspoons
SOUR CREAM	⅔ cup	½ cup	¾ cup	¾ cup	1 cup	1½ cups
ALL-PURPOSE FLOUR	¾ cup	¼ cup	1 cup	1 cup	1½ cups	2 cups
SELF-RISING FLOUR	¾ cup	⅓ cup	1 cup	1 cup	1½ cups	2 cups
BAKING SODA	1 teaspoon	½ teaspoon	1 teaspoon	1 teaspoon	1½ teaspoons	2 teaspoons
BAKING TIME (approx)	1¾ hours	1½ hours	1¼ hours	1¼ hours	1¾ hours	1¾ hours

INGREDIENTS	DEEP 7-INCH HEART SHAPED	DEEP 6-INCH OCTAGONAL	DEEP 8-INCH OCTAGONAL	12-HOLE MUFFIN PAN (⅓ CUP)
DARK CHOCOLATE	4½oz	3oz	4½oz	3oz
COCOA POWDER	¼ cup	3 teaspoons	1 tablespoon	2 teaspoons
WATER	1¼ cups	1 cup	1¼ cups	¾ cup
BUTTER	1½ sticks (¾ cup)	10 tbsp	11 tbsp	1 stick (½ cup)
DARK BROWN SUGAR	1½ cups	1¼ cups	1⅓ cups	1 cup
EGGS (2oz)	3	3	3	2
VANILLA EXTRACT	1 teaspoon	1 teaspoon	1 teaspoon	½ teaspoon
SOUR CREAM	½ cup	½ cup	½ cup	⅓ cup
ALL-PURPOSE FLOUR	¾ cup	⅔ cup	¼ cup	½ cup
SELF-RISING FLOUR	¾ cup	⅔ cup	⅓ cup	½ cup
BAKING SODA	½ teaspoon	½ teaspoon	½ teaspoon	½ teaspoon
BAKING TIME (approx)	1½ hours	1½ hours	1½ hours	30 minutes

WE USED 3-INCH DEEP CAKE PANS WITH STRAIGHT SIDES. BUTTER, EGGS, AND SOUR CREAM SHOULD BE AT ROOM TEMPERATURE FOR BEST RESULTS. BROWN SUGAR SHOULD BE FIRMLY PACKED INTO MEASURING CUP.

1 Preheat oven to 325°F. Grease and line base and side(s) of cake pan with parchment paper, extending paper 2 inches above side(s).

2 Combine broken chocolate, sifted cocoa and the water in saucepan; stir over low heat until smooth. Transfer mixture to a bowl; cool 15 minutes.

3 Add butter, sugar, eggs, extract, sour cream and sifted dry ingredients; beat on low speed with electric mixer until combined. Increase speed to medium; beat about 3 minutes or until mixture is smooth and changed to a paler color. Spread mixture into pan.

4 Bake cake for the time given in chart. Cover cake with foil halfway through baking if cake is over-browning, or lower the oven temperature by 10-20 degrees if cake is over 8 inches.

5 Test cake by inserting a skewer into center of cake; if cooked, skewer will be clean, if there is cake mixture on the skewer, bake cake 10 minutes longer before testing again.

6 Cool cake in pan.

tips This cake is quite soft, and needs to be cooled in the pan before turning out. The cake will keep well for 5 days in an airtight container, or can be frozen for 3 months.

Coconut Cake

INGREDIENTS	DEEP 4-INCH ROUND	DEEP 5-INCH ROUND	SHALLOW 6-INCH ROUND	DEEP 6-INCH ROUND	SHALLOW 7-INCH ROUND	DEEP 7-INCH ROUND	SHALLOW 8-INCH ROUND
BUTTER	5 tbsp	6 tbsp	6 tbsp	1 stick (½ cup)	1 stick (½ cup)	11 tbsp	1 stick + 1 tbsp
COCONUT EXTRACT	½ teaspoon	1 teaspoon	¾ teaspoon	1 teaspoon	1 teaspoon	1½ teaspoons	1 teaspoon
SUPERFINE SUGAR	¾ cup	⅔ cup	⅔ cup	1 cup	1 cup	1½ cups	1¼ cups
COCONUT CREAM	½ cup	½ cup	½ cup	¾ cup	¾ cup	1 cup	1 cup
SELF-RISING FLOUR	⅔ cup	¾ cup	¾ cup	1 cup	1 cup	1⅔ cups	1⅓ cups
EGG WHITES	2	2	2	3	3	4	4
BAKING TIME (approx)	50 minutes	1½ hours	50 minutes	1½ hours	1 hour	1½ hours	1 hour

INGREDIENTS	DEEP 8-INCH ROUND	DEEP 9-INCH ROUND	SHALLOW 10-INCH ROUND	DEEP 10-INCH ROUND	DEEP 12-INCH ROUND	DEEP 14-INCH ROUND
BUTTER	2 sticks + 3 tbsp	2 sticks (1 cup)	2 sticks (1 cup)	3 sticks (1½ cups)	5 sticks (2½ cups)	7 sticks (3½ cups)
COCONUT EXTRACT	2 teaspoons	2 teaspoons	2 teaspoons	3 teaspoons	1 tablespoon	1 tablespoon
SUPERFINE SUGAR	2⅓ cups	2 cups	2 cups	3 cups	5⅓ cups	6⅔ cups
COCONUT CREAM	1¾ cups	1½ cups	1½ cups	2¼ cups	4 cups	5 cups
SELF-RISING FLOUR	2⅔ cups	2¼ cups	2¼ cups	3⅓ cups	6 cups	7½ cups
EGG WHITES	7	6	6	9	16	20
BAKING TIME (approx)	1¾ hours	1 hour	1¼ hours	1½ hours	2¼ hours	3 hours

INGREDIENTS	SHALLOW 4-INCH SQUARE	DEEP 4-INCH SQUARE	SHALLOW 6-INCH SQUARE	DEEP 15 CM (6-INCH) SQUARE	SHALLOW 7-INCH SQUARE	DEEP 7-INCH SQUARE	SHALLOW 8-INCH SQUARE
BUTTER	3 tbsp	6 tbsp	5 tbsp	11 tbsp	6 tbsp	2 sticks (1 cup)	2 sticks (1 cup)
COCONUT EXTRACT	½ teaspoon	1 teaspoon	½ teaspoon	1 teaspoon	1 teaspoon	2 teaspoons	2 teaspoons
SUPERFINE SUGAR	⅓ cup	¾ cup	⅔ cup	1⅓ cups	¾ cup	2 cups	2 cups
COCONUT CREAM	¼ cup	⅔ cup	½ cup	1 cup	⅔ cup	1½ cups	1½ cups
SELF-RISING FLOUR	⅓ cup	1 cup	¾ cup	1½ cups	1 cup	2¼ cups	2¼ cups
EGG WHITES	1	2	2	4	2	6	6
BAKING TIME (approx)	40 minutes	40 minutes	1¼ hours	1½ hours	1 hour	1¾ hours	1¾ hours

INGREDIENTS	DEEP 8-INCH SQUARE	SHALLOW 9-INCH SQUARE	DEEP 9-INCH SQUARE	SHALLOW 10-INCH SQUARE	DEEP 10-INCH SQUARE	DEEP 12-INCH SQUARE
BUTTER	2 sticks (1 cup)	2 sticks (1 cup)	3 sticks (1½ cups)	3 sticks (1½ cups)	4 sticks (2 cups)	7 sticks (3½ cups)
COCONUT EXTRACT	2 teaspoons	2 teaspoons	3 teaspoons	3 teaspoons	1 tablespoon	1 tablespoon
SUPERFINE SUGAR	2 cups	2 cups	3 cups	3 cups	4 cups	6⅔ cups
COCONUT CREAM	1½ cups	1½ cups	2¼ cups	2¼ cups	3 cups	5 cups
SELF-RISING FLOUR	2¼ cups	2¼ cups	3⅓ cups	3⅓ cups	4½ cups	7½ cups
EGG WHITES	6	6	9	9	12	20
BAKING TIME (approx)	1 hour	1¼ hours	1½ hours	1½ hours	1½ hours	3 hours

INGREDIENTS	DEEP 7-INCH HEART SHAPED	DEEP 6-INCH OCTAGONAL	DEEP 8-INCH OCTAGONAL	12-HOLE MUFFIN PAN (⅓ CUP)
BUTTER	2 sticks (1 cup)	1 stick + 1 tbsp	2 sticks + 3 tbsp	1 stick + 1 tbsp
COCONUT EXTRACT	2 teaspoons	1 teaspoon	2 teaspoons	1 teaspoon
SUPERFINE SUGAR	2 cups	1¼ cups	2⅓ cups	1¼ cups
COCONUT CREAM	1½ cups	1 cup	1¾ cups	1 cup
SELF-RISING FLOUR	2¼ cups	1⅓ cups	2⅔ cup	1⅓ cups
EGG WHITES	6	4	7	4
BAKING TIME (approx)	45 minutes	1½ hours	1¾ hours	45 minutes

WE USED 3-INCH DEEP CAKE PANS WITH STRAIGHT SIDES. BUTTER AND EGG WHITES SHOULD BE AT ROOM TEMPERATURE FOR BEST RESULTS. WE USED CANNED COCONUT CREAM.

1 Preheat oven to 325°F. Grease and line base and side(s) of cake pan with parchment paper, extending paper 2 inches above side(s).

2 Beat butter, coconut extract and sugar in bowl with electric mixer until light and fluffy. Transfer mixture to a larger bowl; stir in coconut cream and sifted flour, in two batches.

3 Beat egg whites in bowl (see tips) with electric mixer until soft peaks form. Fold egg whites into coconut mixture, in two batches. Spread mixture into pan.

4 Bake cake for the time given in chart. Cover cake with foil halfway through baking if cake is over-browning, or lower the oven temperature by 10-20 degrees if cake is over 8 inches.

5 Test cake by inserting a skewer into center of cake; if cooked, skewer will be clean, if there is cake mixture on the skewer, bake cake 10 minutes longer before testing again.

6 Cool cake in pan.

tips The egg whites need to be beaten in a narrow bowl so that the beaters are well down in the egg whites to create the necessary volume. If beating large quantities of egg whites, say, more than 10, beat them in 2 or more batches. This cake is quite soft, and needs to be cooled in the pan before turning out. The cake will keep well for 3 days in an airtight container, or it can be frozen for 3 months.

CARROT CAKE

INGREDIENTS	DEEP 4-INCH ROUND	DEEP 5-INCH ROUND	SHALLOW 6-INCH ROUND	DEEP 6-INCH ROUND	SHALLOW 7-INCH ROUND	DEEP 7-INCH ROUND	SHALLOW 8-INCH ROUND
SELF-RISING FLOUR	½ cup	⅓ cup	½ cup	½ cup	½ cup	1 cup	1 cup
ALL-PURPOSE FLOUR	¼ cup	¼ cup	⅓ cup	⅓ cup	⅓ cup	⅔ cup	½ cup
BAKING SODA	¼ teaspoon	¼ teaspoon	½ teaspoon	½ teaspoon	¼ teaspoon	½ teaspoon	½ teaspoon
PUMPKIN PIE SPICE	1 teaspoon	1 teaspoon	1 teaspoon	1 teaspoon	1 teaspoon	3 teaspoons	2 teaspoons
LIGHT BROWN SUGAR	¼ cup	¼ cup	⅓ cup	⅓ cup	⅓ cup	⅔ cup	½ cup
COARSELY GRATED CARROT	¾ cup	¾ cup	1 cup	1 cup	1 cup	2 cups	1½ cups
VEGETABLE OIL	¼ cup	¼ cup	⅓ cup	⅓ cup	⅓ cup	⅔ cup	½ cup
EGGS (2oz)	1	1	1	1	1	3	2
SOUR CREAM	¼ cup	¼ cup	⅓ cup	⅓ cup	⅓ cup	⅔ cup	½ cup
BAKING TIME (approx)	1 hour	1 hour	30 minutes	1 hour	1 hour	1½ hours	1 hour

INGREDIENTS	DEEP 8-INCH ROUND	DEEP 9-INCH ROUND	SHALLOW 10-INCH ROUND	DEEP 10-INCH ROUND	DEEP 12-INCH ROUND	DEEP 14-INCH ROUND
SELF-RISING FLOUR	1 cup	1½ cups	1½ cups	1¾ cups	3 cups	5 cups
ALL-PURPOSE FLOUR	⅔ cup	1 cup	1 cup	1¼ cups	2 cups	3¼ cups
BAKING SODA	½ teaspoon	1 teaspoon	1 teaspoon	1¼ teaspoons	2 teaspoons	3 teaspoons
PUMPKIN PIE SPICE	3 teaspoons	1 tablespoon	1 tablespoon	1 tablespoon	2 tablespoons	2 tablespoons
LIGHT BROWN SUGAR	⅔ cup	1 cup	1 cup	1¼ cups	2 cups	3¼ cups
COARSELY GRATED CARROT	2 cups	3 cups	3 cups	3¾ cups	6 cups	8¼ cups
VEGETABLE OIL	⅔ cup	1 cup	1 cup	1¼ cups	2 cups	3¼ cups
EGGS (2oz)	3	4	4	5	8	13
SOUR CREAM	⅔ cup	1 cup	1 cup	1¼ cups	2 cups	3¼ cups
BAKING TIME (approx)	1½ hours	1¾ hours	1¾ hours	2 hours	2½ hours	2 hours

INGREDIENTS	SHALLOW 4-INCH SQUARE	DEEP 4-INCH SQUARE	SHALLOW 6-INCH SQUARE	DEEP 15 CM (6-INCH) SQUARE	SHALLOW 7-INCH SQUARE	DEEP 7-INCH SQUARE	SHALLOW 8-INCH SQUARE
SELF-RISING FLOUR	¼ cup	½ cup	½ cup	¾ cup	½ cup	1¾ cups	1 cup
ALL-PURPOSE FLOUR	2 tablespoons	⅓ cup	¼ cup	½ cup	⅓ cup	1¼ cups	⅔ cup
BAKING SODA	¼ teaspoon	½ teaspoon	¼ teaspoon	½ teaspoon	½ teaspoon	1 teaspoon	½ teaspoon
PUMPKIN PIE SPICE	1 teaspoon	1 teaspoon	1 teaspoon	2 teaspoons	1 teaspoon	1 tablespoon	3 teaspoons
LIGHT BROWN SUGAR	2 tablespoons	⅓ cup	¼ cup	½ cup	⅓ cup	1¼ cups	⅔ cup
COARSELY GRATED CARROT	½ cup	1 cup	¾ cup	1½ cups	1 cup	3¾ cups	2 cups
VEGETABLE OIL	¼ cup	⅓ cup	¼ cup	½ cup	⅓ cup	1¼ cups	⅔ cup
EGGS (2oz)	1	1	1	2	1	5	3
SOUR CREAM	¼ cup	⅓ cup	¼ cup	½ cup	⅓ cup	1¼ cups	⅔ cup
BAKING TIME (approx)	50 minutes	1¼ hours	1 hour	1¼ hours	45 minutes	1½ hours	1 hour

INGREDIENTS	DEEP 8-INCH SQUARE	SHALLOW 9-INCH SQUARE	DEEP 9-INCH SQUARE	SHALLOW 10-INCH SQUARE	DEEP 10-INCH SQUARE	DEEP 12-INCH SQUARE
SELF-RISING FLOUR	1½ cups	1 cup	1¾ cups	1¾ cups	3 cups	3¾ cups
ALL-PURPOSE FLOUR	1 cup	⅔ cup	1¼ cups	1¼ cups	2 cups	2½ cups
BAKING SODA	1 teaspoon	½ teaspoon	1 teaspoon	1 teaspoon	2 teaspoons	2 teaspoons
PUMPKIN PIE SPICE	1 tablespoon	3 teaspoons	1 tablespoon	1 tablespoon	2 tablespoons	2 tablespoons
LIGHT BROWN SUGAR	1 cup	⅔ cup	1¼ cups	1¼ cups	2 cups	2½ cups
COARSELY GRATED CARROT	3 cups	2 cups	3¾ cups	3¾ cups	6 cups	7½ cups
VEGETABLE OIL	1 cup	⅔ cup	1¼ cups	1¼ cups	2 cups	2½ cups
EGGS (2oz)	4	3	5	5	8	10
SOUR CREAM	1 cup	⅔ cup	1¼ cups	1¼ cups	2 cups	2½ cups
BAKING TIME (approx)	1¾ hours	1 hour	2 hours	2 hours	1¾ hours	3 hours

INGREDIENTS	DEEP 7-INCH HEART SHAPED	DEEP 6-INCH OCTAGONAL	DEEP 8-INCH OCTAGONAL	12-HOLE MUFFIN PAN (⅓ CUP)
SELF-RISING FLOUR	1½ cups	1 cup	1 cup	¾ cup
ALL-PURPOSE FLOUR	1 cup	⅔ cup	⅔ cup	½ cup
BAKING SODA	1 teaspoon	½ teaspoon	½ teaspoon	½ teaspoon
PUMPKIN PIE SPICE	1 tablespoon	3 teaspoons	3 teaspoons	2 teaspoons
LIGHT BROWN SUGAR	1 cup	⅔ cup	⅔ cup	½ cup
COARSELY GRATED CARROT	3 cups	2 cups	2 cups	1½ cups
VEGETABLE OIL	1 cup	⅔ cup	⅔ cup	½ cup
EGGS (2oz)	4	3	3	2
SOUR CREAM	1 cup	⅔ cup	⅔ cup	½ cup
BAKING TIME (approx)	1¾ hours	1½ hours	1½ hours	45 minutes

WE USED 3-INCH DEEP CAKE PANS WITH STRAIGHT SIDES. EGGS AND SOUR CREAM SHOULD BE AT ROOM TEMPERATURE FOR BEST RESULTS. BROWN SUGAR AND CARROT SHOULD BE FIRMLY PACKED INTO MEASURING CUP.

1 Preheat oven to 325°F. Grease and line base and side(s) of cake pan with parchment paper, extending paper 2 inches above side(s).

2 Sift flours, soda, spice and sugar into bowl. Add carrot; stir in combined oil, eggs and sour cream (do not over-mix). Spread mixture into pan.

3 Bake cake for the time given in chart. Cover cake with foil halfway through baking if cake is over-browning, or lower the oven temperature by 10-20 degrees if cake is over 8 inches.

4 Test cake by inserting a skewer into center of cake; if cooked, skewer will be clean, if there is cake mixture on the skewer, bake cake10 minutes longer before testing again.

5 Stand cake in the pan for 10 to 30 minutes, depending on the size of cake, before turning, top-side down, onto wire rack to cool.

tip The cake will keep well for 5 days in an airtight container, or can be frozen for 3 months.

White Chocolate Cake

INGREDIENTS	DEEP 4-INCH ROUND	DEEP 5-INCH ROUND	SHALLOW 6-INCH ROUND	DEEP 6-INCH ROUND	SHALLOW 7-INCH ROUND	DEEP 7-INCH ROUND	SHALLOW 8-INCH ROUND
BUTTER	6 tbsp	6 tbsp	7 tbsp	1 stick (½ cup)	1 stick + 1 tbsp	2 sticks (1 cup)	10 tbsp
WHITE CHOCOLATE	1½oz	1½oz	2oz	5½oz	3oz	4½oz	3oz
SUPERFINE SUGAR	⅔ cup	⅔ cup	⅔ cup	1 cup	1¼ cups	2 cups	1⅓ cups
MILK	⅓ cup	⅓ cup	½ cup	½ cup	⅔ cup	1 cup	⅔ cup
ALL-PURPOSE FLOUR	½ cup	½ cup	¾ cup	¾ cup	½ cup	1½ cups	1 cup
SELF-RISING FLOUR	2 tablespoons	2 tablespoons	¼ cup	¼ cup	¼ cup	½ cup	⅓ cup
VANILLA EXTRACT	¼ teaspoon	¼ teaspoon	½ teaspoon	½ teaspoon	½ cup	1 teaspoon	½ teaspoon
EGGS (2oz)	1	1	1	1	1	2	1
BAKING TIME (approx)	1¼ hours	1¼ hours	1 hour	1½ hours	1¼ hours	1¾ hours	1¼ hours

INGREDIENTS	DEEP 8-INCH ROUND	DEEP 9-INCH ROUND	SHALLOW 10-INCH ROUND	DEEP 10-INCH ROUND	DEEP 12-INCH ROUND	DEEP 14-INCH ROUND
BUTTER	2 sticks (1 cup)	2 sticks + 5 tbsp	2 sticks + 2 tbsp	3 sticks (1½ cups)	5 sticks (2½ cups)	10 sticks (5 cups)
WHITE CHOCOLATE	4½oz	6½oz	5½oz	7oz	12oz	1½lb
SUPERFINE SUGAR	2 cups	2⅔ cups	2⅓ cups	3 cups	5 cups	10 cups
MILK	1 cup	1½ cups	1¼ cups	1½ cups	2½ cups	5 cups
ALL-PURPOSE FLOUR	1½ cups	2 cups	1¾ cups	2¼ cups	3¾ cups	8 cups
SELF-RISING FLOUR	½ cup	⅔ cup	¾ cup	¾ cup	1¼ cups	2½ cups
VANILLA EXTRACT	1 teaspoon	1 teaspoon	1 teaspoon	1½ teaspoons	2½ teaspoons	1 tablespoon
EGGS (2oz)	2	3	3	3	5	10
BAKING TIME (approx)	1¾ hours	2 hours	1¾ hours	2½ hours	3½ hours	4½ hours

INGREDIENTS	SHALLOW 4-INCH SQUARE	DEEP 4-INCH SQUARE	SHALLOW 6-INCH SQUARE	DEEP 6-INCH SQUARE	SHALLOW 7-INCH SQUARE	DEEP 7-INCH SQUARE
BUTTER	5 tbsp	7 tbsp	1 stick (½ cup)	10 tbsp	10 tbsp	2 sticks + 5 tbsp
WHITE CHOCOLATE	1½oz	2oz	2½oz	3oz	3oz	6½oz
SUPERFINE SUGAR	½ cup	⅔ cup	1 cup	1⅓ cups	1⅓ cups	2⅔ cups
MILK	⅓ cup	⅓ cup	½ cup	⅔ cup	⅔ cup	1½ cups
ALL-PURPOSE FLOUR	½ cup	⅔ cup	¾ cup	1 cup	1 cup	2 cups
SELF-RISING FLOUR	2 tablespoons	¼ cup	¼ cup	⅓ cup	⅓ cup	⅔ cup
VANILLA EXTRACT	¼ teaspoon	½ teaspoon	¼ teaspoon	½ teaspoon	½ teaspoon	1 teaspoon
EGGS (2oz)	1	1	1	1	1	3
BAKING TIME (approx)	55 minutes	1 hour	1¼ hours	1¾ hours	1¾ hours	2 hours

INGREDIENTS	SHALLOW 8-INCH SQUARE	DEEP 8-INCH SQUARE	SHALLOW 9-INCH SQUARE	DEEP 9-INCH SQUARE	SHALLOW 10-INCH SQUARE	DEEP 10-INCH SQUARE	DEEP 12-INCH SQUARE
BUTTER	2 sticks (1 cup)	2 sticks + 5 tbsp	2 sticks (1 cup)	3 sticks (1½ cups)	3 sticks (1½ cups)	4 sticks	6 sticks (3 cups)
WHITE CHOCOLATE	4½oz	6½oz	4½oz	7oz	7oz	9½oz	14½oz
SUPERFINE SUGAR	2 cups	2⅔ cups	2 cups	3 cups	3 cups	4 cups	6 cups
MILK	1 cup	1½ cups	1 cup	1½ cups	1½ cups	2 cups	3 cups
ALL-PURPOSE FLOUR	1½ cups	2 cups	1½ cups	2¼ cups	2¼ cups	3 cups	4½ cups
SELF-RISING FLOUR	½ cup	⅔ cup	½ cup	¾ cup	¾ cup	1 cup	1½ cups
VANILLA EXTRACT	1 teaspoon	1 teaspoon	1 teaspoon	1½ teaspoons	1½ teaspoons	2 teaspoons	3 teaspoons
EGGS (2oz)	2	3	2	3	3	4	6
BAKING TIME (approx)	1¾ hours	2 hours	1¼ hours	2½ hours	1¾ hours	3 hours	4 hours

INGREDIENTS	DEEP 7-INCH HEART SHAPED	DEEP 6-INCH OCTAGONAL	DEEP 8-INCH OCTAGONAL	12-HOLE MUFFIN PAN (⅓ CUP)
BUTTER	7 tbsp	2 sticks (1 cup)	2 sticks (1 cup)	2 sticks (1 cup)
WHITE CHOCOLATE	6½oz	4½oz	4½oz	4½oz
SUPERFINE SUGAR	2⅔ cups	2 cups	2 cups	2 cups
MILK	1½ cups	1 cup	1 cup	1 cup
ALL-PURPOSE FLOUR	2 cups	1½ cups	1½ cups	1½ cups
SELF-RISING FLOUR	⅔ cup	½ cup	½ cup	½ cup
VANILLA EXTRACT	1 teaspoon	1 teaspoon	1 teaspoon	1 teaspoon
EGGS (2oz)	3	2	2	2
BAKING TIME (approx)	2 hours	1¾ hours	1¾ hours	50 minutes

WE USED 3-INCH DEEP CAKE PANS WITH STRAIGHT SIDES. EGGS SHOULD BE AT ROOM TEMPERATURE FOR BEST RESULTS.

1 Preheat oven to 325°F. Grease and line base and side(s) of cake pan with parchment paper, extending paper 2 inches above side(s).

2 Combine chopped butter, broken chocolate, sugar and milk in a saucepan; stir over low heat until mixture is smooth. Transfer mixture to a bowl; cool 15 minutes.

3 Whisk in sifted flours, extract and lightly beaten eggs. Pour mixture into pan.

4 Bake the cake for the time given in chart. Cover cake with foil halfway through baking if the cake is over-browning, or lower the oven temperature by 10-20 degrees if cake is over 8 inches.

5 Cake will develop a thick sugary crust during baking (cracks are normal); test for firmness by touching with fingers about 5 minutes before the end of baking time, then, test with a skewer. If cooked, skewer will be clean, if there is cake mixture on the skewer, bake cake 10 minutes longer before testing again.

6 Cool cake in pan.

tip The cake will keep well for 1 week in an airtight container, or can be frozen for 3 months.

Dark Chocolate Cake

INGREDIENTS	DEEP 4-INCH ROUND	DEEP 5-INCH ROUND	SHALLOW 6-INCH ROUND	DEEP 6-INCH ROUND	SHALLOW 7-INCH ROUND	DEEP 7-INCH ROUND	SHALLOW 8-INCH ROUND
BUTTER	1 stick (½ cup)	1 stick (½ cup)	1 stick (½ cup)	11 tbsp	10 tbsp	1 stick + 7 tbsp	1¾ sticks
DARK CHOCOLATE	6oz	6oz	6oz	8½oz	8½oz	12oz	11½oz
INSTANT COFFEE GRANULES	2 teaspoons	2 teaspoons	2 teaspoons	3 teaspoons	2 teaspoons	1 tablespoon	1 tablespoon
WATER	⅓ cup	⅓ cup	⅓ cup	½ cup	½ cup	⅔ cup	¾ cup
LIGHT BROWN SUGAR	⅓ cup	⅓ cup	⅓ cup	½ cup	½ cup	⅔ cup	¾ cup
ALL-PURPOSE FLOUR	½ cup	½ cup	½ cup	¾ cup	⅔ cup	1 cup	1 cup
SELF-RISING FLOUR	2 tablespoons	2 tablespoons	2 tablespoons	¼ cup	2 tablespoons	¼ cup	¼ cup
EGGS (2oz)	1	1	1	1	1	2	2
COFFEE-FLAVORED LIQUEUR	2 tablespoons	2 tablespoons	2 tablespoons	¼ cup	1 tablespoon	¼ cup	¼ cup
BAKING TIME (approx)	1 hour	1½ hours	1½ hours	1¾ hours	1¼ hours	2 hours	2 hours

INGREDIENTS	DEEP 8-INCH ROUND	DEEP 9-INCH ROUND	SHALLOW 10-INCH ROUND	DEEP 10-INCH ROUND	DEEP 12-INCH ROUND	DEEP 14-INCH ROUND
BUTTER	3 sticks + 1 tbsp	3½ sticks (1¾ cups)	3 sticks + 1 tbsp	4 sticks (2 cups)	7 sticks (3½ cups)	11 sticks (5½ cups)
DARK CHOCOLATE	1¼lb	1¼lb	1¼lb	1¾lb	3lb	4½lb
INSTANT COFFEE GRANULES	1½ tablespoons	1½ tablespoons	1½ tablespoons	2 tablespoons	⅓ cup	⅓ cup
WATER	1 cup	1¼ cups	1 cup	1¼ cups	2⅔ cups	4 cups
LIGHT BROWN SUGAR	1 cup	1¼ cups	1 cup	1¼ cups	2⅔ cups	4 cups
ALL-PURPOSE FLOUR	1½ cups	1¾ cups	1½ cups	1¾ cups	3½ cups	5½ cups
SELF-RISING FLOUR	⅓ cup	½ cup	⅓ cup	½ cup	1 cup	1⅓ cups
EGGS (2oz)	3	4	3	4	7	11
COFFEE-FLAVORED LIQUEUR	⅓ cup	⅓ cup	⅓ cup	⅓ cup	1 cup	1⅓ cups
BAKING TIME (approx)	2¼ hours	2½ hours	2 hours	2½ hours	4 hours	3 hours

INGREDIENTS	SHALLOW 4-INCH SQUARE	DEEP 4-INCH SQUARE	SHALLOW 6-INCH SQUARE	DEEP 6-INCH SQUARE	SHALLOW 7-INCH SQUARE	DEEP 7-INCH SQUARE
BUTTER	6 tbsp	1 stick (½ cup)	2 sticks (1 cup)	1 stick (½ cup)	2 sticks (1 cup)	3 sticks (1½ cups)
DARK CHOCOLATE	2oz	6oz	5oz	6oz	13½oz	1¼lb
INSTANT COFFEE GRANULES	1 teaspoon	2 teaspoons	2 teaspoons	2 teaspoons	½ teaspoon	1 teaspoon
WATER	¼ cup	⅓ cup	½ cup	⅓ cup	¾ cup	1 cup
LIGHT BROWN SUGAR	¼ cup	⅓ cup	½ cup	⅓ cup	¾ cup	1 cup
ALL-PURPOSE FLOUR	⅓ cup	½ cup	⅔ cup	½ cup	1 cup	1⅓ cups
SELF-RISING FLOUR	1 tablespoon	2 tablespoons	2 tablespoons	2 tablespoons	¼ cup	⅓ cup
EGGS (2oz)	1	1	1	1	2	3
COFFEE-FLAVORED LIQUEUR	3 teaspoons	2 tablespoons	1 tablespoon	¼ cup	¼ cup	⅓ cup
BAKING TIME (approx)	1¼ hours	1 hour	1¼ hours	1¼ hours	1¾ hours	2 hours

INGREDIENTS	SHALLOW 8-INCH SQUARE	DEEP 8-INCH SQUARE	SHALLOW 9-INCH SQUARE	DEEP 9-INCH SQUARE	SHALLOW 10-INCH SQUARE	DEEP 10-INCH SQUARE	DEEP 12-INCH SQUARE
BUTTER	3 sticks + 1 tbsp	3½ sticks (1¾ cups)	3 sticks + 1 tbsp	4 sticks	4 sticks	4 sticks	8 sticks (4 cups)
DARK CHOCOLATE	1¼lb	1¼lb	1¼lb	1¾lb	1¾lb	1¾lb	3½lb
INSTANT COFFEE GRANULES	1½ tablespoons	1½ tablespoons	1½ tablespoons	2 tablespoons	2 tablespoons	2 tablespoons	⅓ cup
WATER	1 cup	1¼ cups	1 cup	1¼ cups	1¼ cups	1⅔ cups	3 cups
LIGHT BROWN SUGAR	1 cup	1¼ cups	1 cup	1¼ cups	1¼ cups	1⅔ cups	3 cups
ALL-PURPOSE FLOUR	1½ cups	1¾ cups	1½ cups	1¾ cups	1¾ cups	2¼ cups	4 cups
SELF-RISING FLOUR	⅓ cup	½ cup	⅓ cup	½ cup	½ cup	½ cup	1 cup
EGGS (2oz)	3	4	3	4	4	4	8
COFFEE-FLAVORED LIQUEUR	⅓ cup	⅓ cup	⅓ cup	⅓ cup	⅓ cup	½ cup	1 cup
BAKING TIME (approx)	1¾ hours	2½ hours	2 hours	2½ hours	2 hours	2¼ hours	4½ hours

INGREDIENTS	DEEP 7-INCH HEART SHAPED	DEEP 6-INCH OCTAGONAL	DEEP 8-INCH OCTAGONAL	12-HOLE MUFFIN PAN (⅓ CUP)
BUTTER	3 sticks + 1 tbsp	2 sticks + 6 tbsp	3 sticks + 1 tbsp	1¾ sticks
DARK CHOCOLATE	1¼lb	1lb	1¼lb	11½oz
INSTANT COFFEE GRANULES	1½ tablespoons	1 tablespoon	1½ tablespoons	1 tablespoon
WATER	1 cup	1 cup	1 cup	¾ cup
LIGHT BROWN SUGAR	1 cup	1 cup	1 cup	¾ cup
ALL-PURPOSE FLOUR	1½ cups	1¼ cups	1½ cups	1 cup
SELF-RISING FLOUR	⅓ cup	⅓ cup	⅓ cup	¼ cup
EGGS (2oz)	3	2	3	2
COFFEE-FLAVORED LIQUEUR	⅓ cup	⅓ cup	⅓ cup	¼ cup
BAKING TIME (approx)	1½ hours	2 hours	2¼ hours	50 minutes

WE USED 3-INCH DEEP CAKE PANS WITH STRAIGHT SIDES. EGGS SHOULD BE AT ROOM TEMPERATURE FOR BEST RESULTS. THE LIGHT BROWN SUGAR SHOULD BE FIRMLY PACKED INTO THE MEASURING CUP. USE SOFT LIGHT BROWN SUGAR IN THIS RECIPE, NOT SOFT DARK BROWN OR RAW SUGAR.

1 Preheat oven to 325°F. Grease and line base and side(s) of cake pan with parchment paper, extending paper 2 inches above side(s).

2 Combine chopped butter, broken chocolate, coffee, the water and sugar in saucepan; stir over low heat until smooth. Transfer mixture to bowl; cool 15 minutes.

3 Whisk in sifted flours, lightly beaten eggs and liqueur. Pour mixture into pan.

4 Bake cake for the time given in chart. Cover cake with foil halfway through baking if cake is over-browning, or lower the oven temperature by 10-20 degrees if cake is over 8 inches.

5 Cake will develop a thick sugary crust during baking (cracks are normal); test for firmness by touching with fingers about 5 minutes before the end of baking time, then, test with a skewer. If cooked, skewer will be clean, if there is cake mixture on the skewer, bake 10 minutes longer before testing again.

6 Cool cake in pan.

tip The cake will keep well for 1 week in an airtight container, or can be frozen for 3 months.

Fruit Cake

INGREDIENTS	DEEP 4-INCH ROUND	DEEP 5-INCH ROUND	SHALLOW 6-INCH ROUND	DEEP 6-INCH ROUND	SHALLOW 7-INCH ROUND	DEEP 7-INCH ROUND	SHALLOW 8-INCH ROUND
MIXED DRIED FRUIT	10oz	15½oz	15½oz	1¼lb	10oz	2½lb	1lb
MARMALADE	3 teaspoons	1 tablespoon	1 tablespoon	1 tablespoon	3 teaspoons	1½ tablespoons	7 teaspoons
DARK RUM	1½ tablespoons	2 tablespoons	2 tablespoons	¼ cup	1½ tablespoons	½ cup	¼ cup
BUTTER	4 tbsp (½ stick)	6 tbsp	6 tbsp	1 stick (½ cup)	4 tbsp (½ stick)	1¾ sticks	6 tbsp
FINELY GRATED CITRUS RIND	½ teaspoon	½ teaspoon	½ teaspoon	1 teaspoon	½ teaspoon	1½ teaspoons	1 teaspoon
DARK BROWN SUGAR	¼ cup	⅓ cup	⅓ cup	½ cup	¼ cup	1 cup	½ cup
EGGS (2oz)	1	1	1	2	1	3	2
ALL-PURPOSE FLOUR	½ cup	¾ cup	¾ cup	1 cup	½ cup	1½ cups	¾ cup
PUMPKIN PIE SPICE	¼ teaspoon	¼ teaspoon	¼ teaspoon	½ teaspoon	¼ teaspoon	1 teaspoon	¼ teaspoon
BAKING TIME (approx)	1¼ hours	2 hours	1½ hours	2½ hours	1¾ hours	2½ hours	2½ hours

INGREDIENTS	DEEP 8-INCH ROUND	DEEP 9-INCH ROUND	SHALLOW 10-INCH ROUND	DEEP 10-INCH ROUND	DEEP 12-INCH ROUND	DEEP 14-INCH ROUND
MIXED DRIED FRUIT	1lb	2¾lb	1¾lb	4lb	7½lb	7½lb
MARMALADE	1½ tablespoons	2 tablespoons	2 tablespoons	¼ cup	5 tablespoons	½ cup
DARK RUM	⅓ cup	½ cup	⅓ cup	¾ cup	1¼ cups	1½ cups
BUTTER	1 stick + 5 tbsp	2 sticks (1 cup)	10 tbsp	3 sticks (1½ cups)	5 sticks (2½ cups)	6 sticks (3 cups)
FINELY GRATED CITRUS RIND	1½ teaspoons	2 teaspoons	1 teaspoon	2 teaspoons	1 tablespoon	1 tablespoon
DARK BROWN SUGAR	¾ cup	1 cup	¾ cup	1½ cups	2½ cups	3 cups
EGGS (2oz)	3	4	3	6	10	12
ALL-PURPOSE FLOUR	1⅔ cups	2 cups	1¼ cups	3 cups	5 cups	6 cups
PUMPKIN PIE SPICE	1 teaspoon	1 teaspoon	¾ teaspoon	1½ teaspoons	2½ teaspoons	3 teaspoons
BAKING TIME (approx)	3 hours	3½ hours	1½ hours	4 hours	6 hours	5 hours

INGREDIENTS	SHALLOW 4-INCH SQUARE	DEEP 4-INCH SQUARE	SHALLOW 6-INCH SQUARE	DEEP 6-INCH SQUARE	SHALLOW 7-INCH SQUARE	DEEP 7-INCH SQUARE	SHALLOW 8-INCH SQUARE
MIXED DRIED FRUIT	10oz	15½oz	10oz	1¾lb	1¼lb	1lb	1¾lb
MARMALADE	3 teaspoons	1 tablespoon	3 teaspoons	1½ tablespoons	1 tablespoon	1½ tablespoons	1½ tablespoons
DARK RUM	1½ tablespoons	2 tablespoons	1½ tablespoons	⅓ cup	¼ cup	⅓ cup	⅓ cup
BUTTER	4 tbsp (½ stick)	6 tbsp	4 tbsp (½ stick)	10 tbsp	1 stick (½ cup)	1 stick + 5 tbsp	10 tbsp
FINELY GRATED CITRUS RIND	½ teaspoon	½ teaspoon	½ teaspoon	1½ teaspoons	1 teaspoon	1½ teaspoons	1 teaspoon
DARK BROWN SUGAR	¼ cup	⅓ cup	¼ cup	¾ cup	½ cup	¾ cup	¾ cup
EGGS (2oz)	1	1	1	3	2	3	3
ALL-PURPOSE FLOUR	½ cup	¾ cup	½ cup	½ cup	1 cup	1⅔ cups	½ cup
PUMPKIN PIE SPICE	¼ teaspoon	¼ teaspoon	¼ teaspoon	¾ teaspoon	½ teaspoon	1 teaspoon	¾ teaspoon
BAKING TIME (approx)	1 hour	1¾ hours	1½ hours	2½ hours	2½ hours	3 hours	2½ hours

INGREDIENTS	DEEP 8-INCH SQUARE	SHALLOW 9-INCH SQUARE	DEEP 9-INCH SQUARE	SHALLOW 10-INCH SQUARE	DEEP 10-INCH SQUARE	DEEP 12-INCH SQUARE
MIXED DRIED FRUIT	2¾lb	1lb	4lb	4lb	4½lb	7½lb
MARMALADE	2 tablespoons	1½ tablespoons	¼ cup	¼ cup	⅓ cup	½ cup
DARK RUM	½ cup	⅓ cup	¾ cup	¾ cup	1 cup	1½ cups
BUTTER	2 sticks (1 cup)	1 stick + 5 tbsp	3 sticks (1½ cups)	3 sticks (1½ cups)	3 sticks + 6 tbsp	6 sticks (3 cups)
FINELY GRATED CITRUS RIND	2 teaspoons	1½ teaspoons	2 teaspoons	2 teaspoons	1½ teaspoons	3 teaspoons
DARK BROWN SUGAR	1 cup	¾ cup	1½ cups	1½ cups	1¾ cups	3 cups
EGGS (2oz)	4	3	6	6	8	12
ALL-PURPOSE FLOUR	2 cups	1⅔ cups	3 cups	3 cups	3¾ cups	6 cups
PUMPKIN PIE SPICE	1 teaspoon	1 teaspoon	1½ teaspoons	1½ teaspoons	2 teaspoons	3 teaspoons
BAKING TIME (approx)	3 hours	3 hours	4 hours	2¼ hours	3¼ hours	6 hours

INGREDIENTS	DEEP 7-INCH HEART SHAPED	DEEP 6-INCH OCTAGONAL	DEEP 8-INCH OCTAGONAL	12-HOLE MUFFIN PAN (⅓ CUP)
MIXED DRIED FRUIT	2¾lb	2lb	1lb	10oz
MARMALADE	¼ cup	2 tablespoons	2 tablespoons	2 tablespoons
DARK RUM	½ cup	⅓ cup	⅓ cup	¼ cup
BUTTER	2 sticks (1 cup)	1½ sticks (¾ cup)	1 stick + 5 tbsp	6 tbsp
FINELY GRATED CITRUS RIND	1 teaspoon	1 teaspoon	1 teaspoon	1 teaspoon
DARK BROWN SUGAR	1 cup	¾ cup	¾ cup	½ cup
EGGS (2oz)	4	3	3	2
ALL-PURPOSE FLOUR	2 cups	1½ cups	1⅔ cups	¾ cup
PUMPKIN PIE SPICE	1 teaspoon	1 teaspoon	1 teaspoon	½ teaspoon
BAKING TIME (approx)	3½ hours	2¾ hours	3 hours	50 minutes

WE USED 3-INCH DEEP CAKE PANS WITH STRAIGHT SIDES. BUTTER AND EGGS SHOULD BE AT ROOM TEMPERATURE FOR BEST RESULTS; BROWN SUGAR SHOULD BE FIRMLY PACKED INTO MEASURING CUP. USE EQUAL AMOUNTS OF LEMON AND ORANGE RIND TO MAKE CITRUS RIND.

1 Preheat oven to 325°F. Grease and line base and side(s) of pan (see pages 206-7).

2 Mix fruit, marmalade and rum in bowl. Beat butter, rind and sugar in another bowl with electric mixer until combined; beat in eggs, one at a time. Stir butter mixture into fruit mixture; stir in sifted flour and spice. Spread mixture into pan. Tap pan firmly on counter to settle mixture, level top of cake with wet spatula.

3 Bake cake for the time given in chart. Cover cake with foil halfway through baking if cake is over-browning, or lower the oven temperature by 10-20 degrees if cake is over 8 inches.

4 Feel surface of cake; it should feel firm. Remove cake from oven, close oven door, gently push blade of a sharp-pointed vegetable knife straight through center of cake, right to base of pan. Withdraw knife slowly, feel blade with your fingers; if you feel uncooked mixture, return cake to oven for another 15 minutes before testing again. If the blade is free from mixture, the cake is cooked through.

5 Immediately cut off paper around edge(s) of pan. Turn cake, in pan, top-side down onto foil; wrap cake and pan tightly with foil. Cover pan with a towel; cool completely upside down.

tips Cooling cakes upside down will make them sit flat and level for decorating. Fruit cakes will keep indefinitely; the biggest problem is insect infestation. Cake will keep well at room temperature if wrapped in plastic wrap and stored in an airtight container; or freeze, wrapped in plastic wrap in an airtight container.

CAKE PANS

Cut strips of parchment paper to line the inside of the pan, overlapping slightly. Make a ¾-inch fold; snip paper, on an angle, up to the fold.

Lightly grease the pan to hold the parchment paper in place. Position the paper around the side of the pan, with snipped fold at the bottom.

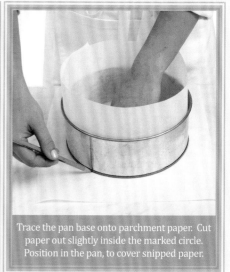

Trace the pan base onto parchment paper. Cut paper out slightly inside the marked circle. Position in the pan, to cover snipped paper.

CHOICE OF CAKE PANS

Cake pans come in all shapes and sizes. Square, rectangular and octagonal shaped pans etc, have sharp corners as opposed to rounded corners; these styles of cakes are better to work with when decorating, as they start off well-shaped. We used 3-inch deep cake pans with straight sides.

Cake pans are made from various metals: our chosen pans are made from a good-quality heavy tin. Aluminium pans are also good as they conduct heat evenly. We avoid pans that have a non-stick surface or are made from flimsy metal, as cakes cooked in these tend to develop a thick crust, which can be quite

tough to bite into – to counter this, reduce the oven temperature by 10 to 20 degrees. Make sure you wash and dry cake pans thoroughly after use – drying them in a low or just-turned-off oven is a good idea. They can develop rust if they're not dried properly after use.

Before you buy a larger than normal cake pan, first measure and check that it will fit in your oven. Cakes do need a little space around them during the baking process to allow for even heat circulation. Some bakeries may be willing to rent out their cake pans, and this is a good option if you're making a one-time-only cake.

PREPARING CAKE PANS

All cake pans must be either greased, greased and floured, or lined to make sure the cakes don't stick. If the recipe requires a long baking time, due to the type or the size of the cake, it's vital to line the pan correctly to insulate the cake, protect the top of the cake from over-browning and to retain the shape of the cake to minimize patching and trimming, especially if the cake is to be iced and decorated.

Large cakes, over 8-inch (20cm), round or square, usually need to be baked in lined pans. The larger the cake, the more lining paper required. For added insulation, use a layer of brown paper on the outside against the side(s) of the pan, and line with parchment paper on the inside of the pan. As a guide, use one layer of parchment paper for cakes that take less than 2 hours to bake, and three layers of

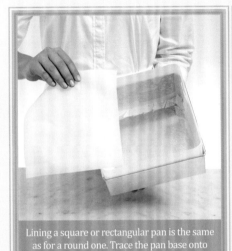

Lining a square or rectangular pan is the same as for a round one. Trace the pan base onto parchment paper; position over snipped paper.

For unusual-shaped pans, use melted butter and a pastry brush to lightly, but evenly, grease the pan. Place in the fridge to set the butter.

Sprinkle the cold, greased pan evenly with flour. Tap and turn the pan to coat it evenly. Tap inverted pan to remove excess flour.

parchment paper for cakes that take 2 to 4 hours to bake. Use a layer of brown paper and three layers of parchment paper (or wax paper) for cakes needing longer than 4 hours to bake.

Lining rectangular, square, octagonal, round or oval cake pans: Cut strips of parchment paper, long enough to encircle the inside of the pan, overlapping the ends slightly, and wide enough to extend 2-inches above the side(s) of the pan. Also, allow for a fold-over at the base of the pan. Fold ¾ inch of the paper over, snipthe paper, on

an angle, up to the fold, making cuts about ¾ inch apart. Lightly grease the inside of the pan with cooking-oil spray or melted butter to hold the lining paper in place. Position the snipped paper around the side of the pan with the snipped fold at the base of the pan. Using the base of the pan as a guide, trace around the base on parchment paper. Cut out paper, cutting slightly inside the marked circle/square to allow for the thickness of the pan. Neatly position the paper in the pan, to cover the snipped paper.

Preparing unusual-shaped pans: Some of the unusual-shaped pans, such as the heart pan, can't be lined efficiently. In this case, grease the pan lightly, but evenly, with melted butter, then refrigerate or freeze the pan to set the butter. Sprinkle a little all-purpose flour all over the greased area, tap and turn the pan so that all the butter is lightly coated with flour. Turn the pan upside down over the sink and knock out any excess flour. If you prefer, line the base of the greased pan with parchment paper, then just grease and flour the side(s) of the pan.

CAKE BOARDS

To cover a square board: Place the board on the back of the covering paper, fold sides of paper over neatly; secure with glue or tape.

Covering a round board (1): Place board on the back of the covering paper; using scissors, snip paper at a slight angle around the board.

Covering a round board (2): Secure snipped paper to board with glue; glue plain paper to the back of the board to cover snipped paper.

To cover a board with ready-to-use fondant (1): Use a pastry brush to evenly coat a paper-covered board with sugar syrup (page 217).

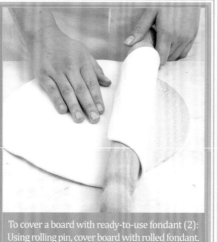

To cover a board with ready-to-use fondant (2): Using rolling pin, cover board with rolled fondant. Smooth with hands and smoothing tools.

To cover a board with ready-to-use fondant (3): Using a sharp knife, trim excess fondant from edge of board; smooth edge(s) with fingertips.

We used wooden cake boards, as wood is strong enough to support the cakes, making them easy to handle and move. They also complement the cake, whether it's single or multi-tiered. They are available from cake decorating shops. If the cake is to be displayed on a stand, you may need to re-think the size of the base board; consider this before starting to decorate. Covered boards can be bought from cake decorating shops. If you want to cover your own, choose a covering that is non-absorbent; cake decorating shops supply this type of paper. We used cardboard cake boards, available from cake decorating shops, for small individual cakes. Occasionally these must be trimmed to fit the base of the cake.

Covering rectangular or square boards: Cut the covering paper about 2-inches larger than the board. Place the board, top-side down, on the back of the paper. Use tape or craft glue to stick the paper to the board. If the paper is thick, cut the corners of the paper as if covering a book. Glue a piece of paper to the back of the board to neaten the appearance.

Covering round boards: Cut the covering paper about 2 inches larger than the board. Place the board, top-side down, on the back of the paper. Snip the paper border, on an angle, all the way around. Fold snipped pieces onto the board and tape or glue in place. Glue a piece of paper to the back of the board to neaten the appearance.

Covering boards with ready-to use fondant: To cover a 12-inch board, knead 1 pound of fondant on surface dusted with a little cornstarch until fondant loses its stickiness. Brush the surface and the side(s) of the board with sugar syrup (page 217). Roll the fondant large enough to cover the board, about $1/8$-inch thick. Use the rolling pin to lift the fondant onto the board; smooth fondant using cornstarched hands. Use smoothing tools to gently smooth the fondant, easing the fondant over the edge(s) of the board. Use a sharp knife to trim the fondant neatly around the bottom edge(s) of the board, then smooth the edge with your fingertip (dipped first into cornstarch). Stand board for 3 hours or overnight, or until the fondant is firm and dry.

PREPARING CAKES FOR COVERING
WITH READY-TO-USE FONDANT

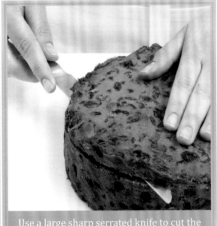

Use a large sharp serrated knife to cut the rounded top off the cake so that it will sit flat when turned upside-down.

Cakes need to be secured to the boards with either royal icing, softened ready-made icing or ganache – royal icing does the best job.

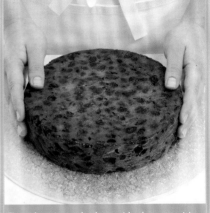

Turn the trimmed cake upside-down; position on the royal icing as soon as it's been applied to the board. Wriggle cake into position.

It's important cakes are properly prepared before using fondant. A poor covering means the cake won't stay fresh for long, and bacteria may contaminate the cake, degrading both the cake and the fondant, not to mention affecting those who eat it. The cakes will keep for up to 2 weeks if covered correctly with an initial layer of ganache or almond paste, then finally covered with ready-to-use fondant so it is airtight. Fruit and some chocolate cakes, if covered and stored correctly, will keep for longer than other cakes. Cupcakes and smaller or cut cakes, will only keep a couple of days. The cakes must be stored in a dust-free area at a cool room temperature. If the weather is humid, it's best to make and keep the cakes in an air-conditioned room.

Trimming cakes: Cakes must first be trimmed before any covering is applied. Most cakes need some trimming to make them flat and a good shape for decorating. We found by cooling heavy cakes, such as chocolate and fruit cakes, upside-down, their own weight flattens them quite a lot, and this should minimize trimming. A cake needs to sit flat and level on its board, and is almost always turned top-side down to cover with fondant. After the cake has cooled and the parchment paper removed, turn the cake top-side up and, using a large serrated knife, cut enough from the top of the cake so it sits flat when turned top-side down. Use a ruler and a small spirit level to get the cake as flat as possible; it's well worth the effort.

Securing cakes to boards: After trimming, cakes need to be secured to their boards so they can be carried safely. Royal icing anchors the cakes well, but if you're not using it to decorate the cakes, then a walnut-sized piece of ready-to-use fondant works well, too. Knead a little cooled boiled water or sugar syrup (page 217) into the fondant until it is soft and spreadable. Spread fondant into the center of the board then position the cake on top; move it around until it's where you want it. Leave to dry out and set – it will hold the cake securely within about 24 hours.

Patching cakes: Once secured to the board, patch the cake if there are any large holes in its surface – this mainly applies to fruit cakes. Use tiny balls of ready-to-use fondant or almond paste to fill the holes (page 216); smooth level with the cake surface, using a metal-bladed spatula, before initially covering with either almond paste, ganache or ready-to-use fondant.

Initial covering: We prefer either ganache or almond paste for the initial covering. Alternatively, you can use just one thick layer of ready-to-use fondant, in which case, triple the quantities of ready-to-use fondant used to cover the cake. After the cake is trimmed, secured and patched, it is then ready for the initial covering.

Initial covering with almond paste: If a cake is to be covered with almond paste, it first needs to be brushed with sugar syrup or warmed sieved jam (page 217). This helps the paste stick to the cake's surface. The almond paste needs to be brushed again with sugar syrup to make the ready-to-use fondant (final covering) stick to the paste.

Initial covering with ready-made icing: You can use a thin layer of ready-to-use fondant (about 1/16-inch-thick) under another thin layer of ready-to-use fondant; brush the cake with sugar syrup before applying the initial layer, then brush that layer with syrup before applying the second (final) layer.

Initial covering with ganache: Apply the initial covering of ganache very thinly, then, if covering with ready-to-use fondant, brush the ganache with sugar syrup so the fondant sticks.

GANACHE

Ganache is a mixture of melted chocolate and cream. It is wonderfully simple to make and versatile to use. It can be used while it's still warm as a glaze over a cake, or even as a sauce with cake. Or, let the ganache partly set, either at a cool room temperature or in the refrigerator, then beat it with a wooden spoon until it's spreadable – making it a perfect filling or frosting. Ganache can be refrigerated for around 30 minutes, or until it becomes thick and spreadable, then whipped with an electric mixer until it increases in volume and becomes fluffy, making it ideal for a frosting or filling.

Ganache will keep in the refrigerator, covered tightly, for about two weeks (stand at room temperature to soften before use), or frozen for 3 months; thaw overnight in the refrigerator, or thaw it in the microwave oven, using short bursts of power.

CHOCOLATE

We used dark- or milk-chocolate when testing the ganache recipe; use whichever type you'd be happy to eat and suits the cake. We prefer not to use chocolate chips, but it will still work in the recipe (right). We don't use high-fat (over 70%) or low-fat chocolate.

Couverture chocolate is expensive, but the results are wonderful. It can be bought online and at some specialty food stores.

White chocolate deserves a special mention as it can be a little tricky to work with – be very careful not to overheat it or it will "split" (turn grainy). We found that by adding more chocolate in proportion to the amount of cream (as compared to milk or dark chocolate) we got better results. Also, we found by chopping white chocolate finely, it melted faster and was less likely to split. We broke the chocolate into pieces straight into the bowl of a food processor, then processed it until finely chopped. If the ganache does split, cool it in the refrigerator, then beat the mixture with an electric mixer; this method hasn't failed us yet. See the finer points of melting chocolate on page 222.

Covering cakes with ganache: This method of using ganache as the initial covering under ready-to-use fondant will result in a well-shaped cake that will taste good, too. Make the ganache recipe (right). Level and trim the cake (page 209), and secure it to the board; patch the cake, if necessary (page 216), and brush lightly with sugar syrup (page 217). Spread a very, very thin coating of ganache all over the cake to hold the crumbs in place and to use as a base for the next layer of ganache (or fondant or frosting). Think of this fine ganache layer as an undercoat. Stand ganache at a cool room temperature until firm to touch. (If the cake is firm, and has no crumbs, this undercoat is not necessary.)

If also using ganache as the second covering, once the undercoat is firm, lightly brush the cake again with sugar syrup, then use a metal spatula to spread a ½-inch layer of ganache over the cake, as evenly as possible. Take your time to get the shape of the cake as perfect as possible; it's worth the effort. Use a straight-sided scraper to smooth the top and side(s) of the ganache covering. Stand the cake at a cool room temperature for about 24 hours, or the until ganache is firm and dry to touch. An air-conditioned room is perfect. If no other covering is to be applied to the ganache-covered cake, it can be refrigerated, if the weather is hot, or stand at a cool room temperature, until needed (up to a week). Bring to room temperature before cutting and serving.

When covering a ganache undercoat with ready-to-use fondant or frosting, brush the ganache lightly, but evenly, with sugar syrup so the next layer will stick. Trim and neaten any rough edges from the surface of the cake so you don't tear the fondant when applying.

(Note: If covering cakes with ganache then ready-to-use fondant, the cake should not be refrigerated as the ganache will absorb the moisture from the fridge, and transfer this to the fondant, making it wet to the touch, sticky and it won't hold its shape.

WHITE CHOCOLATE GANACHE
12 ounces white chocolate
½ cup cream

1 Break chocolate into food processor, process until chocolate is chopped finely.
2 Bring cream to the boil in a small saucepan; remove from heat.
3 Add chocolate to cream; stir until smooth.
4 Cool mixture to room temperature if not being used as a glaze (in which case use while warm and pourable) before beating or whipping to the desired consistency.

Makes enough to cover a deep 8-inch ROUND cake.

DARK OR MILK CHOCOLATE GANACHE
6 milk or dark chocolate
½ cup cream

1 Bring cream to the boil in a small saucepan; remove from heat.
2 Break chocolate into pan with hot cream; stir until smooth.
3 Cool mixture to room temperature if not being used as a glaze (in which case use while warm and pourable) before beating or whipping to the desired consistency.

Makes enough to cover a deep 8-inch ROUND cake.

Note: For a really impressive cake, cut it into layers, as we have done in the step shots, and top the layers with ganache, before covering the cake. You could also layer the cake with butter cream, curd, jam or any type of filling that suits the cake.

You can make the ganache by placing the chocolate and cream in a heatproof bowl over a saucepan of simmering water.

The heat from the water will melt the mixture, stir occasionally until smooth. The water should not touch the bottom of the bowl.

Cool ganache at room temperature or in the fridge, stirring occasionally. Beat ganache with an electric mixer until light and fluffy.

If ganache is the only icing being used on the cake, use a dollop to secure cake to board (or plate); spread ganache with a spatula.

Position cake, or a layer of a split cake, on the board (or plate). Gently push the cake layer to center it or position it as desired.

When layering a cake, spread each layer with ganache. If the weather is hot, refrigerate the layered cake before completing it.

When covering a firm cake (with no crumbs) with ganache, it doesn't need an undercoat; just spread the ganache all over the cake.

Smooth the ganache covering all over with a scraping tool. Take your time to get the shape of the cake as perfect as possible.

Dip the blade of a long-bladed metal spatula into very hot water; dry. Smooth the top of the cake, reheating the blade as necessary.

STACKING AND SUPPORTING TIERS

Throughout this book we've used quite a lot of tall cakes to get the effect we wanted. Sometimes we needed to stack two deep cakes for a really impressive tall cake, other times one deep and one shallow cake stacked together gave us enough height. When stacking and joining same-sized cakes, always stack the shallow cake on top of the deep cake. The charts on pages 190 to 205, listing eight different cake choices, will give you the recipes for making the correct-sized cakes. You can buy the cakes, but make sure you buy deep cakes, or you might have to stack three shallow cakes to achieve the height.

Joining uniced cakes: Cakes can be joined using either jam or ganache. Use any jam you like to join the cakes, one that will complement the flavor of the chosen cake or cakes (page 217). Sometimes it's pleasantly surprising to mix and match two or three different-flavored cakes. If joining different-flavored cakes, attach each cake to its own board (page 209), so that the cakes are easy to separate at serving time using a long-bladed metal spatula.

Trim the tops of the cakes to be joined, so they will sit flat on each other (page 209). Join the cut surfaces of the cakes with jam or ganache to minimize any crumbs escaping. Secure the cake to the board (page 209).

Once joined to the board(s), patch the cakes, if necessary (page 216); brush with sugar syrup and apply the initial covering of almond paste, ready-to-use fondant or ganache and dry overnight or until dry to touch. Apply the second (final) layer to the cakes and leave overnight or until dry (this may take 2 days). You are now ready to support and stack the cakes.

Supporting tiers: Thick wooden skewers are used to support the weight of the upper tiers. Measure the diameter of the board under the next cake tier. Lightly mark this area in the center of the tier below. (This is to ensure the next tier is centerd on top of the bottom tier, otherwise the weight of the tiers will not be evenly distributed, which can cause heavy cakes to tilt and look unbalanced.) Insert the skewers, pointy end down, right through to the cake board about ½ inch in from the marked area to make neat holes in the bottom cake.

Remove the skewers, then push them into the same holes, blunt-side down, through to the board. Mark each skewer level with the surface of the cake tier (note which skewer came from which hole). These skewers will support the next tier, so it's important to have no gaps where the tiers join. Use a hacksaw, pruning shears or a strong serrated knife to cut the skewers as straight as possible, so they are level with the top of the cake tier. Push the skewers into their correct position, cut-side down. (It's best to do this one skewer at a time, so that each skewer is returned to its original hole.) Repeat the skewering process with all the tiers, except the top tier. We use three skewers for each round cake and four skewers for each square cake between each tier. Skewers can be inserted into uniced cakes, if they are to be stacked then iced, as with the *Silhouette Spectacular, page 162* (cakes must be on boards if using skewers).

Stacking cakes: Once the skewers have been inserted into the cakes, the tiers can be stacked on top of each other. Stack and secure the next tier onto the center of the cake below with royal icing or ready-to-use fondant softened with some cooled boiled water. Carefully sit the next tier of the cake on top of the skewers, pressing down gently to secure the bottom of the cake board to the iced cake below. Continue stacking all the tiers in the same way, being careful not to damage the covering when skewering and stacking. Fill any gaps between the tiers, where the cakes join the boards.

Filling any gaps: If a cake is to be covered with ganache or a similar frosting, gaps will be easy to cover. If the cakes are covered with ready-to-use fondant, sometimes decorations or an edging around the tiers will cover any small gaps. To fill larger gaps, and keep the cake airtight, tint some royal icing the same color as the icing covering the cake, and pipe a line of icing around the cake; use your finger to blend the icing around the cake.

At serving time, remove the top tier of the cake by sliding a long metal-bladed spatula under the board to remove it from the tier below. Remove all the skewers when cutting and serving the cake.

note: Except for the bottom cake, which is positioned on a board that is 4-6 inches larger than the cake (or, if being displayed on a cake stand or plate, should be positioned on a board of similar size), each tier is positioned on a wooden board that is the same size as the cake. This is to minimize any gaps between the tiers – these boards should not be visible at all.

Transporting cakes: Tiered cakes can be very heavy – especially if fruit or chocolate cakes are used. Often it takes two people to carry a stacked tiered cake (and one to direct where you're walking and positioning the cake). Transporting a tiered cake can be a problem – it's large, it's heavy and you'll need to anchor the cake for its journey in the car (do not transport it on the car seat). A thin piece of sponge rubber is usually enough to hold the cake still. Allow plenty of headroom for the cake. The only other way of handling and transporting multi-tiered cakes is to assemble the tiers at the venue. This is often impractical to do.

The *Wedding Cake Wonder* (page 120), uses a wooden dowel to secure the cakes in position. Many cake professionals use this method if the cake is three or more tiers. You can use the same technique for any cake in this book over three tiers, if you like (we used a ½-inch dowel, cut to below the height of the cake). You need to drill holes through the centers of all the cake boards.

You also need an undrilled wooden cake board about 2-4 inches smaller than your largest board; this is glued onto the bottom of the largest board, and is used to give height beneath the board, so you can get your fingers under it and lift it off the bench (and out of the car). Glue the dowel into the hole in the largest board and allow to dry. The cakes (attached to their drilled boards) are pushed down over the dowel. These cakes still need to be joined with icing, stacked and supported in the usual way with skewers.

Push pointed ends of skewers into center of cake right through to touch the board, keeping them straight. This makes a neat hole.

Remove the skewers, one at a time, then push back into the cake, blunt-side down. Mark the skewers close to the cake surface.

Use a serrated knife to cut the skewer at the mark; discard pointed end. Replace skewer into cake. It's best to do one skewer at a time.

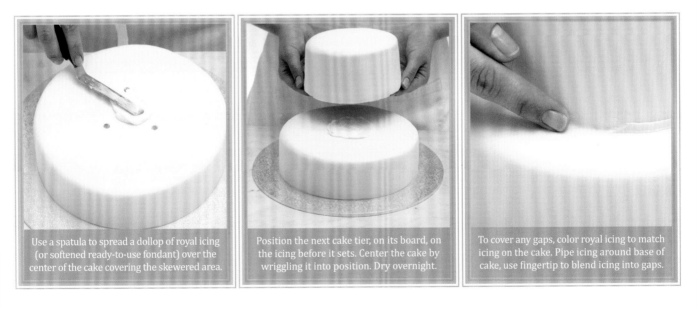
Use a spatula to spread a dollop of royal icing (or softened ready-to-use fondant) over the center of the cake covering the skewered area.

Position the next cake tier, on its board, on the icing before it sets. Center the cake by wriggling it into position. Dry overnight.

To cover any gaps, color royal icing to match icing on the cake. Pipe icing around base of cake, use fingertip to blend icing into gaps.

READY-TO-USE FONDANT

This is a great product and very forgiving for the amateur cake decorator. As with anything, you will get better at handling fondant with practice. It's available in 1 pound packets from supermarkets (usually found among the baking goods), and is found in much larger quantities from cake decorating shops and some craft supply stores. We have specified the amount of this fondant you will need for each recipe. We have presumed you have initially covered the cake with either almond paste, ganache or a thin layer of ready-to-use fondant (page 209), so we have specified only enough fondant to make a thin layer over the initial covering. Should you want to use ready-to-use fondant as the only covering on a cake, you will have to triple the quantity called for in each recipe. In most cases, cakes covered with fondant need to be left to dry for about 2 days – the time depends on the weather. If the weather is humid or wet and the fondant is not drying out, put the cake in a small room, such as a bathroom or laundry, with a fan heater. Don't have the fan too hot or blowing directly onto the cake, just in case there is dust in the heater. The hot air will soon dry out the fondant. If possible, work in air-conditioning when cake decorating, as it makes the processes so much easier. Some cakes in this book need to be decorated with the ready-to-use fondant unset so patterns can be imprinted on it; others require it to be firm or completely set. Follow individual recipe instructions.

Coloring ready-to-use fondant: Use good quality food colorings for best results (not the liquid dyes found in supermarkets). Always start with a tiny dab of the coloring (use a skewer or toothpick), work it through a small ball of the fondant with your fingers until it is evenly colored. Determine the depth and strength of the coloring before adding any more and kneading it through the rest of the fondant. Some cake decorating suppliers stock ready-made fondant already colored – this saves a lot of time and effort.

To cover a cake with ready-to-use fondant: Brush the initial covering on the cake well, and evenly, with sugar syrup before you roll out the fondant. Cut off as much fondant as you need; re-wrap the remaining fondant to exclude air or a crust will develop, which will spoil the smooth texture of the fondant.

Knead fondant, working coloring in, on a surface dusted lightly with a little cornstarch until fondant is smooth and loses its stickiness. Then use a little cornstarch on both the work surface and your hands, to handle the fondant when rolling it out. It's important you don't use too much cornstarch, as it will dry out the fondant, which will cause cracks to occur in the fondant when you cover the cakes. Cover any rolled icing with plastic wrap or a vinyl mat while not working with it to prevent it from drying out. Roughly measure up the side of the cake, across the top and down the other side so you have an idea of how large to roll the fondant (the fondant will stretch once you pick it up and while you're placing it over the cake). Use your hand to press the fondant out first to a manageable thickness in the shape of the cake (circle, square), then start rolling from the center of the fondant outwards; don't roll over the edge of the fondant. Use a rolling pin to roll the fondant to the correct size and thickness (about $1/8$-inch, for the final cover). The fondant can be rolled between sheets of parchment paper, or use a non-stick mat that's suitable for rolling out fondant. The mats can be bought from cake decorating

Use a toothpick to dab a little coloring onto the fondant. Knead on a lightly cornstarched surface to work the coloring through evenly.

Roll out the fondant on a lightly cornstarched surface. Roll from center to the outside edge turning and easing the fondant to fit the cake.

Gently roll fondant around rolling pin. Hold the pin with one hand while supporting the fondant with the other. Lift fondant over cake.

shops and some craft stores. When rolling, try to keep the fondant the shape you need, to match the shape of the cake, and the same thickness all over; do this by gently stretching and rotating the fondant around as you roll. Never turn the fondant over when rolling it out. Roll the fondant around the rolling pin, then lift the fondant over the cake. Dust your hands lightly with cornstarch, and mold and smooth the fondant around the shape of the cake, gently easing out any folds in the fondant. Make sure the fondant feels as if it is clinging to the cake and there are no air pockets under the fondant. Using the plastic smoothing tools, smooth the edges and corners of the cakes neatly. Use a small sharp pointed knife to carefully trim away excess fondant from around the base of the cake. Scraps of fondant will keep well for months if they're wrapped tightly in plastic wrap to exclude the air. If you're making a tiered cake, incorporate the scraps into the next batch of fondant. If air bubbles develop in the fondant during kneading, use a fine pin or fine needle to burst the bubbles, then gently smooth the fondant with your fingers, the bubble and the hole from the pin will soon disappear.

HOME-MADE FONDANT

If you really want to make your own fondant, it's easy to make, but not as easy as buying it.

3 teaspoons powdered gelatin
2 tablespoons water
2 tablespoons glucose syrup
2 teaspoons glycerine
1 pound confectioners' sugar

1 Combine gelatin, the water, glucose and glycerine in a small saucepan. Stir over medium heat, without boiling, until gelatin is dissolved. Remove from the heat; cool until liquid is barely warm.

2 Meanwhile, finely sift confectioners' sugar into a medium bowl. Add warm liquid; stir until mixture becomes too stiff to stir.

3 Use your hand to work ingredients into a ball, then turn the fondant onto a surface dusted with more sifted confectioners' sugar. Knead icing until smooth. Enclose icing in plastic wrap to keep airtight.

Makes 1 pound

tips Keep fondant at a cool room temperature for 2 days, or in the fridge for 1 week. It can also be frozen for 3 months; thaw overnight in the fridge. Knead fondant on a surface dusted lightly with cornstarch to return it to its correct consistency.

Lower the fondant onto cake surface, unrolling it from the rolling pin at the same time. The fondant will stretch a little at this stage.

Lightly cornstarch your hands. Quickly smooth top of the cake, then smooth side(s) of cake, easing the fondant around the shape of the cake.

Trim excess fondant from base of the cake. Burst any air bubbles with a fine pin. Use smoothing tools to smooth fondant. Neaten the cake base.

ALMOND PASTE

Almond paste, often referred to as marzipan or marzipan paste, is the traditional undercoat for rich fruit cakes, which are then usually covered with ready-to-use fondant. Almond paste is easy to make, however, it can be bought ready-made from cake decorating suppliers, supermarkets and some craft supply shops; price is a good guide to quality. Ideally, almond-paste covered cakes need to stand for at least one day (depending on the weather – longer if the weather is humid) at room temperature to set (dry) before they are covered with ready-to-use fondant. This gives a firm, manageable surface for the final layer. Roll out the paste on a surface lightly dusted with sifted pure icing sugar.

Covering cakes with almond paste:
Trim and level the top of the cake, so it will sit flat on the board (pages 209). Secure the cake to the board, top-side down. Use tiny balls of almond paste to patch any large holes in the surface of the cake; smooth the paste with a small metal-bladed spatula. Roll thin ropes of almond paste, thick enough to fill any gaps where the cake joins the board; gently push the paste around and under the base of the cake to fill any gaps, then smooth the paste with a spatula.

There are two methods for covering cakes with almond paste. Cakes 8-inches or less are easily covered with one large piece of almond paste. Larger cakes are better covered using strips of almond paste for the side(s), and a square, rectangular or round shape cut-to-size, to cover the top of the cake. Brush sugar syrup over cake before covering.

To cover a large cake: To cover the sides of the cake, measure up the side of the cake to determine its height then around the cake. Brush the cake all over with sugar syrup. Roll a piece of paste into a long strip, trim to fit around the side(s) of the cake; do this in about four batches, depending on the size of the cake. Position the strips of paste around the side(s) of the cake. If you like slightly rounded corners on a square or rectangular cake, wrap strips of paste around the corners, joining strips somewhere along the side of the cake. If you prefer sharper corners, take the strips to the corner edge, use your fingers to mould the joins together at each corner.

To cover the top of the cake, use the base of the cake pan as a guide, and roll out a piece of paste large enough to cover the top of the cake. Use your hands or a rolling pin to lift the paste into position on the cake. Use your fingers to mold the seams together. Smooth the paste with cornstarched hands, then use the smoothing tools to smooth the paste. Using a small sharp knife, trim around the base of the cake to neaten.

Use small pieces of almond paste to fill and patch any holes in the cake's surface; smooth level with the cake, using a metal spatula.

Roll long thin pieces of almond paste thick enough to cover gap around the base where it sits on the board. Smooth with a spatula.

Roll paste on lightly cornstarched surface until large enough to cover cake; lift paste onto cake, smooth icing over cake with hands.

ALMOND PASTE

2⅓ cups confectioners' sugar
1 cup ground almond
2 tablespoons brandy
1 egg yolk
1 teaspoon strained lemon juice

1 Sift confectioners' sugar and ground almonds into a large bowl; discard any lumps. Stir in remaining combined ingredients.
2 When mixture becomes too stiff to stir, use your fingers to press the ingredients together. Turn paste onto surface dusted with extra sifted confectioners' sugar; knead gently until paste becomes smooth and pliable.
3 Wrap paste in plastic wrap to keep airtight until required.
Makes 1 pound

tips Almond paste will keep well in the refrigerator for 2 weeks or frozen for several months. Thaw the frozen paste in the refrigerator overnight. If you're covering cakes with almond paste before ready-to-use fondant, you will need the same quantity of almond paste as the ready-to-use fondant specified in the recipes.

SUGAR SYRUP

This can be bought from cake decorating shops, but it is quick, easy and inexpensive to make at home. This is used to brush onto the cake's surface before initially covering with almond paste, ready-to-use fondant or ganache (to make them stick). The syrup is then brushed over the initial covering before the final layer of ready-made icing, or ganache, is applied.

1 cup superfine sugar
1 cup water

1 Combine sugar and the water in a small saucepan; stir over high heat, without boiling, until sugar is dissolved.
2 Bring syrup to the boil; boil, uncovered, for 5 minutes without stirring. Cool.
3 Pour syrup into a screw-top jar, store in the fridge for up to 4 weeks.

JAM

Rather than brushing or joining the cakes with sugar syrup, you can use jams, conserves or jellies combined with complementary liqueurs or spirits instead. As a guide, for a deep 8-inch cake you will need ¼ cup jam and 1 tablespoon liqueur. Warm jam in a small bowl over a small saucepan of simmering water; strain the jam while it's warm into another small bowl, then stir in the liqueur. Alternatively, warm the jam in a microwave safe bowl, strain it, then add the liqueur. Make sure the combinations of flavors marry well with the cake itself.

Here are some ideas:
Apricot jam and Grand Marnier or
  Cointreau or limoncello
Orange marmalade and whisky
Raspberry or strawberry jam and Framboise
Plum jam and brandy
Fig jam and rum or brandy
Redcurrant jelly and brandy

When the cake feels smooth and even, trim around the base. Use smoothing tools to make the paste as even and flat as possible.

To cover a large cake, 9 inches or more (round, square or rectangular), cut manageable strips of paste large enough to cover side(s).

Mold the joins together with cornstarched fingers. Use the cake pan as a guide to cut out a piece of paste to cover top of the cake.

BUTTER CREAM

Butter cream, also known as vienna cream, is a popular, easy-to-make frosting to use on cakes. We've left our recipe unflavored, but if you want, you can use any extract, essence or grated citrus rind you like to flavor it. You can use either confectioners' sugar (also known as regular icing sugar) or pure icing sugar (with no added cornstarch).

It's important to have the butter at room temperature, not melted or too soft. Use a small narrow mixing bowl, so that the beaters of the electric mixer can get well-down into the mixture.

The best way to cover a cake with butter cream is to spread a thin layer all over the cake, then refrigerate the cake to set the butter cream; this, in turn, will capture any loose crumbs. Apply the remaining butter cream to the cake, spreading it as evenly as possible.

Coloring the butter cream: Butter cream will always have a slightly yellow tinge to it from the butter content. This is quite tricky to counteract, especially if you want to color the butter cream pink, as it is inclined to end up turning an apricot/salmon color. You can buy a whitening agent from cake decorating suppliers, which will fix the problem. Beat this in before adding any coloring.

Use a skewer or toothpick to dab a tiny amount of coloring onto the butter cream. Use a wooden spoon to mix the coloring through the butter cream evenly before adding any more. Cakes covered with butter cream can be stored in the fridge for up to 24 hours. Return cake to room temperature before serving.

tips Colored butter cream will usually change color within a few hours. It's a good idea to color a small amount and let it stand overnight to see what happens. Some colors darken, others become lighter. Butter cream will keep for about a week in the fridge. Allow it to come to room temperature before beating it again either with a mixer or a spoon. If it's beaten when it's too cold, it will separate. If this happens, let the mixture come to room temperature, then drain off and reserve the liquid. Beat the remaining butter mixture with an electric mixer until it becomes smooth, then beat in the reserved liquid.

BUTTER CREAM
1 stick (½ cup) softened butter
1½ cups confectioners' sugar
2 tablespoons milk

1 Beat the butter (and any flavoring, if using) in a small narrow bowl with an electric mixer until the butter is as white as possible. (This will result in a whiter butter cream, which will give you better results when coloring it.)
2 Gradually beat in half the sifted confectioner's sugar, then the milk, then the remaining sifted confectioner's sugar.
3 Beat until the butter cream is smooth and spreadable. Keep scraping down the side of the bowl during beating.

To make a chocolate butter cream:
Sift ⅓ cup cocoa powder in with the icing sugar.

Makes enough to cover a deep 8-inch cake.

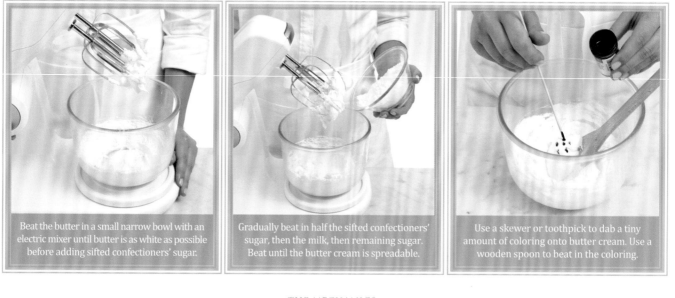

Beat the butter in a small narrow bowl with an electric mixer until butter is as white as possible before adding sifted confectioners' sugar.

Gradually beat in half the sifted confectioners' sugar, then the milk, then remaining sugar. Beat until the butter cream is spreadable.

Use a skewer or toothpick to dab a tiny amount of coloring onto butter cream. Use a wooden spoon to beat in the coloring.

FLUFFY FROSTING

We love this frosting, it looks and tastes wonderful. It can be flavored with any extract or essence and, because it's so white, it will happily take on any color. We always stick to pastel colors when we use this frosting. If you want a strong-colored frosting, however, such as red, this recipe won't work, as you need to add so much coloring that it softens the frosting, and it won't set.

Once all the syrup has been added, start beating in the coloring, a tiny dab at a time to control the color. Scrape down the side of the bowl and the beaters to ensure the coloring is evenly distributed throughout the frosting.

We used a candy thermometer in the recipe below, but it's not essential, just boil the sugar syrup until it's thick with heavy bubbles; it should not be colored. Remove from the heat and let the bubbles subside, then test the thickness of the syrup by dropping 1 teaspoon of it into a cup of cold water. The syrup should form a ball of soft sticky toffee.

Have the cake ready to be frosted as the frosting will begin to set quite quickly as it cools down. The frosting will be glossy for a few hours, then it will become dull and meringue-like in appearance and taste.

FLUFFY FROSTING
1 cup superfine sugar
⅓ cup water
2 egg whites

1 Stir sugar and the water in a small saucepan over high heat, without boiling, until sugar is dissolved. Boil, uncovered, without stirring, about 5 minutes or until syrup reaches 240°F on a candy thermometer. Remove from heat, allow the bubbles to subside.

2 Begin to beat the egg whites in a small bowl with an electric mixer on a medium speed towards the end of the syrup's cooking time. Keep beating the egg whites while the sugar syrup reaches the correct temperature, or the egg whites will deflate.

3 With the mixer on medium speed, slowly pour in the hot syrup in a thin, steady stream; if the syrup is added too quickly, the frosting will not thicken. Once all the syrup is added, continue beating on medium to high speed for about 10 minutes or until the mixture is thick and stands in stiff peaks; the frosting should be barely warm at this stage. Use the frosting immediately.

Makes enough to cover a deep 8-inch cake.

Using a candy thermometer: Candy thermometers must be heated to boiling point before placing into boiling syrup, otherwise the thermometer can break. Put the thermometer into a small saucepan of cold water, bring it to the boil. When the syrup begins to boil, put the thermometer into the syrup. Leave it in the syrup until the temperature required is reached, then return it to the pan of boiling water; turn the heat off and cool the thermometer before cleaning and drying it. Digital thermometers are easier to use; they are simply placed into the boiling syrup.

When making syrup: Stir sugar and the water over heat until the sugar dissolves; any grains of sugar on the side of the pan should be brushed down into the liquid using a wet pastry brush. When the sugar is dissolved, bring the syrup to the boil; once the syrup is boiling, stop stirring. Any stirring at this point will cause the sugar to recrystallize and turn grainy, and you will have to start all over again.

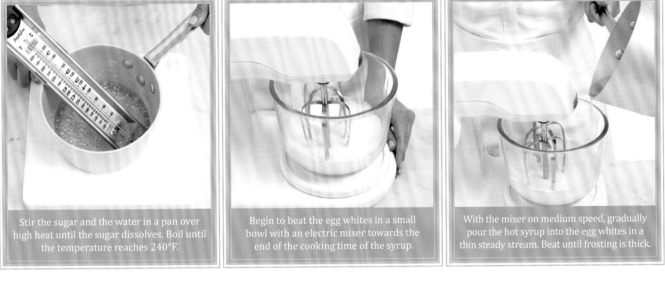

Stir the sugar and the water in a pan over high heat until the sugar dissolves. Boil until the temperature reaches 240°F.

Begin to beat the egg whites in a small bowl with an electric mixer towards the end of the cooking time of the syrup.

With the mixer on medium speed, gradually pour the hot syrup into the egg whites in a thin steady stream. Beat until frosting is thick.

ROYAL ICING

All cake decorators mainly use royal icing for piping. It's easy to make, but a little harder to achieve the right consistency for whatever you're using it for. Using royal icing for piped flowers requires the stiffest consistency; while piping dots and lines etc, requires the softest consistency; piping shells, stars, basket weave and leaves etc, needs a medium consistency. The amount of confectioners' sugar to use is determined by the size of the egg white and the consistency required. Getting the icing just right is a matter of experience.

We use an electric mixer for the quantity given in our recipe. Smaller quantities can be mixed in a cup using a teaspoon. A teaspoon, or even less, of egg white is good to work with, especially for finer piping. A lot of cake decorators make royal icing by hand, not using an electric mixer, as this gives good results and minimizes the development of air bubbles.

It's most important to keep this icing away from the air, as it soon develops a crust, making it unusable for piping – tiny bits of crust will block the piping tubes. Cover the surface of the icing closely with plastic wrap, then a damp cloth, just to be sure.

ROYAL ICING
1½ cups confectioners' sugar, approximately
1 egg white
¼ teaspoon strained lemon juice

1 Sift the confectioners' sugar through a fine sieve.
2 Lightly beat the egg white in a small bowl with an electric mixer until mixture is just broken up – do not whip into peaks. Beat in the confectioners' sugar, a tablespoon at a time, to get the required consistency.
3 When icing reaches the right consistency, mix in the juice using a wooden spoon.

tips Beat the egg whites slowly, just to break them up. You don't want to turn them into meringue, or add air bubbles – air bubbles are hard to get rid of and will affect the look of your icing and the way in which it comes out of the piping tube. An air bubble can cause a piped line of icing to break. Sifting confectioners' sugar through a very fine sieve is important, as any tiny lumps will block fine piping tubes.

If properly covered and sealed, royal icing will keep at a cool room temperature or in the fridge for several days. Beat it with a wooden spoon to bring it back to the correct consistency before using it again. Keep a wooden spoon aside just for beating royal icing. Regularly-used wooden spoons absorb fat from sweet and savory foods, and the last thing you need in royal icing is any trace of fat.

You can buy a royal icing mix from cake decorating suppliers; this works well and is very convenient to use.

Coloring royal icing: Because the icing is white it will take on any coloring. Good quality colorings are expensive, but they are concentrated, so a little goes a long way. They are also quite stable – in other words, the color usually doesn't change much on standing. Use a toothpick or a skewer to dab a little coloring onto the icing. Mix the coloring through with a wooden spoon, scraping down the side of the bowl often.

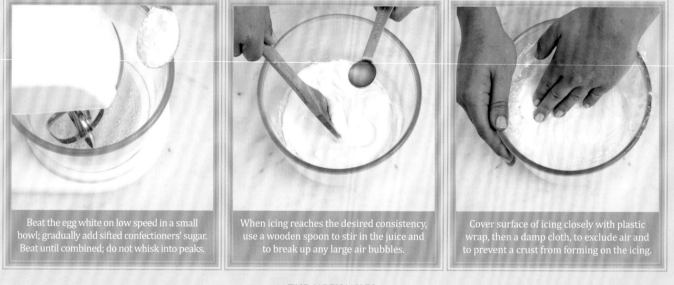

Beat the egg white on low speed in a small bowl; gradually add sifted confectioners' sugar. Beat until combined; do not whisk into peaks.

When icing reaches the desired consistency, use a wooden spoon to stir in the juice and to break up any large air bubbles.

Cover surface of icing closely with plastic wrap, then a damp cloth, to exclude air and to prevent a crust from forming on the icing.

PIPING BAGS AND TUBES

Paper piping bags: You will find paper piping bags incredibly useful, especially if you're working with different colored icings in small quantities. They can be used for piping ganache and butter cream as well as royal icing. You can make your own, using parchment paper, or wax paper, though parchment paper is the stronger of the two. You can also buy large paper triangles suitable for making larger piping bags; these are available from cake decorating shops, craft supply shops and shops that supply chefs and cooks.

Basic piping used for dots, lines, loops, snail trails and so on (page 224); don't really require the use of a piping tube. Fill a paper piping bag ½ or ¾ full with royal icing – whichever feels comfortable in your hand. Gently squeeze the icing down to the tip of the bag; fold the top of the bag over to enclose the icing. Use a pair of sharp scissors to snip the tiniest tip from the base of the bag, then do a test run to see if enough icing comes out of the hole to suit whatever it is you want to pipe. If not, snip another tiny piece from the bag until

you get the opening just right. You can use piping tubes in these bags too; the tubes do give you more control over piped icing. If you're using piping tubes, use two thicknesses of parchment paper to make the bags stronger when piping. Follow the steps below to making paper bags: with practice you will become quick at making them in no time.

Disposable plastic piping bags: These can be bought from supermarkets in a useful medium size. You need to use piping tubes with these bags, unless you're doing some simple piped work like dots or writing (in which case, put the icing in the bag and snip the tip from the bag until the opening is of the correct size). Some boxes of bags may include a kit of a few plastic piping tubes; these are good for some piping, but not for any fine work.

Fabric piping bags: These come in a wide range of sizes, from quite small to very large. The small ones are usually used for cake decorating, either with a piping tube inserted in the opening, or fitted with a piping screw (also known as a 'coupler'), which secures

the piping tube to the outside of the piping bag, making it a simple process to change tubes (to pipe a different decoration) or to use the tube with a different colored icing. Larger piping bags are usually fitted with large tubes; these are suitable for piping whipped cream, meringue and butter-based frostings. After use, wash the bags in warm water and leave to dry over a bottle.

Piping tubes: These are available in many sizes, either made from plastic or metal. We prefer metal tubes, they're more expensive than plastic but will last a lifetime. Wash in warm water, using a small paint brush around the tip to clean them thoroughly. Whatever you do, don't clean out leftover mixture by poking your finger through the end of the tube, as it can get stuck, which is particularly painful if it's a sharp fluted tube. Smaller diameter tubes and fluted tubes are delicate and can, with rough handling, easily become distorted, which will affect the outcome of your piping. So treat your tubes with care and store them properly.

Cut a perfect square from baking paper, fold it in half diagonally. Use a sharp knife to cut paper along the fold to make two triangles.

Hold apex of triangle towards you, wrap one point of triangle around to form a cone. Wrap remaining point around to make bag.

Wriggle the points of the triangle together until they line up perfectly. Staple the bag to secure the three points in place.

CHOCOLATE

There are several ways to melt chocolate, regardless of the color. We prefer to use a glass, china or ceramic bowl when melting chocolate over a pan of simmering water as these bowls heat slowly, and melt the chocolate gently. Stainless steel bowls also work, but be aware that metal conducts heat rapidly, which can cause the chocolate to overheat if it's not watched carefully.

Seizing: This occurs when water comes in contact with the chocolate, it causes it to turn hard and grainy, making it impossible to work with. You will have to start again with another batch of chocolate. It only needs the tiniest amount of water to seize.

Melting in a medium saucepan: Place a medium heatproof bowl over a pan of simmering water; don't let the water touch the base of the bowl as this can overheat the chocolate. Stir occasionally. Remove the bowl from the pan as soon as the chocolate is smooth, to prevent it from overheating.

Melting in the sink: Another method that is easy and mess-free is to put the chocolate into a bowl – we use a stainless steel bowl for this method. Stand the bowl in a sink of hot tap water, or a larger bowl of hot water. Stir occasionally until the chocolate is smooth. This method takes a little longer, but it's fail-proof. The water should come about half-way up the side of the bowl.

Melting in a microwave oven: This works well if you don't overheat the chocolate. Check your instruction manual for the best directions. Usually 50% or 75% power is right for melting chocolate. Place chocolate in a microwave-safe bowl, then microwave it using short bursts of power. Check every 20 seconds by pressing it with a spatula – it

Melt in a sink: Place chocolate in a stainless steel bowl in a sink (or a larger bowl) half-filled with hot tap water; stir occasionally.

Melt over a saucepan: Place chocolate in a glass bowl over a pan of simmering water; don't let water touch bowl; stir occasionally.

Melt in the microwave: Place chocolate in a microwave-safe bowl; heat on medium heat. Stir often, as it holds its shape when melted.

Stir chocolate away from the heat until smooth. Microwaved chocolate will hold its shape, so test by pressing with a spoon.

To make curls: Spread melted chocolate thinly, but evenly, onto a cold surface such as marble or stainless steel; stand until almost set.

For long curls, use a sharp long-bladed knife, holding the blade at a 45° angle on surface, drag the knife over chocolate to make curls.

could be melted even though it has retained its shape. Don't let the tiniest drop of water near the chocolate or it will seize. Never cover or partially cover chocolate – or the bowl it is in – while it's melting, as condensation will form under the lid or covering, and drops of moisture will fall into the chocolate – and it will seize and be useless.

Making chocolate curls: There are quite a few ways to make curls, all of which will make different-sized and shaped curls. The classic way is to spread melted chocolate evenly over a cold surface, such as marble, a stainless steel bench top or a flat oven tray; leave it at room temperature until it is almost set; this shouldn't take long – up to 10 minutes. Drag the blade of a large sharp knife, held at about a 45 degree angle, across the chocolate to make curls. It is important the chocolate is at the right stage. If the chocolate is not set enough, it will not curl and if the chocolate is set too much, the curls will break.

Another way to make simple small chocolate curls is to scrape a vegetable peeler along the side of a block of chocolate. A cheese slicer is good if you want larger curls. Make the curls from the back of a whole block of chocolate. Place the chocolate block, flat-side up, on a board and place your hand on the surface to warm it very slightly. Drag the slicer over the chocolate block. You may have to re-warm the chocolate with your hand several times during the process. If you want large chunky curls, spread melted chocolate onto a cold surface and drag an ice-cream scoop across the surface of the almost-set chocolate.

Piping chocolate: A small paper piping bag (page 221) is the best to use when piping chocolate. Cut a small snip off the end and you can pipe messages or shapes directly onto a cake, or onto baking paper – the chocolate dries quickly and can be lifted straight onto the cake. You almost always have to pipe more than you need as breakages will occur.

For short chunky curls (1): Allow the melted chocolate to almost set then hold the tip of an ice-cream scoop on the surface.

For short chunky curls (2): Firmly drag the ice-cream scoop over the surface of the chocolate using an even pressure.

For large curls: Soften back of chocolate by holding your hand on the surface for about a minute. Drag cheese slicer across chocolate.

For smaller chocolate curls: Slightly warm the chocolate block; drag the blade of a sharp vegetable peeler evenly down the side.

To pipe chocolate (1): First make a paper piping bag (page 221), then half-fill the bag with melted chocolate; fold over top of bag.

To pipe chocolate (2): Snip a tiny tip from the piping bag. Pipe chocolate, holding bag at a 45° angle. Pipe freehand or use a pattern.

PIPING TECHNIQUES

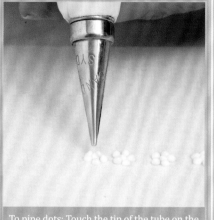

To pipe dots: Touch the tip of the tube on the surface while holding bag upright. Squeeze to make dot, stop squeezing, pull tube straight up.

To make forget-me-nots using a plain tube: Pipe five dots in a circle, then finish with one dot in the center of each circle.

Snails' trail (1): Using a plain tube, hold bag at a 45° angle, touch down with tube squeezing bag to make a teardrop of icing.

Snails' trail (2): Gradually reduce pressure on bag, lifting tube slightly. Touch tube on surface, stop squeezing, making a tiny trail.

Straight lines (1): Using a plain tube, hold bag at a 45° angle, touch tube down, squeeze bag to make and anchor a dot of icing.

Straight lines (2): Keep pressure on bag by squeezing gently. Lift tube up from anchor point, piping evenly, towards where it ends.

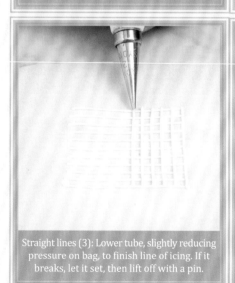

Straight lines (3): Lower tube, slightly reducing pressure on bag, to finish line of icing. If it breaks, let it set, then lift off with a pin.

Stars (1): Using a fluted tube, hold the bag upright, squeeze the bag, keeping tip of tube barely above surface; pipe a star shape.

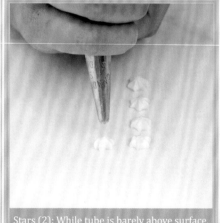

Stars (2): While tube is barely above surface, gradually reduce, then stop squeezing the bag. Pull tube up without leaving a point.

We used royal icing and a number 2 plain (writing), number 8 fluted (shell) and number 22 (basket weave) tube on these two pages. Piping is not difficult, it just takes practice.

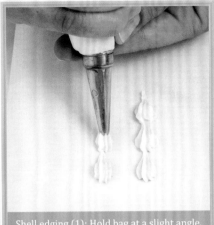

Shell edging (1): Hold bag at a slight angle. Touch tip of fluted tube on surface, squeeze bag, lifting tube slightly to make a shell shape.

Shell edging (2): Gradually reduce pressure on the bag to make a short tail on the shell. Start a new shell shape at the end of this tail.

To pipe a rope: Using fluted tube, touch tube on surface, squeeze bag and lift tube at same time, moving clockwise in a small tight circle.

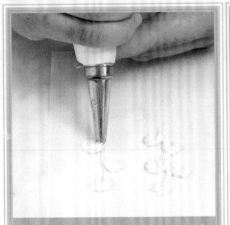

Feather and fan (1): Hold bag almost upright, touch fluted tube down on surface, squeeze bag, and twist tube to pipe a question mark.

Feather and fan (2): Reduce pressure on bag as you pipe to make the tail of the question mark. Repeat on other side to make pattern.

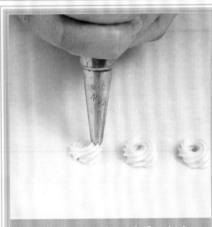

Candle holders: Touch tip of a fluted tube on surface squeezing the bag at the same time, and moving the tube in a circular pattern.

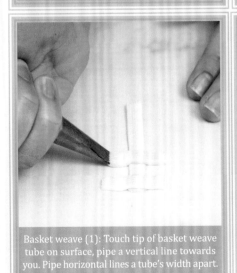

Basket weave (1): Touch tip of basket weave tube on surface, pipe a vertical line towards you. Pipe horizontal lines a tube's width apart.

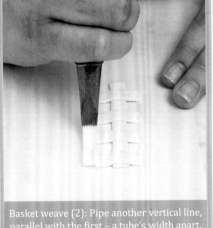

Basket weave (2): Pipe another vertical line, parallel with the first – a tube's width apart, barely covering ends of the horizontal lines.

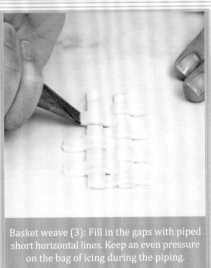

Basket weave (3): Fill in the gaps with piped short horizontal lines. Keep an even pressure on the bag of icing during the piping.

MAKING BOWS

We've used bows to decorate some of the ribbons on the cakes in this book. Here's how to make them.

Sewing a tailored bow (1): Fold a length of ribbon to make four loops. Stitch in the center of bow to hold loops together.

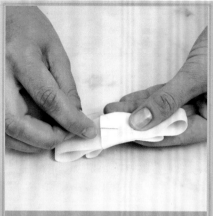

Sewing a tailored bow (2): Sew a small strip of ribbon into position in the center of the bow to cover and neaten the looped ribbon.

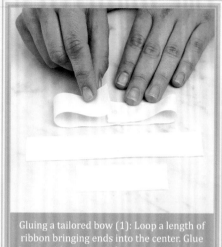

Gluing a tailored bow (1): Loop a length of ribbon bringing ends into the center. Glue into position using a glue gun or craft glue.

Gluing a tailored bow (2): Loop a smaller length of ribbon, secure ends in center with glue. Glue smaller loop onto larger loop.

Gluing a tailored bow (3): Glue a small strip of ribbon over the center of the double bow to cover and neaten the middle of the bow.

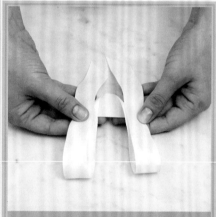

Tying a simple bow (1): Make two loops from a length of ribbon. Leave enough ribbon for tails – make these as long as you want them.

Tying a simple bow (2): Cross the loops over; bring the top loop under bottom loop then through the hole under the bottom loop.

Tying a simple bow (3): Pull the tops of the loops at the same time to make the bow even and roughly the size you want it to be.

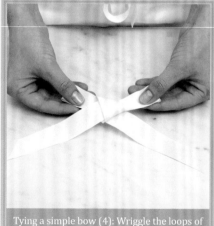

Tying a simple bow (4): Wriggle the loops of the bow until they are the same length, and the bow and its center are as you want them.

GUM PASTE

Many different shapes can be made using this paste. It's easy to make, and keeps for several days at room temperature, wrapped in plastic wrap to keep airtight. It can be bought in cake decorators' shops, however, we found the home-made paste best to work with, as the shapes dried and stayed firmer longer than those made with bought paste.

Gum paste, also called flower or petal paste, can be molded into cute 3D shapes, etc. – such as animals, people, or toys, which can then be wired to stand up on the cake.

The paste can also be rolled out thinly, and cutters used to cut out petals and other shapes. Petals are often dried separately, then assembled into buds and flowers by using royal icing to secure petals together, or by wiring the petals together with floral wire.

Work with small amounts of paste only, as once it's exposed to air it dries out quickly. Plastic wrap is perfect for enclosing pieces of paste to keep it airtight. Most cut-out shapes need further shaping, so keep unshaped cut-outs under plastic wrap, or a piece of vinyl, until you're ready to use them. Everything made using modeling paste needs to be dried. This takes varying amounts of time depending on the weather and the thickness of the paste. As a guide, thin petals will dry in a few hours; more solid shapes, for example letters ½-inch thick, may take two days to dry out completely.

Many shapes are wired and positioned in the cake. Because of health reasons, don't insert the wired shapes into the cake until the day of the function as, once pierced, the cake's seal is no longer intact and bacteria may enter. A more hygienic way to insert decorations is to use flower spikes: these hollow, inert plastic spikes are pushed into the cake and used to hold the decoration in place. Fresh flowers can also be positioned in spikes; add a couple of drops of water to keep the flowers fresh during the celebration.

GUM PASTE

2 teaspoons powdered gelatin
1½ tablespoons water
2 teaspoons glucose syrup or corn syrup
1½ cups confectioners' sugar

1 Sprinkle gelatin over the water in a heatproof cup; stand cup in small saucepan of simmering water, stir until gelatin is dissolved. Stir in glucose.
2 Sift icing sugar into medium bowl; stir in gelatin mixture then, when mixture becomes too stiff to stir, use your hand to combine the ingredients.
3 Knead on surface dusted with extra sifted icing sugar until smooth and elastic. Wrap tightly in plastic wrap to keep airtight.

Makes 8 ounces

Coloring gum paste: Since the paste is white it colors easily. Start with a small dab of coloring, applied to a small ball of paste, to determine the strength of the coloring. Once you're happy with the color, tint the amount of paste you need. Shapes made from gum paste can be painted once they're dried out, use food coloring for this.

Wiring shapes made from modeling paste: This must be done as soon as the shape is established. Wire is usually dipped in flower glue and pushed into the shape, then allowed to dry.

FLOWER GLUE

1 tablespoon tylose powder
2 tablespoons water

1 Combine ingredients in a screw-topped jar; shake well, stand overnight (lumps will dissolve overnight).
2 Stir in a little more water to bring the glue to the consistency of unbeaten egg white; shake well.

tips This glue must be made at least 12 hours before using. It keeps indefinitely at room temperature, but will thicken on standing. Return it to the consistency of unbeaten egg white by stirring in a little more water each time you use it.

Sift confectioners' sugar into a medium bowl; pour in combined liquids. Stir with a wooden spoon until mixture becomes difficult to stir.

Work the ingredients together. Turn paste onto surface dusted with sifted confectioners' sugar; knead until smooth. Enclose in plastic wrap.

Keep paste covered with plastic wrap or a piece of vinyl to stop it from drying out. Only work with small quantities at a time.

CAKE
Patterns

SECOND TIER FROM BOTTOM

LATTE LACE CAKE (PAGE 132)

BOTTOM TIER

TOP TIER (LARGER)

SECOND TIER FROM TOP

MIDDLE TIER (SMALLER)

WEDDING CAKE POPS
(PAGE 142)

Thank You

Thank You

Thank You

Thank You

Thank You

Thank You

Thank You

Thank You

BRIDAL MOSAIC SQUARES
(PAGE 168)

BUCKLE UP BABY CAKES
(PAGE 172)

BOOTIES FOR BABY (PAGE 180)

BOOTIES FOR BABY
(PAGE 180)

BOOTIES FOR BABY (PAGE 180)

EQUIPMENT

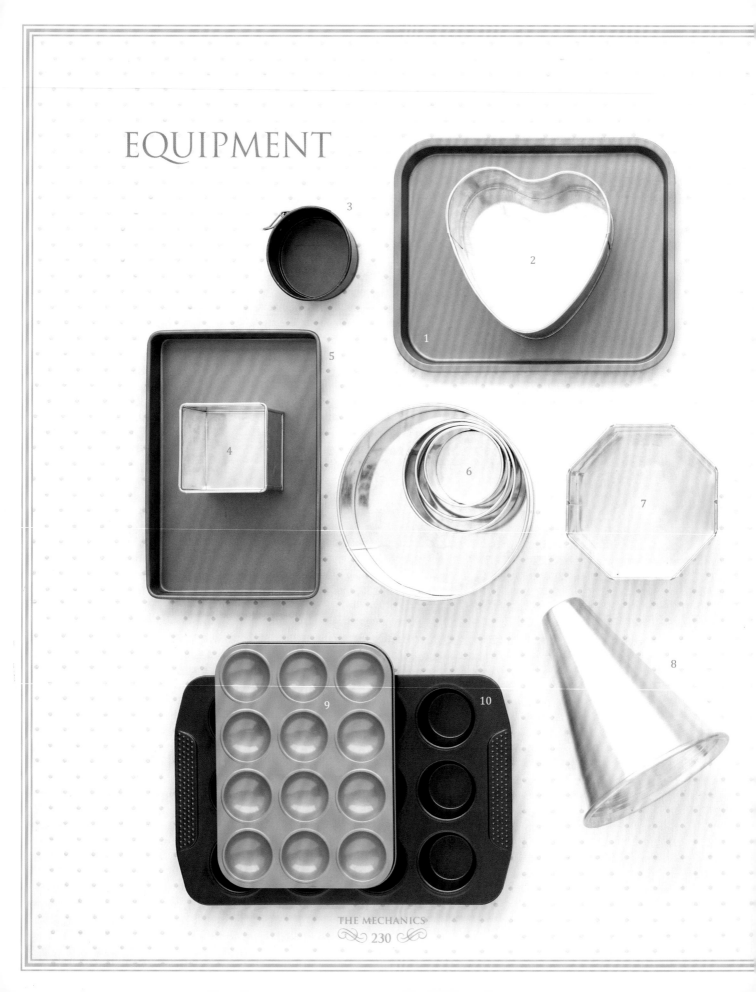

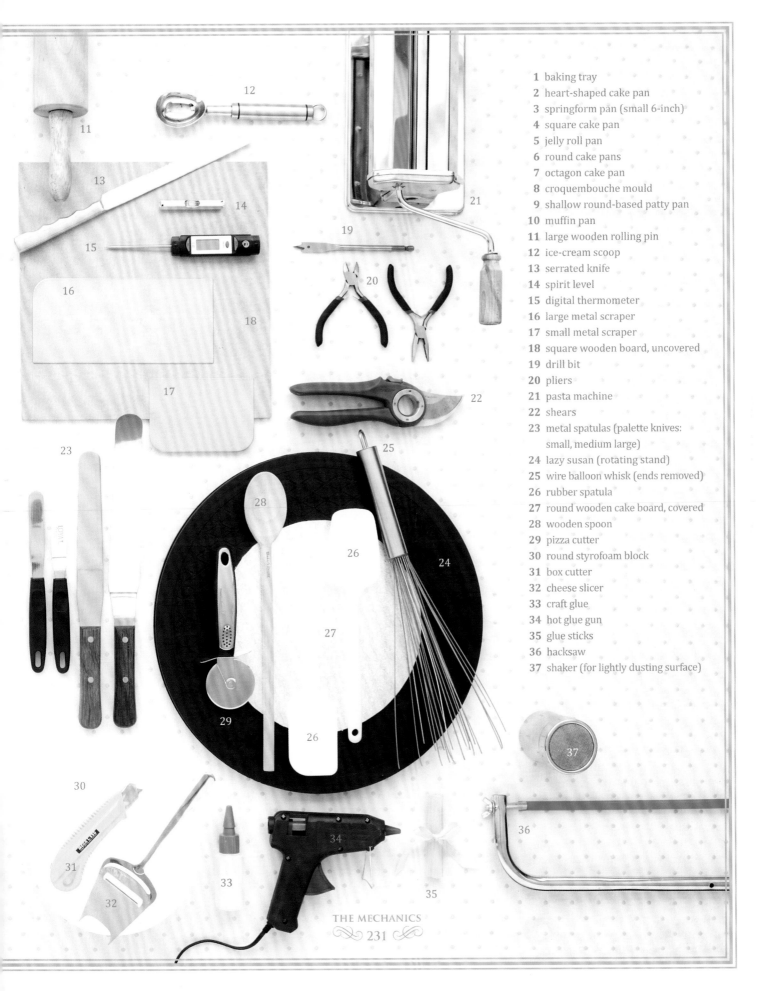

1 baking tray
2 heart-shaped cake pan
3 springform pan (small 6-inch)
4 square cake pan
5 jelly roll pan
6 round cake pans
7 octagon cake pan
8 croquembouche mould
9 shallow round-based patty pan
10 muffin pan
11 large wooden rolling pin
12 ice-cream scoop
13 serrated knife
14 spirit level
15 digital thermometer
16 large metal scraper
17 small metal scraper
18 square wooden board, uncovered
19 drill bit
20 pliers
21 pasta machine
22 shears
23 metal spatulas (palette knives:
   small, medium large)
24 lazy susan (rotating stand)
25 wire balloon whisk (ends removed)
26 rubber spatula
27 round wooden cake board, covered
28 wooden spoon
29 pizza cutter
30 round styrofoam block
31 box cutter
32 cheese slicer
33 craft glue
34 hot glue gun
35 glue sticks
36 hacksaw
37 shaker (for lightly dusting surface)

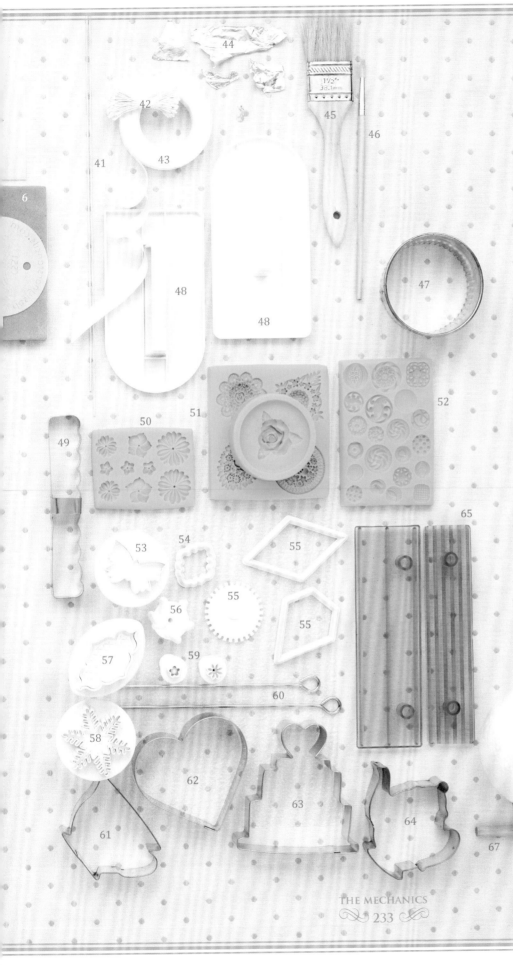

1 fondant cutter/embosser **2** ball tool (large) **3** frill tools **4** ball tool (small) **5** alencon lace stencil **6** blue modeling sponge (flower mat) **7** filigree damask stencil **8** textured acrylic rolling pin (patchwork) **9** small non-stick rolling pin **10** textured acrylic rolling pin (swirl) **11** textured acrylic rolling pin (filigree) **12** lollypop candy sticks (cake pop sticks) **13** large wooden skewers **14** toothpicks **15** acrylic measures (various sizes) **16** stencil (coffee) **17** petal veiner **18** plastic ruler **19** number cutters **20** eyelet cutters **21** luster dust **22** petal dust **23** food coloring (concentrated paste not liquid) **24** metal blossom cutters **25** magnolia cutters **26** peony cutter **27** round cutter **28** rose petal cutter **29** plain metal piping nozzles **30** plastic star nozzle **31** piping bags **32** tweezers **33** square cutter **34** vinyl mat **35** pearl-headed pins **36** patchwork cutter trellis **37** diamond-sided patchwork cutter **38** small scissors **39** cupcake wrappers (decorative cupcake wrappers) **40** tape measure **41** floral wire **42** stamens **43** white florist's tape **44** gold leaf **45** pastry brush **46** artist's fine paint brush **47** round fluted cutter **48** smoothing tools **49** frill cutter **50** silicone mold (small flower) **51** silicone molds (floral pendant) **52** silicone mold (beads & buttons) **53** veined butterfly plunger cutter **54** scalloped cutter **55** patchwork set **56** leaf cutter **57** plaque plunger cutter **58** snowflake plunger cutter **59** blossom cutter plunger **60** metal skewers **61** teacup cutter **62** heart-shaped cutter **63** wedding cake cutter **64** teapot cutter **65** strip cutter **66** sytrofoam ball **67** wooden dowels

GLOSSARY

acrylic measures clear rulers that come in different widths; used to cut icing ribbons to specified widths for cakes. Often come in a set of 5 widths.

almond meal also known as ground almonds; nuts are powdered to a coarse flour-like texture.

almond paste similar to marzipan, but is less granular and contains less sugar (see also marzipan).

baking powder a raising agent consisting of two parts cream of tartar to one part baking soda.

ball tool a plastic stick with a ball of different sizes at either end. Is used to thin ready-made icing when making flower petals, and to smooth curves and rounded ends. There are a number of sizes available.

Baking soda used as a leavening agent in baking.

blossom cutters tiny cutters used to make small flowers; come as 3, 4 or 5 petals.

brushes artist's paint brushes and make-up brushes are excellent when brushing cakes, models, flowers and other decorations with glitter, powder or dusts, or painting colors, water or sugar syrup onto cakes. Larger-sized brushes are also useful for brushing crumbs off cakes or dried icing from boards.

butter use salted or unsalted (sweet) butter; one stick of butter (4 ounces) is equal to ½ cup.

cake boards often made from masonite and covered in a thick non-absorbable paper, silver or gold colored. Come in myriad sizes, usually round or square, occasionally octagonal. If displaying on a cake board, rather than a plate, the base board is often 4-6 inches larger than the cake, so it can be lifted and transported without fingers poking holes in the icing. The remaining cakes are placed on cake boards of the same-size. If displaying on a cake plate, the base board should be the same size as the cake.

chocolate

dark also known as semi-sweet or luxury chocolate; made of a high percentage of cocoa liquor, cocoa butter, and a little added sugar.

milk mild and very sweet; similar in make-up to dark with the difference being the addition of milk solids.

white contains no cocoa solids but derives its sweet flavor from cocoa butter. Very sensitive to heat so watch carefully when melting.

cocoa powder also known as cocoa; dried, unsweetened, roasted and ground cocoa beans (cacao seeds).

dutch cocoa is treated with an alkali to neutralize its acids. It has a reddish-brown color, a mild flavor and is easy to dissolve in liquids.

coconut

desiccated dried, unsweetened, finely shredded coconut.

extract produced from coconut flavoring, oil and alcohol.

flaked dried, flaked coconut flesh.

shredded strips of dried coconut.

cornstarch often used as a thickener, here we use it to roll out ready-to-use fondant and gum paste.

coupler this device lets you quickly change piping tubes without changing the bag. It has two parts; the base sits on the inside of the bag with the end poking out; the piping tube is then placed over the part poking out and the ring is twisted or screwed over the tube to lock it in place.

cream we use heavy or whipping cream, unless otherwise stated. Look for a brand free of additives, unlike commercially thickened cream, and a minimum fat content of 35%.

sour a thick cultured soured cream.

cream cheese commonly known as Philadelphia or Philly, a soft cow's-milk cheese.

cream of tartar an acid ingredient in baking powder; keeps frostings creamy and improves volume when beating egg whites. Helps prevent sugar from crystallizing when used in candy making.

cutters come in many sizes, shapes, styles, plunging etc. Used to cut ready-made icing and modeling paste into different shapes.

dragées these minuscule (⅛ to ¹³/₆₄ inch) metallic-looking-but-edible confectionery balls are available in silver, gold or various colors. Also known as cachous.

edible dust, glitter, powders are available from cake decorating suppliers. Used to add details and highlights to cakes.

embossing tools are pressed or rolled onto soft ready-to-use fondant leaving a print of the design. Textured mats are also a type of embossing tool.

filigree an intricate type of lace work done using royal icing. Is very delicate and breaks easily.

floral wire also known as florist's or craft wire. A covered flexible wire that comes in different thicknesses. The higher the number of the gauge (eg 33-gauge) the finer the wire and the finer the wire the more delicate and flexible it is (used for smaller pieces); the lower the number of the gauge (eg 18-gauge) the thicker the wire (used for making large sugar flowers). Also used to bind petals when making flowers, or to position shapes or flowers into cakes. The wire itself may be uncovered or wrapped in white or green florist's tape. Available from craft and cake decorating suppliers in cut lengths and on spools. When we ask for a length of wire, we mean 14 inch lengths.

florist's tape from craft and cake decorating suppliers. Wrapped around flower stems to provide a seal when placing fresh flowers on cakes. Also used to cover wooden dowels, or to cover floral wire when making flowers from gum paste, etc, to hold the petals in place.

flour

rice very fine, almost powdery, gluten-free flour; made from ground white rice.

self-rising plain flour sifted with baking powder in the proportion of 1 cup flour to 2 teaspoons baking powder. Also called self-raising flour.

flower cutters used to cut small flower shapes (see blossom cutters).

flower spikes are hollow plastic spikes that are pushed through the icing into the cake. Used to position wired flowers and other decorations, thus keeping the floral wire out of the cake. This is a safe, hygienic way to add embellishments to the cake. Fresh flowers can also be positioned in spikes; add a couple of drops of water into the spike to keep the flowers fresh during the celebration.

foam pad Provides a nonstick soft surface when working with ready-to-use fondant and gum paste to make flower petals, etc. Also provides a soft base when pushing cutouts out of plunger cutters.

food coloring dyes used to change the color of foods.

concentrated pastes, which is what we used throughout this book, are the easiest to use, though are a little more expensive.

liquid dyes the strength varies depending on the quality. Useful for pastel colors only, as adding large amounts of liquid coloring will break down most icings. Also useful for painting icing sculptures.

powdered colorings are best for primary colors or black.

frilling tool usually comes as part of a 'modeling' kit. Used to frill the edges of ready-to-use fondant.

gelatin a thickening agent. Available in sheet form, known as leaf gelatin, or as a powder. Three teaspoons of powdered gelatin (7g or one envelope) is roughly equivalent to four gelatin leaves. We used powdered gelatin throughout this book.

glucose syrup also known as liquid glucose; a clear, thick liquid made from corn.

glycerine a sweet, colorless liquid that retains moisture and adds sweetness to cakes. It also softens ready-to-use and royal icings.

golden syrup a by-product of refined sugarcane; pure maple syrup or honey can be substituted.

gum paste also known as flower modeling paste and pastillage. Sets very hard, and is used to make all types of decorations for cakes.

hazelnuts also known as filberts; a plump, grape-sized, rich, sweet nut. *meal* known as ground hazelnuts.

jam also known as preserve or conserve; most often made from fruit. When heated and mixed with a little water, it can be used as a glaze to cover cakes, this acts as a glue helping the initial covering of the cake stick to the cake's surface. Strain the jam mixture before spreading over the cake to remove any solid pieces of fruit.

marzipan an almond and sugar paste used to cover cakes, as a filling in Danish pastries or sculpted into a variety of shapes to be eaten as candy or used as cake decorations. After kneading, it has the consistency of dough and can be rolled, shaped, cut or molded (see also almond paste).

metal spatula also known as a palette knife. Come in small, medium and large. The larger ones have flexible steel blades. There are two types, straight-bladed, and offset or crank, which is used for getting into tight areas the flat straight blade can't.

mixed fruit consists of a mixture of golden raisins, dark raisins, currants, mixed peel and sometimes glacé cherries.

mixed spice a blend of ground spices usually consisting of cinnamon, allspice and nutmeg.

modeling tools are used to draw, frill, shape, imprint, stencil, hollow or cut

soft icing when making decorations for cakes. Can be found singly, but are also available in kits.

muslin a loosely-woven cotton fabric. Tie cornstarch in a square of muslin and use to lightly dust the work surface when kneading and rolling ready-made icing.

nougat a confectionery made from honey, nuts and egg whites. The nougat we are most familiar with is the chewy white confectionery studded with nuts, however, it can be either soft and chewy or crunchy.

nutmeg dried nut of an evergreen tree native to Indonesia; it is available in ground form or you can grate your own with a fine grater.

parchment paper a silicone-coated paper primarily used for lining baking pans and trays so cakes and biscuits won't stick, making removal easy.

petal cutters various metal or plastic cutters in the shape of flower petals. Available as a kit for specific flowers, which also include the veining tool.

piping bags

disposable bags are made of clear plastic. Discard after each use. Only available in one size and come in packs; available from supermarkets.

paper piping bags are made from baking paper (silicone or parchment paper) and discarded after each use. Used for small amounts of icing, writing, flooding (runouts), etc. See page 221 for directions on how to make them.

polyester bags are lightweight, flexible and reusable. Wash in hot soapy water after each use and dry, standing over a soft drink bottle. Are available in many different sizes.

piping tubes small metal or plastic cone shapes with various openings used to produce many different designs when icing or frosting is pressed through them. Smaller ones are quite fragile and must be treated carefully, otherwise they can be bent or squashed out of shape.
basket weave tubes are used for woven designs. They have both a smooth and a ribbed side, which pipe wide stripes.
drop flower tubes are the easiest to use and produce small flower shapes, either plain or swirled.
leaf tubes have a 'V' opening and are used to pipe leaves with pointy ends.
ruffle tubes have a teardrop tip, and are used to pipe bows, ribbons scallops and ruffles.
rose tubes have an opening that is wide at one end and narrow at the other. It's not only used for piping roses – daisies, carnations, pansies, etc, may also be piped with this tube.
round tubes are used for outlining details, filling and writing. Also piping dots, balls, beads and filigree, etc.
star tubes are used to pipe shells, stars, rosettes and flowers.
pizza cutter used to cut through ready-made icing. The blade presses down vertically, rather than dragging, through the icing, which gives a clean, sharp cut.
plunger cutters have a plunger on top: push to cut the shape, then push to release the cut shape. Doesn't damage the shape as it pushes it out.
powders and dusts are also known as petal, pearl, sparkles, blossom tints and lustres.
quilting tools also known as tailor's or stitching wheels. Used to create 'stitches' on ready-made icing. Wheels are removable so the stitching can be of different lengths.
raisins dried sweet grapes.
raspberries known as the 'king of the berries'; cylinder-shaped, about $^5/_8$-$^3/_4$ inches long, with a deep red color and a sweet flavor. Also available black or yellow in color. Are fragile and spoil rapidly, so check for mildew when buying. Also available frozen.

ready-to-use fondant A popular, sweet tasting icing with a dough-like consistency when kneaded. Is used to cover cakes and make decorations. Roll on a surface dusted lightly with cornstarch; don't use too much cornstarch, as the icing will dry and crack when lifted over the cake.
rolling pins come in a variety of sizes; use large ones to roll out the icing, use medium and smaller ones to thin out icing for decorations. They can be made of wood, granite, non-stick plastic, etc.
royal icing is a mixture of egg white and pure icing sugar. Pure icing sugar has no softener (cornstarch) so it sets very hard. Do not use confectioners' sugar or soft icing sugar for this. Is the best to use when securing cakes to their boards. Instant mixes (just add water) are available from cake decorating suppliers.
scrapers can be either plastic or metal (stainless steel). Used to scrape excess ganache off the side of a cake, or to remove excess royal icing off stencils. Plastic scrapers are useful when cleaning up, to scrape any leftover icing stuck to the bench top.
skewers are used in cake decorating to support the cake tiers, they are not the same as the skewers used in kebabs, etc. They are much thicker so they are able to support the weight of the cakes stacked above. They are pointed at one end to push all the way through the cake before cutting down to size.
smoothers these plastic paddles with handles are used to smooth ready-made icing, and remove air bubbles after the icing has been positioned on the cake. When smoothing the icing you need to use the two plastic paddles together; they give the cake a smooth, shiny, appearance.
stamens (the reproductive part of the flower, usually found in the center). Most often sold double-ended, which are either cut in half before using, or are pulled through a hooked wire and folded up in a bunch. May also be found single-ended. Used to make flower centers.
styrofoam is a tightly-packed polystyrene foam that resists moisture. It is available

in different-shaped blocks from cake decorating and craft supply stores.
sugar
brown a very soft, fine sugar retaining molasses for its flavor.
confectiononers' also known as powdered sugar; granulated sugar crushed together with a small amount of added cornstarch.
pure icing this sugar is also known as confectioners' sugar or powdered sugar, but it has no cornstarch added; this means it is very lumpy and it has to be sifted well before use.
superfine also known as finely granulated table sugar.
white a coarse, granulated table sugar.
sugar syrup also known as simple syrup, is brushed all over the surface of a cake before applying the initial covering of ganache, almond paste or ready-to-use fondant. It sticks the initial covering layer to the cake and sticks the final layer to the initial layer. It also stops the cake from drying out. It may be flavored with alcohol, if you like.
textured mats see embossing tools.
tylose powder when mixed into royal icing, almond paste, ready-to-use fondant or modeling paste, tylose powder creates a strong paste that dries very hard. Used when something is required to set in a certain position.
vanilla
bean the tiny black seeds impart a luscious vanilla flavor.
extract made by extracting the flavor from the vanilla bean pods.
veining tool also known as a leaf veiner. Plastic molds that leave an imprint of a leaf when pressed on ready-to-use fondant. Available in kits along with matching flower petal cutters.
wooden dowels or dowel rods, are used to support cakes over three tiers so they can be carried and transported safely. Cut with a small hacksaw to the size required (just below the height of the cake).

CONVERSION CHART

MEASURES

All cup and spoon measurements are level. The most accurate way of measuring dry ingredients is to weigh them. When measuring liquids, use a clear glass or plastic measuring cup with a pouring spout.

We use large eggs with an average weight of 2oz/60g.

DRY MEASURES

IMPERIAL	METRIC
½oz	15g
1oz	30g
2oz	60g
3oz	90g
4oz (¼lb)	125g
5oz	155g
6oz	185g
7oz	220g
8oz (½lb)	250g
9oz	280g
10oz	315g
11oz	345g
12oz (¾lb)	375g
13oz	410g
14oz	440g
15oz	470g
16oz (1lb)	500g
24oz (1½lb)	750g
32oz (2lb)	1kg

LIQUID MEASURES

IMPERIAL	METRIC
1 fluid oz	30ml
2 fluid oz	60ml
3 fluid oz	100ml
4 fluid oz	125ml
5 fluid oz	150ml
6 fluid oz	190ml
8 fluid oz	250ml
10 fluid oz	300ml
16 fluid oz	500ml
20 fluid oz	600ml
32 fluid oz	1000ml (1 litre)

LENGTH MEASURES

⅛in	3mm
¼in	6mm
½in	1cm
¾in	2cm
1in	2.5cm
2in	5cm
2½in	6cm
3in	8cm
4in	10cm
5in	13cm
6in	15cm
7in	18cm
8in	20cm
9in	23cm
10in	25cm
11in	28cm
12in (1ft)	30cm

OVEN TEMPERATURES

The oven temperatures in this book are for conventional ovens; if you have a fan-forced oven, decrease the temperature by 10-20 degrees.

	°F (Fahrenheit)	°C (Celsius)
Very slow	250	120
Slow	300	150
Moderately slow	325	160
Moderate	350	180
Moderately hot	400	200
Hot	425	220
Very hot	475	240

Metric/imperial conversions are approximate only. Measurements for cake pans are approximate only; using same-shaped cake pans of a similar size should not affect the outcome of your baking. We measure the inside top of the cake pan to determine sizes.

INDEX

STERLING
New York

An Imprint of Sterling Publishing
387 Park Avenue South
New York, NY 10016

© 2013 by ACP Magazines Ltd

This 2013 edition published by Sterling Publishing by arrangement with ACP Books.

ISBN 978-1-4549-1016-9

Distributed in Canada by Sterling Publishing
c/o Canadian Manda Group, 165 Dufferin Street
Toronto, Ontario, Canada M6K 3H6

For information about custom editions, special sales, and premium and corporate purchases,
please contact Sterling Special Sales at 800-805-5489 or specialsales@sterlingpublishing.com.

Manufactured in the China

2 4 6 8 10 9 7 5 3 1

www.sterlingpublishing.com